Social Protection Goals in East Asia

The book examines the conceptual, economic, and fiscal impact(s) of the Social Protection Floor (SPF) initiative of the International Labor Organisation (ILO) and other policy influencers by first critically examining the methodologies used by the international agencies to estimate the fiscal costs of designated minimum package(s) of social protection programs. The book also briefly reviews the methodologies used and usefulness of the Social Protection Index (SPI) of the Asian Development Bank (ADB).

Second, the book analyses strategies and specific initiatives used by the selected East Asian countries (China, India, Indonesia, the Philippines, Thailand, and Vietnam), designed to progress towards the social protection goals underlying the Social Development Goals (SDGs) adopted by the United Nations in September 2015, and endorsed by the countries covered in this book.

Finally, the book provides a framework for generating fiscal space to fund the social protection programs and initiatives. The country chapters utilise this framework in the context of each specific country to suggest generating fiscal space.

Mukul G. Asher is Professorial Fellow, Lee Kuan Yew School of Public Policy at the National University of Singapore. He specialises in social security and public financial management issues in Asia. He has published widely in national and international journals, and authored or edited more than fifteen books. He is on the Editorial Board of several journals, including the *Journal of the Economics of Ageing* and *Poverty & Public Policy*. He has been a consultant to multilateral organisations such as the IMF, The World Bank, Asian Development Bank, and the World Health Organization. He has led Executive Training Programs for officials of several countries, including Indonesia, India, Sri Lanka, and Kazakhstan. He served as Chairman of the 5th State Finance Commission of Haryana State in India from May 2016 to September 2017.

Fauziah Zen is Senior Economist at the Economic Research Institute for ASEAN and East Asia (ERIA). She is also a faculty member at the Faculty of Economics and Business, University of Indonesia, and a visiting professor at Hitotsubashi University, Japan. She has been working with the governments of East Asia in the fields of public finance, infrastructure and connectivity, disaster management, and social protection.

Astrid Dita is an independent researcher working on issues related to public finance, fiscal decentralisation, infrastructure, and social protection in Indonesia. She is consultant to various international organisations such as Asian Development Bank, World Bank, and AusAID. She obtained her Masters in Economics from University of Indonesia.

Routledge-ERIA Studies in Development Economics

For a full list of titles in this series, visit www.routledge.com/Routledge-ERIA-Studies-in-Development-Economics/book-series/ERIA

Social Protection Goals in East Asia

Strategies and Methods to
Generate Fiscal Space

**Edited by Mukul G. Asher,
Fauziah Zen, and Astrid Dita**

LONDON AND NEW YORK

First published 2018
by Routledge
2 Park Square, Milton Park, Abingdon, Oxon OX14 4RN

and by Routledge
605 Third Avenue, New York, NY 10017

First issued in paperback 2020

Routledge is an imprint of the Taylor & Francis Group, an informa business

British Library Cataloguing-in-Publication Data
A catalogue record for this book is available from the British Library

Library of Congress Cataloging-in-Publication Data
A catalog record for this book has been requested

ISBN 13: 978-0-367-50422-9 (pbk)
ISBN 13: 978-1-138-29296-3 (hbk)

Typeset in Galliard
by Apex CoVantage, LLC

To our constant inspirations
Isaac and Maya
M.G.A
Sarah Sabila
F.Z
Debbie Retnoningrum
A.D

Contents

Figures

Tables

Contributors

Mukul Asher is Professorial Fellow at the Lee Kuan Yew School of Public Policy, National University of Singapore. He specialises in social security and public financial management issues in Asia. He has published widely in national and international journals, and has authored or edited more than fifteen books. He is on the editorial boards of several journals, including the *Journal of the Economics of Ageing* and *Poverty & Public Policy*. He has been a consultant to multilateral organisations such as the IMF, The World Bank, Asian Development Bank, and the World Health Organization. He has led executive training programs for officials of several countries, including Indonesia, India, Sri Lanka, and Kazakhstan. He served as Chairman of the 5th State Finance Commission of Haryana State in India from May 2016 to September 2017.

Astrid Dita is an independent researcher working on issues related to public finance, fiscal decentralisation, infrastructure, and social protection in Indonesia. She is consultant to various international organisations such as Asian Development Bank, World Bank, and AusAID. She obtained her Masters in Economics from University of Indonesia.

Jin Feng is Professor of Economics at Fudan University and Associated Dean of Faculty of Economics. She is also a researcher in the Employment and Social Security Research Center of Fudan University and Fudan Development Institute. Her publications and research interests focus on social security reforms, health insurance, health care and elderly care in China. She is serving on the boards of Gerontological Society of Shanghai, Chinese Women Economists Society.

Krzysztof Hagemejer has worked with the International Labour Organization (ILO) for more than two decades and was Chief of Policy Development and Research in its Social Security Department. He is now affiliated to ICRA foundation and Collegium Civitas in Poland, and currently serves as Honorary Professor in Hochschule Bonn-Rhein-Sieg, Germany. He has advised the Polish government on pension design and policies as well as social policy monitoring and evaluation.

Aniceto C. Orbeta, Jr. is Senior Research Fellow at the Philippine Institute for Development Studies. He was a Visiting Researcher at the Asian Development Bank Institute. He has extensive experience in economic modelling, developing and setting up monitoring systems, as well as evaluating programs and policies.

Srawooth Paitoonpong is Senior Research Fellow at Human Resources and Social Development Program, Thailand Development Research Institute. He also serves as the Chairman of Thailand National Advisory Council for Labour Development. He has more than four decades of experience in social protection issues, particularly in Thailand.

Phacharawadee Tasee is Researcher at the Thailand Development Research Institute. She is a fellow of the Asia Pacific Leadership Program in East-West Center, Hawaii. She obtained her Masters of Economics from the National Institute of Development Administration, Thailand.

Nguyen Thi Lan Huong is Senior Expert and Former General Director of Institute of Labour Science and Social Affairs, Ministry of Labour, Invalids and Social Affairs, Viet Nam.

Yutika Vora is an independent researcher working on issues related to social protection, public sector governance and public finance in Asia. She is a consultant to multilateral organisations and non-governmental organisations. She has been working on examining challenges in implementing rural development programs and on improving public service delivery.

Pimrumpa Waisuriya is Researcher at the Thailand Development and Research Institute. She conducts policy research in human resource and social development issues. She obtained her Masters of Economics from the National Institute of Development Administration, Thailand.

Fauziah Zen is Senior Economist at the Economic Research Institute for ASEAN and East Asia (ERIA). She is also a faculty member at the Faculty of Economics and Business, University of Indonesia, and a visiting professor at Hitotsubashi University, Japan. She has been working with the governments of East Asia in the fields of public finance, infrastructure and connectivity, disaster management, and social protection.

Foreword

The year 2015 represented an important milestone in economic development for the world and for the Association of Southeast Asian Nations (ASEAN). As the timeline for Millennium Development Goals (MDGs) of the United Nations (UN) ended in 2015, the UN officially launched the 2030 Agenda for Sustainable Development (ASD). In the same year, the ASEAN Economic Community (AEC) was also established, with the aim of achieving the ASEAN Community Vision 2025. This vision emphasises five characteristics; one of which is a Resilient, Inclusive, People-Oriented, and People-Centred ASEAN. There are 17 Sustainable Development Goals (SDGs) under the ASD, 169 targets, and 304 proposed indicators to be monitored.

Traditional social protection floor objectives are an integral part of the ASD. This is reflected in Goals 1 (no extreme poverty), 2 (zero hunger), 3 (good health and well-being), 5 (gender equality), and 10 (reduced inequalities). Thus, social protection is an integral element to support a strong and solid ASEAN Community Vision 2025, as well as the ASD goals.

While the ASD has been adopted globally, there are intense discussions on how the social protection goals, including progress towards a social protection floor (SPF), can be adopted at the national level. It is recognised by the ASD that social protection needs to be approached and implemented in various ways, in the context of the country's development priorities and capabilities. The implications for planning, managing, monitoring, as well as fiscal adjustment, vary from country to country. In general, the challenges will be greater for middle-income countries, especially those with ageing populations.

This volume comes at the right time, as countries have just begun to focus on how to adopt the ASD for their specific contexts. The countries have been reviewing the baselines and benchmarks, to achieve their own social protection targets. This is particularly relevant for the East Asia region, where construction of robust social protection systems is still a work in progress. But the region is becoming globally more integrated, and expectations of people concerning the benefits from the social protection systems are rising.

East Asian economies have adopted different methods and time frames in designing and implementing social protection systems. This book portrays and critically discusses the process, taking into account how public policy responds to the dynamics of global trends, including MDGs, and the ASD. Achieving the social protection goals of ASD requires funding, primarily from the states, but also by households and other sectors. The mix of the funding sources may differ from program to program and from country to country.

This current work contains case studies of countries with the largest populations in East Asia – China, India, and Indonesia – and the emerging economies of the Philippines, Thailand, and Vietnam. These represent an important contribution to the comparative analysis of how Asian countries are devising innovative methods to progress towards the social protection goals of the ASD and to fund their social protection systems.

This compilation is a product of ERIA's project in Fiscal Year 2015: "Social Protection Floor from the Perspectives of Developing East Asia," which focused on methodologies used by the international community to design and to cost SPF; and the need for designing context-specific social protection goals, programs, and systems; as well as generating fiscal space to fund them.

ERIA would like to thank the contributing authors, and especially the editors, for their efforts in producing this timely volume, and thereby contributing to the literature on comparative analysis of social protection systems in Asia.

Shujiro Urata
October 2017

Acknowledgements

The impetus for this edited volume was provided by the launch of the Agenda for Sustainable Development (ASD) by the United Nations in 2015; and by the growing awareness of the need for construction of robust and sustainable social protection systems as an integral component of development strategies. Accordingly, this volume focuses on how the selected Asian countries plan to progress towards social protections goals contained in the ASD; and on critical assessment of analytical fiscal and economic techniques for the social protection floors (SPFs).

It is with a sense of humility and gratitude that we welcome this opportunity to acknowledge various organisations and individuals who have contributed to the production of this book.

The editors would like to express sincere appreciation to the leadership of the Economic Research Institute for ASEAN and East Asia (ERIA) for intellectual and funding support, enabling research on social protection issues in Asia to be undertaken on a longer-term basis. The Chief Economist of ERIA, Professor Fukunari Kimura, has been very supportive of our research efforts. We owe a particular debt of gratitude to Professor Shujiro Urata, for his support in facilitating publication of this volume by Routledge.

The current book is a result of a collective effort of the contributors, the editors, supporting staff, and others who assisted in various ways. We have been privileged to be a part of this collective effort. We have benefited from constructive discussion with our colleagues from ERIA, National University of Singapore, University of Indonesia, International Labour Organisation, the governments of respective countries represented in case studies, as well as our students.

The editors are pleased to acknowledge efforts by Sandy Maulana and Nitya Shukla in preparing the manuscript for publication. Meilawati ensured that our administrative and logistics requirements were met efficiently and pleasantly. We would also like to thank the Routledge editorial and production team who, as always, undertook their responsibilities in a professional and efficient manner.

Mukul Asher, Fauziah Zen, and Astrid Dita

October 2017

1 Approaches and fiscal space generation for social protection floor goals

An overview

Mukul Asher, Fauziah Zen, and Astrid Dita

1. Introduction

This book project was conceived when the global community under the aegis of the United Nations and its agencies was in the final stages of deliberating on the global goals for mitigating various risks faced by persons of all ages throughout the lifecycle. In September 2015, the United Nations was able to achieve consensus to formally launch the 2030 Agenda for Sustainable Development (ASD). The ASD aims at "transforming our world", a far more ambitious and long-term project (particularly as geo-economic and geo-socio-political uncertainties have become more pronounced) than the relatively narrowly defined areas underlying the Millennium Development Goals (MDGs) that it replaced (UNIRISD, 2016).

The ASD contains 17 goals, 169 targets, and 304 proposed indicators, requiring data collection and reporting calling on institutional, fiscal, economic, and political management capacities beyond what most low- and middle-income countries that are the intended target group possess or are willing to allocate resources and energies to. The estimated total investment to attain the ASD by 2030 is between USD 90 trillion and USD 120 trillion, not including costs of transitioning to new set of policies.[1] This is a formidable sum under any circumstances, but more so under the subdued medium-term global growth and global trade prospects (IMF, 2016).

There are also indications, at least in the near term, that there is and will be considerably less enthusiasm among major countries for cooperative global solutions to address economic, social, political, and ecological challenges, including willingness to find resources for them, and engaging in knowledge-transfer. Nevertheless, there has been increasing acceptance in most countries of the need to make social protection policies, programs, and schemes consistent with high, sustainable, and broad-based economic growth, while advancing development goals such as gender equality, and more equitable access to public amenities and services.

Translating the above acceptance into an integrated set of policies, even for a narrow area such as social protection, will be a major challenge. Understanding how select East Asian countries are approaching this challenge was the main motivation for this volume.

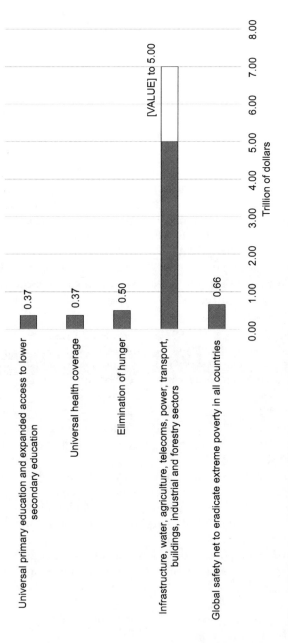

Figure 1.1 Projected costs for achieving sustainable development goals annually

Source: adapted from Sustainable Development Goals, Council of Foreign Relations

2. Key conceptual areas

This section discusses three different conceptual areas. First, a sub-section on *Social Protection Floor (SPF)* provides a brief overview of how SPF is defined in the literature, the distinction between SPF as an instrument and as an outcome to be achieved, as well as a brief discussion of whether the SPF goals should be mandated or if they should be approached in the context of each specific country.

The second sub-section is on the *Social Protection Indicator (SPI)* developed by the Asian Development Bank (ADB). This sub-section briefly explains the methodology used in constructing SPI, and its strengths and limitations. The appropriate use of the SPI for social protection policies is also discussed.

Third, a separate sub-section discusses a *Framework for Generating Fiscal Space*. It focuses on economic growth, conventional and unconventional revenues, and expenditure management, all as having potential to generate fiscal space. This is linked to the East Asian country studies. It should be stressed that a framework is to organise thinking about an issue in context-specific manner. It should not be regarded as a blueprint to be followed. Insufficient recognition of this distinction could lead to inappropriate policy advice, and often to sub-optimal policy choices.

2.1 Social Protection Floor (SPF)

The Social Protection Floor (SPF) concept or approach to progress towards aspirational goals of social protection has been popularised by the International Labor Organization (ILO). This approach is based on the premise of social protection services as a basic human right. However, the definitions of the SPF approach adopted by countries are varied because of differences in ideological and political preferences and capacity to social policies. The SPF approach has evolved over time from establishing a social safety net during economic crisis to more elaborate social protection designs drawing from social risk management (Drolet, 2014).

Recommendation No. 202 of ILO adopted in June 14, 2012, has defined the minimum basic social security guarantees. They are:

- access to a nationally defined set of goods and services, constituting essential healthcare, including in the case of maternity;
- basic income security for children, at least at a nationally defined minimum level, providing access to nutrition, education, care, and any other necessary goods and services;
- basic income security, at least at a nationally defined minimum level, for persons in active age who are unable to earn sufficient income, including in cases of sickness, unemployment, maternity, and disability;
- and basic income security, at least at a nationally defined minimum level, for persons in old age.

The intent of the ILO's Recommendation for the SPF is to define sets of basic social security guarantees over a person's lifetime that secure protection aimed at preventing or alleviating poverty, vulnerability, and social exclusion (ILO, 2012). This suggests that the SPF is designed to provide a minimum level of various types of social protection services for the population. Its aim is not to lower the higher level of social protection status already achieved by some countries, or to replace existing programs that already exhibit higher social protection outcomes. Each country can devise its own strategies and programs, and measures for each of the elements of the SPF, and new funding and sharing of financing between stakeholders is undertaken. Thus, the SPF is better regarded as a set of aspirational goals to progress towards than a blueprint, though the ILO and many other organisations approaching social protection from a rights-based approach continue to use the word 'guarantees'.

As noted, the ASD contains 17 goals, 169 targets, and 304 proposed indicators. Sequencing and priorities, and the generation of fiscal, institutional, and organisational capacities to achieve desired progress are left to each individual country. The SDG goals are voluntary and aspirational (not guarantees), with each country choosing its pace and methods of progress towards the goals that suit its policy objectives, political economy, and economic and organisational capabilities.

There is a probability that multiple goals and targets could detract the integration from close-linked sectors to achieve social protection objectives of the ASD. For instance, sufficient and targeted efforts in basic infrastructure and education will leverage the achievement in the health sector, and the combination of appropriate efforts from the three sectors could result in better household welfare than what individual outcomes would achieve.

To deliver and track SDGs' progress, the UN has issued guidelines and templates for the SGDs' implementation and monitoring framework.[2] Some countries have set up specific institutions tasked to help monitor and integrate SDG goals into decision-making and implementation. Thus, the National SDG Secretariat in Indonesia under the National Development Planning Agency; the National Committee on Sustainable Development in Thailand chaired by the Prime Minister; and a group within India's NITI Aayog are the designated agencies in these countries. Also in India, some state governments such as Haryana have also set up SDG agencies. While there is no global monitoring agency for the SDGs, the UN and its agencies are anticipated to perform research and advocacy functions and keep the progress of the SDGs as an integral element of the global development agenda.

SDG's progress at a global level will thus be significantly affected by the evolution of capabilities and the influence of the UN and its agencies. At the national level, it is the commitment of national level leadership to more citizen-centric public amenities and services – combined with effectively empowering citizens to obtain more productive livelihoods – that will directly or indirectly drive progress towards SDG goals.

The priorities, sequencing and specific initiatives undertaken by each country concerning the SDGs, will understandably vary. Constructing baseline data series of acceptable quality and regularly monitoring progress towards the benchmarked indicator of various social protection and other SDG goals will be required to signal solid commitments towards the goals. The UN and other multilateral agencies, such as the Asian Development Bank and the World Bank, could consider augmenting domestic capabilities regarding meeting of the prerequisites for the SDGs by individual countries.

The countries will also need to be aware of fiscal implications of SDG commitments, including potential contingent liabilities: (1) the need for spending less (lower expenditure by different government agencies for a given quality and quantity of a good, service, or asset): (2) spending well (improving the relationships between monetary expenditure and physical inputs, and the outputs obtained); (3) and spending wisely (spending to meet societal needs and improving household welfare) in a fiscally constrained environment to obtain value-for-money from the social protection initiatives. The IMF's study on 'Achieving More with Less' may be instructive in this regard (IMF, 2017).

The SDGs include goals to be achieved by 2030 that are consistent with the SPF recommendations of the ILO. These include eliminating extreme poverty and hunger, good health and well-being, and reduced inequalities – including those relating to gender.[3]

2.2 Social protection indicator

This sub-section briefly reviews the SPI developed by the Asian Development Bank (ADB). The material in this sub-section is predominantly obtained from ADB (2016), *The Social Protection Indicator: Assessing Results for Asia* (https://www.adb.org/sites/default/files/publication/192966/spi-asia-2016.pdf).

The ADB regards the SPI as a unique tool which provides social protection statistics and measurement in Asia. Its underlying premise is that good quality data on social protection, updated at regular intervals, could help policymakers make better policy and implementation decisions concerning social protection systems.

The SPI is a relative indicator. The numerator is based on dividing total expenditure on social protection by a country by total *potential* beneficiaries of social protection. The denominator of the SPI is GDP per capita. Thus, if the numerator exhibits a lower growth rate than the denominator, the value of the SPI would decrease, and vice versa. It is for this reason that the ADB's 2016 report presents a country's SPI as being equivalent to a percentage of GDP per capita.

Table 2.1 in ADB (2016) reports that the highest SPI for 2012 in Asia and the Pacific was 11.9 for Japan; the overall average for the region was 3.1. Among the countries included in this volume, only China (4.3) and Vietnam (4.0) exhibited scores above the overall average. The others, in descending order of SPI values, were Thailand (2.9), the Philippines (2.2), India (1.3), and Indonesia (1.2).

The ADB disaggregates the SPI into the corresponding SPIs for social insurance, social assistance, and labour market programs, with further sub-groups under each of the three programs. Such comparisons could permit a comparison of the social protection expenditure share of a particular program (e.g., pensions or child allowance) with the potential beneficiaries covered.

ADB (2016) states three benefits of the SPI. First, the SPI provides an estimation of how much is spent on social protection by the countries, how many potential beneficiaries are reached by all the programs, as well as by each sub-group of programs.

Second, the SPI emphasises social protection systems, rather than excessively focusing on one group or sub-groups of social protection programs. The system-perspective is needed, as there has often been excessive preoccupation, including in the East Asian countries included in this volume, with a particular social protection scheme or program impeding policy coherence and coordination.

Third, as the SPI is estimated at increasingly disaggregated levels, distributional and gender impacts of sub-groups of social protection programs could become more evident. This, in turn, could facilitate better understanding of the social protection gaps and limitations of the current policies and programs.

Fourth, the SPI estimates, undertaken at periodic intervals, could also provide an indication of the intertemporal progress in social protection by countries.

The SPI represents one of the useful tools on social protection available to policymakers, organisations, and researchers. However, its limitations should also be viewed in a given country-specific context. These limitations, which have been deduced from the ADB's 2016 report (ADB, 2016) may be grouped as follows:

1. Data constraints: the SPI is quite data intensive. This becomes even more pronounced once the SPI estimates are made on a disaggregated basis. The quality of data for the Asia-Pacific group of countries is uneven. The estimates of potential beneficiaries and other such elements of the SPI are also of uneven quality, including the consistency of comparative data for each country over time, as well as for groups of countries. These limitations help explain why ADB (2016) provides SPI values for 2012.

    However, this large gap presents challenges for policy deliberations for many countries, including those covered in this volume, regarding the conditions and circumstances in 2017 and moving forward.

2. Limited scope to accommodate linkages among sub-groups in the SPI and to track outcomes on household welfare: The SPI is a relative indicator which aggregates different sub-groups comprising of social insurance, social assistance, and labour market programs. These cover a limited number of programs and schemes in each area. However, a country may undertake initiatives such as improving public hygiene and health, or time and energy saving initiatives for women (like replacing indoor pollution-creating bio-mass for cooking with cleaner liquified petroleum gas) which could improve household welfare by reducing disease burden and malnutrition. Thus, interlinkages between various protection measures and outcomes are not captured in the SPI.

    It is not suggested that the SPI attempt to capture all potential linkages and outcomes on household welfare. These are, however, stated to caution users of the SPI not to interpret it in a mechanical manner, but to use it to devise innovative and context-specific social protection measures or initiatives designed to improve household welfare.

3. The SPI does not take into account social protection activities of the sub – national governments. In countries such as India, Indonesia, China the SPI is therefore likely to be understated.

2.3 Generating fiscal space: a framework

An important issue in delivering social protection for the people is the creation of the needed fiscal space to fund the programmes. This section discusses a framework for analyzing the generation of fiscal space. Funding refers to the proportion of GDP required to be generated by the government. This should be contrasted from financing methods used to generate funds.

Heller (2005) has defined fiscal space as "the availability of budgetary room that allows government to provide resources for a desired purpose without any prejudice to the sustainability of government's financial position". This is a broad and rather vague definition, with varying interpretations possible. The World Bank Group (2015, Chapter 3), in discussing how to generate fiscal space and use it in the developing countries, adopts the definition of fiscal space as the "availability of budgetary resources for a specific purpose . . . without jeopardizing the sustainability of the government's financial position or sustainability of the economy". The focus of the World Bank Group (2015, Chapter 3) study is on fiscal space generation and use among a cross-section of countries for short-term counter-cyclical fiscal policy to cope with macro-economic shocks, such as those generated by the 1997–1998 East Asian financial crisis, and by the 2008 global crisis.

The above study identifies fiscal rules imposing specified numerical targets on budgetary aggregates; stabilisation and reserve funds which involve setting aside revenue from commodity booms or fiscal and balance of payments surpluses; and medium-term expenditure frameworks (MTEFs) designed to link budgetary plans and allocations on the one hand and growth and other strategic objectives on the other in a multi-year flexible framework.

An alternative approach (e.g., Ortiz et al., 2015) to the concept of fiscal space stems from the advocacy perspective for significantly expanding social sector programs, without considering design, implementation, and actual outcomes of the ongoing social sector programs. Such studies simply enumerate various sources from which the government can obtain higher revenue, and assert that government expenditure be reallocated, usually from the defense sector (expenditure inappropriately asserted to be without merit) to the social sector (inappropriately asserted to be "investment").

Three key questions are usually missing from such studies, which is not surprising as they typically emphasise an advocacy role rather than focus on a rigorous and nuanced analysis of existing programs and social security organizations. The *first* missing question is that whether society's resources devoted to current social sector (and other) programmes bring commensurate benefits to the society. The success of a typical subsidy program is when conditions giving rise to its need are substantially mitigated, and therefore over time the subsidy expenditure and beneficiaries are reduced. Instead, the usual assumption is that more expenditure and more beneficiaries are, by definition, desirable. This is not to suggest that subsidies or public expenditure on social programmes are undesirable or unwarranted, but that there is need for rigorous analysis of the programmes and of the social sector organisation implementing them. In many subsidy programmes, entry of beneficiaries is encouraged for a variety of economic, political, and social reasons, but exit often necessitates difficult political choices and is therefore given little emphasis.

The *second* missing question is the need for trade-offs among different sources of government revenue required to generate fiscal space. Thus, foreign assistance, which is not sustainable in the long run, is often advocated in such studies as one of the options for generating fiscal space.

The *third* is the neglect of context-specific factors, including political economy and societal priorities reflected through governments and other stakeholders. An example of this includes advocating shifting defense expenditure to social sector programmes; reducing fiscal incentives; and proposals for eliminating shifting of tax bases to low tax jurisdictions. Reallocating public expenditure, without increasing funding, does not improve or create fiscal space.

Analysts concerned with broader development issues focus on how additional fiscal revenue and expenditure can be generated from such avenues as reprioritisation and efficiency enhancements of and effectiveness of expenditures, domestic revenue mobilisation, budgetary deficits, and in selected countries in the short run from development assistance. These analyses emphasise how the additional resources are used for obtaining better societal outcomes from specific government spending such as on education or health; and how government spending can help in enhancing broad-based economic growth. This suggests that developmental aspects rather than short-term stabilisation aspects are emphasised in such definitions of fiscal space.

Thus Roy, Heauty, and Letouze (2007) adopt the following definition of fiscal space:

> Fiscal space is the financing that is available to the government as a result of concrete policy actions for enhancing resource mobilisation, and the reforms necessary to secure the enabling governance, institutional, and economic environments for these policy actions to be effective, for a specified set of development objectives.

Some analysts such as Asher (2005) have argued that greater competence and willingness in generating nonconventional revenue resources can help generate fiscal space. Such sources include using state assets, both physical and financial, more productively; gaining revenue from state-created property rights in a transparent and economically desirable manner; and willingness to use non-tax revenue, including appropriate cost recovery and user charges; and surpluses of regulatory bodies. State assets include land owned by the state, mining, the telecommunication spectrum, and other rights such as the air-space above and the area within and below public sector properties, including railways and bus stations, and accumulated balances in various funds, including pension funds.

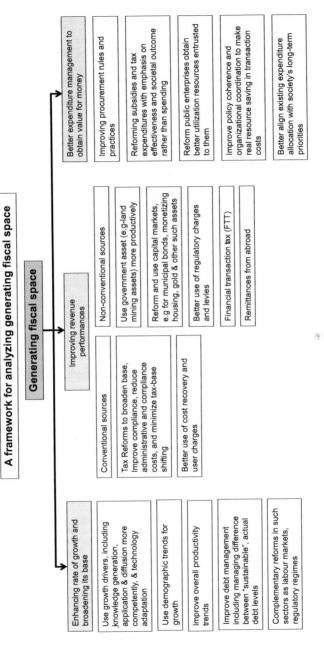

A framework for analyzing generating fiscal space

Generating fiscal space

Enhancing rate of growth and broadening its base

Use growth drivers, including knowledge generation, application & diffusion more competently, & technology adaptation

Use demographic trends for growth

Improve overall productivity trends

Improve debt management including managing difference between "sustainable", actual debt levels

Complementary reforms in such sectors as labour markets, regulatory regimes

Improving revenue performances

Conventional sources

Tax Reforms to broaden base, improve compliance, reduce administrative and compliance costs, and minimize tax-base shifting

Better use of cost recovery and user charges

Non-conventional sources

Use government asset (e.g-land mining assets) more productively

Reform and use capital markets, e.g for municipal bonds, monetizing housing, gold & other such assets

Better use of regulatory charges and levies

Financial transaction tax (FTT)

Remittances from abroad

Better expenditure management to obtain value for money

Improving procurement rules and practices

Reforming subsidies and tax expenditures with emphasis on effectiveness and societal outcome rather than spending

Reform public enterprises obtain better utilization resources entrusted to them

Improve policy coherence and organizational coordination to make real resource saving in transaction costs

Better align existing expenditure allocation with society's long-term priorities

Figure 1.2 A framework for analyzing the generation of fiscal space

Source: constructed by Mukul Asher July 12, 2015

Willingness to charge for publicly organised (but not necessarily produced) goods and services (such as water and electricity) also involves taking responsibility for effectiveness in delivering these goods and services, increasing the accountability of the government. This is perhaps one of the factors constraining many authorities to use cost recovery and user charges more extensively. For those who may require assistance, use of utility vouchers, combined with block pricing, where per unit pricing increases with usage, merits serious considerations. Progress on the pre-conditions necessary for using such methods, including installing of effective metering systems, is essential if fiscal costs are to be managed.

Broadly, generation of fiscal space might be achieved by: 1. enhancing rate of growth and broadening its base; 2. improving revenue performance; 3. better expenditure management to obtain value for money (Figure 1.2). In enhancing the growth rate and broadening its base, one may use growth drivers such as human capital, use demographic dividends, improve overall productivity, improve debt management, and conduct pro-growth structural reforms. To improve revenue performance, one may use both conventional and non-conventional sources, the prior including tax reforms, and the latter including asset securitisation and other means of better asset utilisation. The last is on better expenditure management, where one may obtain significant value from improving procurement rules and practices, reforming subsidies both above and below the line, and reforming public enterprises.

Having elaborated the framework above – to ensure sufficient and sustainable funding for attaining desirable social protection goals – it is crucial to expand the decision-making horizon of policymakers and stakeholders beyond the typical recipes from policy advocates, and constraints of political economy in their respective countries.

3. Country experiences

This section provides key findings from the country experiences/lessons for with social protection policies, and possible lessons which may be instructive.

3.1 Analytical and cost projection aspects of social protection floors

The chapter titled "Review of approaches to assess the sustainability of social protection floors" is authored by Krzysztof Hagemejer. The author posits that there seems to be already widespread and growing agreement that provision of social protection – meant as putting in place various instruments through which all those in need have guarantees of income security and affordable access to necessary healthcare – is an economic and social necessity. Furthermore, the author states that is why many international standards, agreements, and documents recognise that in civilized world everybody should have right to such guarantees (such as recent ILO Recommendation No. 202, Sustainable Development Goals or joint ILO, World Bank and WHO call for universal social protection, including universal healthcare).

Social protection measures require sustainable financing – creating and maintaining adequate fiscal space at the national level. Fiscal space will be adequate only within policy space that is supportive for social protection and which includes social and political willingness to allocate requisite resources as the available resources have many claimants.

Good governance of social protection at all stages – planning policies, policy reforms, and implementation – requires continuous monitoring of its performance and finances, including long-term projections and simulations of cost and benefits of different social protection programs and overall social protection systems. These projections and simulations should take into account demographic trends, including demographic ageing. However, one has also to include – and it is much more challenging methodologically – economic impacts of social protection in the longer term on human capital, productivity, and growth. Investments in social protection may enhance human capital, productivity, and growth allowing an expanding fiscal envelope, creating additional fiscal space for further improvements of social protection coverage and adequacy. But this cannot be assumed, and empirical evidence in a specific context is essential if this argument is used to significantly expand social protection programs in any country-specific context.

After examining the concepts of social protection systems and its floors (i.e., Social Protection Floor or SPF), as well as briefly reviewing the social protection sustainability and affordability debate, this chapter reviews different aspects of methodologies needed to assess sustainability of social protection. Availability of good quality statistics on social protection expenditure, financing, coverage, and adequacy is a precondition for empirical evidence-based governance of any public expenditure programs; thus attention is drawn to existing challenges to social protection statistics existing at national and international levels. Existing statistical standards in this area are discussed, as well as initiatives in this respect of various international organisations. These data limitations should make policymakers cautious when embracing ambitious social protection initiatives which commit current and future fiscal resources.

The chapter then turns to the debate on the need go beyond pure static accounting when assessing financial sustainability of public expenditure and discusses various challenges associated with incorporating projection results into inter-temporal government accounts. And finally, this chapter includes a review of ILO social budgeting methodology and its applications to assess additional fiscal costs of social protection measures, leading to progress towards social protection floors in different countries. In Thailand, Vietnam, Philippines, and Indonesia such studies were undertaken by the ILO in the initial years of this decade. These are reviewed in the respective chapters.

This chapter is supplemented with an extensive list of literature devoted to the methodological questions of financial governance of social protection systems, bearing on the sustainability and affordability debate. The chapter, however, does not contain any quantitative estimates of national and/or fiscal costs of SPF. This is deliberate, as a robust methodology, widely adaptable, for such estimates is still a work in progress. The author of the chapter thus implicitly cautions against taking assertions about fiscal costs of SPF at face value. Healthy skepticism, and more context-specific empirical estimates, including using "stress tests" (simulation studies) for various underlying assumptions, are warranted. This is particularly important as several prominent advocacy groups for such floors or for particular components of them (such as the ILO and HelpAge International) have been among those providing such estimates.

The chapter provides authoritative, nuanced discussion of the formidable requirements and challenges faced by those engaged in the task of projecting fiscal and other costs of individual SPF measures, and for the SPF as a whole.

3.2 China

The chapter titled "Social protection programs in China: an assessment" is authored by Jin Feng. Social protection is considered to be both a social and an economic imperative in China. A comprehensive social protection system has been developed in China, consisting of social insurance programs, social assistance programs, and labor market policies. The chapter presents structure and administrative framework of social protection system in China from a life-cycle perspective. There are eight categories of programs in the system: 1. compulsory education for children, 2. minimum living security scheme for both rural and urban residents (MLSS), 3. social insurance for urban employees, 4. labor market policies for urban employees, 5. resident pension in rural and urban areas, 6. aged care subsidy for rural and urban residents, 7. resident health insurance in rural and urban areas, 8. housing security for urban residents. The percentage of GDP dedicated to social protection expenditures (not including education, social insurance, and housing security) was 2.37 percent in 2012. Social insurance expenditure was 4.76 percent of GDP in 2013.

Following ILO's concept of SPF, the chapter assesses three most crucial programs in SPF in China, which are MLSS, Resident Pension Schemes, and Resident Health Insurance Schemes. Based on literature reviews, statistical summaries, and simulation methods, the following findings are presented:

a.   As one of the largest cash transfer programs in the developing world, MLSS has played a substantial role in reducing poverty. However, identification of the poor is always a problem, as in many other countries. Recipients are reluctant to exit the program, since obtaining MLSS benefits is often associated with other preferential programs. Decentralisation of the social expenditure responsibility of local governments has resulted in potential regional imbalances in the MLSS.

b.   Due to significant government subsidy, the Resident Pension Scheme in both rural and urban areas expanded rapidly. The scheme provides a universal protection floor to alleviate old age poverty. Despite the impressive progress in reaching universal coverage, the scheme suggests limitations in terms of adequacy of the benefits, in incentive structuring for participation, and in fiscal sustainability. The basic pension is about 10 to 25 percent of consumption per capita, varying among regions. The potential to raise the benefit lies in expanding coverage of formal urban social insurance and a slower increase of pensioners in the resident pension system.

c. Resident Health Insurance Schemes involve large amounts of government subsidy. There are a number of studies evaluating the effects of resident health insurance. Some find that resident health insurance increases the utilisation of formal medical services. However, supply-induced demand issues and the low reimbursement rate provided by the schemes limit the demand for healthcare, especially the demand from rural residents.

In the future, China will continue improving the system as well as increasing expenditures on social protection. Future improvements will, however, be in a less favorable environment than in the past: China's economy is slowing down and growth of fiscal revenue is declining. The chapter considers the following ways to further develop the social protection system in China: reprioritising public spending to increase social expenditures, exploring alternative fiscal resources (including dividends from stated owned enterprises and foreign exchange reserves), increasing fiscal capability of local governments, and improving efficiency in delivery of social protection.

3.3 *India*

The chapter by Mukul Asher and Yutika Vora titled "Social protection system in India: an assessment of the recent initiatives" examines the nature of these initiatives and places them in the context of Agenda for Social Development (ASD), Social Protection Floor (SPF), and generation of fiscal space. The authors discuss the existing programs for healthcare, social protection for children, working population and older people, and initiatives for employability and livelihoods in India.

The chapter focuses particularly on the new initiatives undertaken since Prime Minister Modi's government assumed responsibilities in 2014. The Pradhan Mantri Jan Dhan Yojana (PMJDY) is an innovative scheme to qualitatively expand financial inclusion and using technology to link pension payments, subsidies, and other benefit payments in a secure and reliable manner. The Atal Pension Yojana (APY) combines elements of defined benefit and defined contribution from the government for pensions, primarily for informal sector workers. The MUDRA (Micro Units Development Refinance Agency) facilitates provision of credit to small enterprises in India, to help realise potentials for self-employment and to generate additional jobs in micro and small enterprises.

Under the umbrella of Skill India, the Pradhan Mantri Kaushal Vikas Yojana (PMKVY) is also an innovative program for skilling of the existing and future labour force. In addition, initiatives exist such as the Swachch Bharat Mission (SBM), to improve public and private hygiene and cleanliness, with potentially positive impact on health indicators. Substituting cleaner fuel for biomass through PMUY represents an Indian context-specific initiative to improve the health and nutrition of women and children, and to facilitate women in earning additional income with the time and energy saved. The Mission Indradhanush (MI) is a health initiative to immunise all pregnant women and children against vaccine-preventable diseases.

The authors emphasise that these initiatives are context-specific. A clear linkage needs to be established between a specific initiative and its impact on socio-economic indicators, given the peculiar characteristics of the country. The federal structure, with diffusion of responsibilities for design, implementation, and evaluation of the programs between the Union government and the States, diverse socio-economic characteristics, informal nature of the labour force, and the nature of poverty all pose considerable challenges for policy coherence. To overcome these challenges, the chapter emphasises the need for good-quality "plumbing" of these social protection schemes for better expenditure management and targeting, hence for better outcomes from a given level of expenditure.

The new approach has facilitated taking advantage of seemingly small initiatives (such as ensuring all schools are equipped with toilets for girls) with disproportionate contribution to outcomes. The use of technology-enabled platforms in design and delivery of social protection services has also been strengthened. The Aadhar card (using technology for a biometric identification system) and its linkage with Jan Dhan Yojna, facilitating direct benefit transfers to bank accounts of the beneficiaries of the social protection programs, are key components of the post-2014 social protection initiatives.

The new approach has led to better policy coherence and greater experimentation with different organisational structures, including different combinations of public–private–civil society–social enterprise sectors in delivery and feedback loop, as well as in evaluation of social protection programs.

The chapter suggests India will need to generate between 2 to 4 percent of GDP of additional fiscal space by the year 2030 to fund pensions alone. If other social protection elements are included, the fiscal needs will be higher. The chapter then discusses the use by the Indian government of various components of the Generating Fiscal Space Framework (Figure 1.2) to generate fiscal space for its social protection initiatives. The following, in particular, are being adopted to generate additional fiscal space: procurement reforms to achieve savings; widening of the tax base through data analytics and other digital-based techniques; monetising government's physical assets; and more strategic use of public infrastructure and social investment. Many newer initiatives have co-contribution by the beneficiaries as an integral part of the scheme.

The chapter urges more integrated, outcome-oriented social protection initiatives, and a system-oriented view of such initiatives in the Union and State governments. The authors urge higher investment in constructing social protection databases, data analytics, and encouraging policy-relevant research in social protection; they also advocate linking it with public policies and with public financial management. They suggest that establishment of a national center for research on ageing merits serious consideration. The authors also emphasise that a change in mind-set and attitudes of all stakeholders, including that of the households themselves, is required so that the attributes needed for India to emerge as an upper-middle-income country can be progressively reflected in behaviour.

3.4 Indonesia

The chapter on Indonesia, titled "Social protection system in Indonesia: an assessment" was authored by Fauziah Zen and Astrid Dita. In early years, social protection in Indonesia was mainly intended for civil servants and armed forces personnel. It was not until the 2004 Law on National Social Security System (*Sistem Jaminan Sosial Nasional*, SJSN) was issued that the government started to view social protection through a more comprehensive point of view, where the law mandates social insurance to be universal and mandatory.

The integration process – from previously fragmented programs into a unified, universal, and mandatory program under the SJSN umbrella – has proved to be challenging. The challenges include differences in mechanisms and benefits between the old programs and the new one. There are problems of capacity to handle nationwide programs. There is a large imbalance between supply and demand of social protection services, especially in the health sector, and at the same time many regions have their own programs – particularly for healthcare, adding to the complexity of delivering social protection services.

The chapter finds that both social insurance and social assistance programs face some common constraints: the problems of low coverage (both legal and effective), inequality due to disparity across regions or income levels, database problems, and flaws in program design. Low legal coverage is related to fiscal capacity, implementation capacity, and database effectiveness. Effective coverage mainly rests on fiscal capacity and the capacity of fund managers (in case of SJSN) to invest in better portfolios. The equality issues arise from the fact that the country has uneven distribution of population (60 percent live on Java Island, whose area is less than 10 percent of Indonesia), geographical challenges, insufficient level of connectivity, diverse knowledge/education levels and thus uneven beneficiary literacy and awareness of options, as well as diverse income levels, including within the low-income group.

The program's design for the National Health Insurance (Jaminan Kesehatan Nasional, JKN) has some unresolved issues. Zero co-payment induces excessive demand, low waiting time incentivises the unhealthy to join rather than the healthy, no exit barrier creates deficits for the system, and very low premiums result in low health-service estimated costs. On the other hand, the future program of the national pension (Jaminan Pensiun, JP) will be run as an annuity income stream for the pensioners and their heirs, making the estimation of future liabilities complex and unpredictable; it is also set up as a Defined Benefit program, which will pose huge risks in times of ending of the current favourable demographic dividend phase. Additionally, the programs are prone to political intervention; for example, the cumulative balance in one's mandatory old-age savings account (Jaminan Hari Tua, JHT) can be fully withdrawn by unemployed workers one month post-layoff, which reduces the stability of BPJS Labor's portfolio management, as well as feeding into an existing short-term mindset that erodes the virtue of old age income securities.

There are ongoing discussions on how Indonesia could best adopt the SPF. The current programs are relatively wide in scope, despite missing some elements of ILO's SPF. Meanwhile, the government of Indonesia is now struggling to achieve universal social protection coverage – particularly for healthcare as mandated by the SJSN Law – and the first year(s) of the implementation have been proven to be very costly. However, there is clear potential for cost efficiency by improving programs design and strengthening the system. The stated cost efficiency may free up fiscal space, and by then the government can move forward to look at the possibility of enhancing the current systems by adding additional relevant programs.

3.5 Philippines

The chapter "Social protection system in the Philippines: an assessment" by Aniceto C. Orbeta, Jr., provides a summary of the developments in the social protection system in the Philippines with particular attention to the provision of the social protection floor (SPF) described in ILO (2012). It also provides an assessment of how the current social protection system is able to meet the basic social protection guarantees proposed in the SPF, namely, universal healthcare, social protection for children, social protection for the working age population, and social protection for the elderly.

The chapter is appreciative of the Philippine Government's initiative to invest in an empirically driven database for poor households to help improve effectiveness of programs targeted at them.

On the provision of universal healthcare, the main development is the expansion of the sponsored program where government pays the health insurance premiums of the poor using revenues from recently the so-called "sin taxes." This earmarked source of financing has contributed significantly to its socio-political and financial sustainability.

On social protection for children, the main development is in the Pantawid Pamilyang Pilipino Program (Pantawid), the Philippine version of the conditional cash transfer program. Pantawid has continuously expanded and is currently covering more than 4 million households. Many consider this as already covering virtually all poor households. It is now the third largest CCT program in the world in term of households covered. If the heated debate every time its budget is presented in Congress is used as a gauge, the sustainability of the program is uncertain, since much of the financing comes from the government budget. The program owes its size and sustained implementation to the strong support given by the executive department. Its consistent performance in delivering its primary objectives, as shown by the two waves of rigorous evaluations of the program, likewise, may help in its continuation in the future.

In the case of the working age population, the chapter argues that by law almost every risk group and population group – including household help and informal sector workers – is covered. With respect to risk, the only remaining unresolved issue is the provision of unemployment insurance. With respect to coverage, the weakness lies in terms of actual coverage. For instance, the proportion of contributing members among private wage and salary workers (whose contributions are supposed to be mandatory) was only around 40 percent in 2013. Given this, it is not surprising that the coverage of voluntary members, including self-employed workers, non-working spouses, household helpers, and overseas Filipino workers, is even lower.

On the social protection for the elderly, the main development is in the social pensions program, which provides monthly pensions of PHP 500 to indigent seniors 60 years and older. Recently, the actual coverage of the social pension was expanded from 77 years and older to 65 years and older, nearer to the statutory covered population of 60 and older.

The chapter reviews recent SPF proposals. It is suggested that while many of the proposals are straightforward, others need refinements. A case in point is the proposal to subsidise the premiums of Social Security System coverage of informal sector workers. It is argued in this paper that maybe it would be more productive to expand first the coverage of wage and salary workers, which is currently low, before turning attention to the informal sector workers. There is a need to demonstrate that the system can cover its main mandatory target population before pushing for expansion of coverage of the more problematic voluntarily covered population.

3.5 Thailand

The chapter on Thailand, "Social protection system in Thailand: an assessment," has been authored by Srawooth Paitoonpong et al. The chapter analyses social protection programs in Thailand, with a view to improving their outcomes and coherence. It also discusses fiscal implications of selected social protection measures as projected by a joint UN-TRG study undertaken during the 2011–2013 period (henceforth referred to as Schmitt et al., 2013). It also suggests avenues which could be explored to generate additional fiscal resources.

One of the indications of Thailand's success in social development is that the out-of-pocket expenditure as a share of national health expenditure is only around 12 percent – a quarter of Vietnam's share. Thailand has achieved universal health coverage, though uneven levels of benefits and quality of care across groups remain as challenges.

Thailand's social protection system – encompassing healthcare, children, working age population, the elderly, and disabled – has several sub-components. The chapter argues that coverage in areas other than healthcare and education remains low. Thus, in the SSS, Thailand's social insurance organisation, only about one-tenth of the informal workers are covered. The chapter then discusses the UN/RTG team's study results, as detailed in Schmitt et al. (2013). The healthcare component was excluded, as the study team concluded that since universal coverage has been achieved, no additional steps are necessary. The study focused on additional costs of measures to implement child support grants, maternity allowance, sickness benefit to informal workers, vocational training expansions, and higher benefits to the disabled. These constitute only a limited set of social protection measures. So estimated additional costs should be viewed in this context.

The chapter broadly agrees with the UN/RTG Joint Team recommendations. The report maintains that social protection has a problem of interpretation of the terms "adequate", "minimum", "basic", "essential", and so forth, and since these terms have no clear meaning, they may be interpreted in many divergent ways, making it hard to define the scope of social protection. As such, the extension of more social protection to workers in the informal sectors should be finite, otherwise it may face the problem of moral hazard because of the lack of efficient registration and a good distribution system. It is recommended therefore that before taking further action on these recommendations, more study and planning should be done on the implementation of the programs.

The chapter notes that improving and extending skills training to 20 percent of workers in the informal economy will incur relatively high costs, while there has not been a study on the demand for or need of these workers. Without knowing the real demand for training, program overlaps and wasted resources are likely. Furthermore, the report recommended that fiscal space must be carefully studied and projected, and indicators updated, particularly at the time of a crisis or political instability.

The chapter also emphasises that, in the context of social protection or SPF, looking at the coverage and financing issues is not enough: they deal with only the quantitative aspect of social protection. Indeed, there are quite a few pitfalls in SP implementations, beyond fiscal space and/or sustainability. The pitfalls include the quality as well as the inequality of social protection, management, accessibility, governance, and even political instability. Some examples of social protection's qualitative problems in Thailand include: 1) inequality in the health insurance system; 2) inequality in pension systems; and 3) schooling quality.

The chapter projects the additional fiscal costs (not including infrastructure costs) of the above set of measures as between 0.5 percent and 1.2 percent of GDP by 2020 (Schmitt et al., 2013). It then projects that a low scenario would entail a rise in the government deficit until 2014, and a high scenario untill 2017, but then there will be fiscal surplus in 2020, the end of the projection period. It should be emphasised that the study had assumed that Thailand's government budget would be in surplus from 2013 as compared to a deficit equivalent to 3.1 percent of GDP in 2012. But the Thailand Budget in Brief for the fiscal year 2016 projects a deficit equivalent to 0.8 percent of GDP.[4] The above projections therefore need to be carefully re-evaluated before proceeding with any social protection initiatives.

The chapter suggests that tax reforms, management improvement, and development of a participatory welfare system can be sources for revenues for expanding fiscal space. It does not link these suggestions explicitly with social protection.

3.6 Vietnam

"Social protection system in Vietnam: an assessment", by Nguyen Thai Lan Huong, analyses its social protection system in the context of global initiatives for social protection and suggests options for reforming the system, including how to generate additional funding for the programs. Vietnam's buoyant economic performance and tradition of emphasising social protection have been instrumental in its rapidly improving poverty levels, primary and secondary education attainment, improved health status, and other social indicators.

The chapter argues, however, that there are five factors which Vietnam needs to consider as it aspires towards substantial socio-economic progress. The need for social protections could be impacted first by ongoing rethinking about the pace and type of future globalisation. Vietnam has successfully integrated with the global economy, so this aspect is particularly relevant for the country. Second is the need for adjustment to the rapid ageing of the population, creating social protection structures, including for healthcare for those older than 75 years.

Third, Vietnam's economy has remained largely informal, that is, without formal employer-employee relationships. Four out of five workers are not covered by social insurance schemes for pensions. Healthcare coverage is around 70 percent, but relies primarily on government subsidies. The challenge of designing, implementing, and financing social protection schemes for informal sector workers will continue to be formidable.

Fourth, relatively high and variable inflation rates in Vietnam complicate the task of maintaining real value of various pension and other benefits. Thus, between 2010 and 2015, the official inflation rate ranges from a low of 0.6 percent in 2015 to a high of 18.9 percent in 2011.[5]

Fifth, Vietnam's population remains especially vulnerable to climate change as most of the population lives in low-lying river basins of coastal areas.

The chapter then details the progress of recent initiatives of the government of Vietnam towards healthcare, social assistance, social insurance, and unemployment labor market programs. The government has come to regard social protection as an integral part of economic growth and development. Vietnam's revised 2013 constitution states that all citizens have a right to social protection. The effort will henceforth be directed to putting substance into this provision. It has announced plans for universal health coverage by 2020.

The chapter identifies the main gaps in Vietnam's SPF as unequal access to healthcare among the population; continuing high out-of-pocket healthcare costs (48 percent); low coverage for healthcare, social insurance, and other programs; and implementation inefficiencies. Generating employment opportunities is also proving to be a challenge, especially with subdued growth and global trade prospects, and lower employment intensity due to disruptive technologies.

The chapter then discusses *additional* costs till 2030 of a limited set of social protection measures projected by the UN, MOLISA/ILSSA Team, using the rapid assessment methodology of ILO. This very limited exercise, while useful, needs to be considered with other age-related factors affecting pension, health-care, social assistance, and other expenditure.

The projections for the broadest set of selected options (Option 3) puts additional costs at 1.43 percent of GDP in 2015, while Vietnam's tax-to-GDP ratio is around 20 percent. The projections discussed in the chapter leave unexplained rather curious results of additional costs of Option 3 falling from 1.43 percent of GDP to only 0.63 percent by 2030, only around two-fifths of the total. This suggests that any such studies, in addition to the usual disclaimer that they are not substitutes for more systematic actuarial and fiscal projections which should include full economic costs, should be subjected to rigorous scrutiny by the research community. For expanding fiscal space, the chapter suggests increasing the number of taxpayers, increasing the number of citizens contributing to social insurance, increasing the government retirement age, reforming government expenditure, and improving the performance of the banking sector and state enterprises. The linkages between these suggestions and the social protection system are, however, not yet explored.

4. Concluding remarks

The adoption by the global community of the UN-initiated ASD in 2014 reflects the acceptance – at least in principle – that measures to progress towards desirable social, cultural, and environmental goals should form an integral part of growth and development strategies of individual countries. Aspirational goals of the ASD are much broader than the social protection goals contained in the ILO's advo-cacy of the SPF, but the social protection components of the ASD, unlike the ILO's SPF, do not use the term 'guarantees'. The ASD, therefore, leaves greater scope for innovation and creativity in structuring context-specific social protec-tion initiatives than the ILO's SPF.

The above acceptance of the need to progress towards more robust social protection systems is constrained by subdued prospects for medium-term global economic and trade growth. However, even as economic and fiscal capacities are constrained, the need and expectations of the population for social protec-tion have been increasing, and therefore, more competence, governance, and management of social protection policies and organisations responsible for their outcomes are needed.

It is in the above context that this volume provides case studies of select East Asian countries on their approach and specific measures to progress towards ASD and SPF goals, and on how they have been utilising Generating Fiscal Space Framework (Figure 1.2) for funding social protection.

As has been summarised in the earlier sections, the case studies suggest that select East Asian countries have taken diverse approaches to the ASD and SPF goals to suit their context, priorities, institutional and organisational capacities, and their ability to generate additional fiscal space without departing from prudent macroeconomic and fiscal policies, and without adversely affecting future growth and development prospects. That is, both the protection and promotion aspects of social protection need to be appropriately combined, with requisite attention to changing mind-sets and attitudes to accomplish it.

A common finding of the case studies is that social protection policies need to be designed, implemented, and evaluated, with a resulting feedback loop to improve their outcomes, in a more professional and data-driven empirical evidence–based manner. Institutional structures and system of data gathering, analysis, and communication, appropriate for each country, therefore merit serious consideration. This is needed to enhance the quality of public debate and of resulting public policy decisions on social protection.

It may be useful to express our views on the advocacy of unconditional basic income to all citizens as a citizenship right. The BIEN (Basic Income Earth Network) defined it as a "periodic cash payment unconditionally delivered to all on an individual basis, without means-test or work requirement".[6]

Revival of such a proposal appears to be a response to the fear of increasing technology-driven job automation in the future, where human jobs would be taken over by robots and artificial intelligence. Superficially this may sound attractive, but on deeper analysis, such an approach should not be adopted in, at least, the selected East Asian countries covered in this volume. The chapter on India has indicated that the Indian government considers such a proposal as useful for discussion but not for implementation.

In June 2016, such a proposal, which would end all other social protection programs and replace them with a basic income guarantee, was put to a vote in Switzerland, a high income country (according to the IMF, its per capita income at current exchange rates was USD 79,242 in 2016) with a relatively small population of 8.4 million. The overwhelming majority (77 percent) rejected the proposal.

There are several considerations that are relevant when considering the basic income proposal, particularly in low and middle-income countries and in countries with large populations, such as China, India, and Indonesia.

First, the emphasis on the individual as the unit of benefit rather than the household could seriously erode family and community as risk-coping and risk-sharing methods currently extensively used in these countries.

Second, funding of this proposal would result in significantly higher fiscal expenditure which will need to be funded. There are likely to be incentive effects on work effort, saving, investment, and occupational choices. Their extent needs to be verified from country to country. Moreover, a country establishing such a program could attract cross-border persons, given that borders have become porous, adversely affecting social and political stability, and cultural ethos.

Third, a key requirement for the basic income proposal is that all current social protection programmes be ended. The political economy of East Asian countries included in this volume (and indeed most countries globally) would not permit this. This will create distortions, and additional fiscal costs, with adverse incentive effects.

The editors therefore urge that the East Asian countries focus on how to progress towards the aspirational goals of the ASD and the SPF in their own context-specific manner, and not misdirect their efforts towards a proposal more suited to very industrially advanced high-income countries.

Notes

1 www.cfr.org/global-governance/sustainable-development-goals/p37051
2 https://sustainabledevelopment.un.org/index.php?page=view&type=400&nr=2013&menu=35
3 https://sustainabledevelopment.un.org/sdgs
4 Thailand Government. 2016. Thailand Budget in Brief 2016. Available online at www.bb.go.th/budget_book/e-Book2559/FILEROOM/CABILIBRARY59/DRAWER01/GENERAL/DATA0000/inBrief2016.pdf
5 www.statista.com/statistics/444749/inflation-rate-in-vietnam/
6 http://basicincome.org/basic-income/

References

ADB (2016). *The Social Protection Indicator: Assessing Results for Asia*. Manila: Asian Development Bank.

Drolet, J. (2014). *Social Protection and Social Development: International Initiatives*. Berlin: Springer.

International Monetary Fund (IMF). (2016). *World Economic Outlook: Subdued Demand: Symptoms and Remedies*. Washington, DC: IMF.

International Monetary Fund (IMF) (2017). *Fiscal Monitor: Achieving More With Less*. Washington, April. Available at www.imf.org/en/Publications/FM/Issues/2017/04/06/fiscal-monitor-april-2017

Schmitt, V., T. Sakunphanit, and O. Prasitsiriphol (2013). *Social Protection Assessment Based National Dialogue: Towards a Nationally Defined Social Protection floor in Thailand*. Bangkok: ILO and the United Nations Country Team in Thailand (UNCTT).

2 Review of approaches to assess the sustainability of social protection floors

Krzysztof Hagemejer

1. Introduction

In some parts of the world and in important quarters of the global debate, there is widespread agreement that the provision of social protection – meaning, putting in place various instruments through which all those in need have guarantees of income security and affordable access to necessary healthcare – is an economic and social necessity. That is why many international standards and agreements recognise that in the civilised world, everyone should have the right to such guarantees.

The most important agreement is Recommendation No. 202 in 2012 of the International Labour Organization (ILO) concerning floors of social protection (International Labour Conference, 2012). The ILO, World Health Organization, and the World Bank, joined by other organisations, in 2015 agreed on promoting universal social protection, including universal healthcare.

The most recent of these international agreements is the adoption of the United Nations General Assembly of the Sustainable Development Goals in September 2015. Actually, significant number of targets associated with different development goals – either explicitly or implicitly – require expansion of social protection systems and establishing social protection floors. One of the targets under Goal 1 of ending poverty in all its forms everywhere by 2030 is: 'Implement nationally appropriate social protection systems and measures for all, including floors, and by 2030 achieve substantial coverage of the poor and the vulnerable'. The target of substantial coverage for 2030 is rather moderate compared to the universal coverage objective promoted widely. Also, 'coverage of the poor and vulnerable' is difficult to measure. As the two main objectives of social protection are to (1) prevent and (2) reduce poverty and vulnerability, the coverage of those who are still poor and vulnerable, despite having access to social protection, is a measure which may rather indicate failures of social protection than its effects; and misses completely those whose poverty and vulnerability were prevented or significantly reduced, thanks to their social protection coverage.

In addition to the above target, implementing social protection measures and policies is also indispensable to achieve number of other goals – eliminating hunger, achieve desired access to education, health, other social services or achieve decent employment. All these can be achieved by wide range of policies, but such range must include social protection measures.

However, despite all the above normative standards and agreed goals and targets, majority of the world's population, particularly in Africa and Asia, still lacks comprehensive social protection coverage. This lack of coverage is often explained on the grounds of affordability, particularly in lower income countries, whereas explanation lies in lack of sufficient policy space for social protection in many countries.

Social protection instruments are mainly redistributive mechanisms through which society, by means of general taxation and social security contributions, finances the benefits and services of those who – according to nationally prede-fined entitlement conditions – need them. The maximum scale of possible redis-tribution is determined in the first place by the resource envelope available now (Figure 2.1) and in the future (Figure 2.2) – that amount of resources which can be collected through taxes and contributions in the shorter and longer run.[1]

In the shorter run, fiscal envelope can be also modified by the country's net lending or borrowing as well as through grants received from the rest of the world. The size of the overall fiscal envelope is determined by the willingness of society to pay taxes and contributions (which depends on the quality of public services provided, accountability and transparency of public finance, as well as the degree of democratisation of the budgeting process). It also depends on the abil-ity and capacity of the government to collect taxes and contributions, and enforce existing legislation.

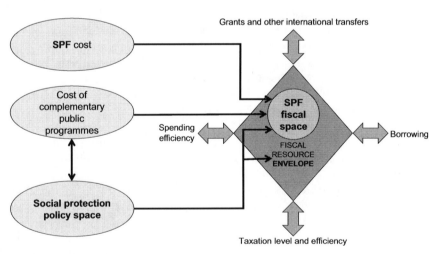

SPF = Social Protection Floor.

Figure 2.1 Fiscal space and policy space for social protection (short and medium term)

Note: SPF = Social Protection Floor
Source: author

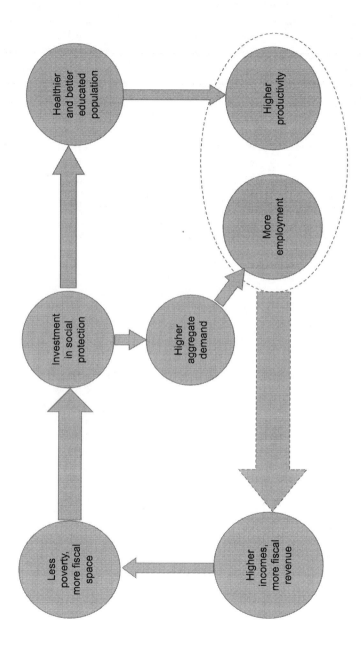

Figure 2.2 Sustainability of social protection (long run)
Source: author

In the global arena, the size of the overall fiscal envelope depends also on external actors as well as on the ability of the government to take autonomous decisions and not bow to the pressures of external forces. These external actors are the international bodies with which countries have some commitments such as the International Monetary Fund (IMF), the World Bank, or the European Union, and the private institutions acting at the global financial markets, rating agencies, and others.

The second group of actors are those who shape the policy space for public redistributive policies in general and for public social protection in particular. Much depends on the attitudes prevailing in society towards redistribution and the poor. In those parts of the world where the majority (or just ruling elites in non-democratic environments) believe that poverty arises due to lack of sufficient efforts of those who fall into poverty, there is no support for public financing of programmes redistributing resources to those in need. Also, if the poor belong mainly to ethnic or social groups seen by the majority or the ruling elite as inferior for whatever reasons, the support for redistribution and social protection is limited.

The role of external actors in shaping the policy space may also prove to be crucial. On the one hand, there are plenty of examples of international financial institutions directly recommending certain types of social protection programmes and directly discouraging government from adopting other ones. Individual donor countries also often pursue very specific policies, and signal that they are willing to fund certain types of programmes but not the others.

The international coalition of international organisations and multilateral and bilateral donors formed after the 2009 financial crisis played a very important role in broadening the policy space for social protection in many developing countries. In the end, however, it is the domestic actors – civil society included – who should play a dominating role in shaping the policy space for social protection and in the design, implementation, monitoring, and evaluation of social protection policies.

Good governance of social protection requires continuous monitoring of its performance and finance, including long-term projections and simulations of cost and benefits of different social protection programmes and of overall social protection systems. These projections and simulations should take into account demographic trends, including ageing. The economic impact of social protection in the longer term on human capital, productivity, and growth should also be included, but this is much more challenging methodologically (Gassman et al., 2012).

The static picture presented in Figure 2.1 should be converted into a more dynamic long-term approach, sketched on Figure 2.2, where investment in social protection could enhance human capital, productivity, and growth, allowing the fiscal envelope and the fiscal space to expand for further improvements of social protection coverage and adequacy.

2. Social protection floors of social protection systems: concept and issues

In 2001, the International Labour Conference prioritised taking all measures to ensure access to social security by all and initiated a global campaign for social security for all. The ILO Social Security Department, in cooperation with other multilateral organisations and some bilateral donors, undertook intensive research on new policies in developing countries, opportunities for financing basic social security in poorer countries, strategies to provide basic social security for all, and gradually built comprehensive social protection systems in accordance with the requirements of existing ILO standards.

As a consequence, the concept of basic social security guarantees ensuring minimum income security and affordable access to essential healthcare services to all in need of protection was born, regardless of their status on the labour market, as part of the wider two-dimensional development strategy of social security. The second dimension of national strategies should aim to ensure and maintain a scope and level of social security within national priorities and available resources, and in coordination with other policies addressing development objectives, which citizens will consider as appropriate and adequate.

The aim of ILO Recommendation No. 202 concerning national floors of social protection is to provide guidance to ILO member states on how to build a set of basic social security guarantees (social protection floors, or SPFs) as part of their overall social security systems and how to develop national strategies and policies aimed at achieving and maintaining this set of basic guarantees while at the same time ensuring higher levels of security to the greatest possible number of residents as soon as possible.

SPFs are defined by each country as a set of minimum social security guarantees aimed at preventing or at least alleviating poverty and social exclusion as well as reducing vulnerability to the impacts of various social and economic contingencies.

The Recommendation also introduces a catalogue of fundamental principles, which should guide the policy of social security (not only in relation to the basic guarantees). Although many of these principles had been codified by earlier ILO standards, they appear here for the first time in such a clear and full form.

Therefore, the Recommendation giving the states full responsibility for the implementation of its provisions requires adherence to, inter alia, the following principles:

1. Social security should be universal in its outreach and based on social solidarity.
2. Entitlements to individual benefits should be defined by laws and regulations.
3. Benefits should be adequate and predictable.
4. Rules for granting benefits should respect the rights and dignity of persons protected, foster social inclusion, and should not discriminate against anyone (i.e., ensure equal treatment but at the same time take into account the specific needs of different groups).

Often, the practice of introduced programmes in many countries differs from the above rules. Many are pilot programmes whose main purpose is to study their economic and social impacts more than the provision of social security, or the programmes planned for a limited period of time in which internal arrangements govern the entitlement to benefits and not the law. The rights and dignity of the actual and potential beneficiaries are often not fully respected by the applicable procedures for targeting benefits.

The Recommendation encourages ILO member states to establish the basic guarantees defined by each country as soon as possible and as a priority. They should ensure that over their life cycle, every person in need would have access to essential healthcare and basic income security. Guarantees defined at the country level should provide as a minimum

1.   availability and accessibility of essential healthcare services;
2.   minimum income security for children;
3.   minimum income security for the unemployed and those who cannot work because of sickness, disability, maternity, etc.; and
4.   minimum income security for older persons.

Paragraph 7 of the Recommendation says: 'these guarantees should be ensured at least to all the inhabitants of the country and to all children, in accordance with international commitments of the country and national law'. This provision is not quite clear and is a trade-off outcome of a difficult discussion on the extent to which immigrants of varying legal status, as well as refugees, should be covered by those basic guarantees. The phrase 'all children' expresses the intention that all the children in the area that is the responsibility of the government of a given country should be covered by the basic social security guarantees irrespective of their legal status (including, for example, children of refugees and illegal migrants).

It is recommended that the laws and regulations define the basic social security guarantees. At the same time, each country, in accordance with its preferences, circumstances, and means, should choose ways, institutions, mechanisms, and specific types of benefits through which these guarantees are implemented.

When it comes to defining the desired level of guarantees, the Recommendation leaves this to individual states. However, it requires, among other things, that the financial consequences of using necessary healthcare services do not increase the risk of poverty, and that the levels of minimum income guarantees allow a dignified life. The financing should come from national resources, but the countries without sufficient economic and fiscal capacities should in principle be able to count on international cooperation and the support of their efforts.

It is recommended that member countries regularly monitor their social security schemes, particularly in the implementation of basic guarantees. The monitoring issue is of major importance. The main obstacle is the lack of regularly collected administrative and survey data in many countries, which would allow measuring social security coverage in all its dimensions: scope of benefits and services provided, extent of access to those benefits and services, as well as levels of benefits and quality of services available. There are no internationally accepted statistical standards similar to existing ones in this area, which allow measuring unemployment or other social and economic phenomena. This lack of data made it difficult to adopt clear social protection targets as part of the new post-2015 sustainable development framework, as it is nearly impossible to define adequate indicators that could be effectively calculated for all the countries. For that reason, the ILO, World Bank, and other multilateral and bilateral partners started intense collaboration aimed at improving the available statistical information as well as developing sets of indicators within the framework of the newly established Social Protection Interagency Collaboration Board. This would help countries measure their progress in extending social protection coverage and its effectiveness.

3. International statistical approaches to measure current and past costs and coverage of social protection systems

The 1957 'Resolution concerning the development of social security statistics' adopted during the Ninth International Conference of Labour Statisticians gives detailed guidelines on the social security system data and information that should be made available from both administrative and survey sources. While European and some non-European OECD (Organisation for Economic Co-operation and Development) countries seem to meet the requirements of this Resolution, in most countries, information on their overall social protection/security system is not collected by national statistics organisations or any other institution. This means that in many instances, consolidated social protection data is not available and, where it is available, is unlikely to be consistent with data from other countries, rendering any cross-country analysis or comparability problematic.

Information is available only from institutions implementing the various social protection programmes and, in many cases, some of the crucial information is not extracted from the records and accounts on a regular basis or may not be available at all (such as disaggregated data by sex and age, administration cost, and others). Moreover, many household surveys do not include regular modules on social protection programmes, which would make it possible to estimate coverage and effects of social protection systems in the income distribution of the countries. In order to address this deficit, various international agencies use a range of different and, in some cases, parallel approaches to collect, synthesise, and analyse social protection provision and expenditure.

A similar challenge refers to the scope of nationally and internationally collected statistics on social protection policies/programmes. It is difficult to gather consistent information that can be used in comparative analyses for indicators such as the total population covered by the different programmes and their main demographic and socio-economic characteristics, the level of benefits and quality of services provided, the benefit costs and costs of administration, sources of financing, the contribution the programmes make to household incomes, and estimates of how they affect the income distribution by changing (or not changing) poverty and inequality indicators.

Social protection/security programmes in any country are usually provided through a large number of different programmes of varying sizes and administered by different government agencies, non-governmental organisations, and private sector entities. The availability of standardised information regarding key policy characteristics of these different programmes, such as their costs, financing sources, number of people directly and indirectly covered, levels, frequency, and quality of the provision offered requires that these institutions keep records of programme activities, inputs, outputs, and outcomes according to standardised guidelines.

Assessing the coverage, gaps, and impacts of social protection/security programmes and their overall system requires, in addition to information from administrative sources, information collected through household surveys (e.g., income and expenditure/household budget surveys and labour force surveys) including questions on the coverage of contributory and non-contributory programmes, information on recipients of specific existing benefits and programmes, the nature of the benefits, periodicity, and amounts/values of benefits.

The United Nations (UN) has adopted the Classification of the Functions of Governments (COFOG), which breaks down government expenditures according to their purpose independently from the nature of the administrative unit in charge of this expenditure. 'Social Protection' is one of the functions used in COFOG. Under COFOG, the term is used to cover the following sub-functions: 'sickness and disability', 'old age', 'survivors', 'family and children', 'unemployment', 'housing', 'social exclusion not elsewhere classified', and some other related categories. Healthcare is a separate function and not included under 'social protection'.

The ILO, OECD, European Union, and the International Monetary Fund (IMF) adopt social protection definitions and programme classifications in their expenditure/financing international databases that are informed by COFOG's general classification, but with some important variations. It is also worth mentioning country-specific methodologies that have been used to measure social protection/security expenditures and financing in comprehensive ways (e.g., Japan and Germany).

The System of National Accounts (SNA) recommends the use of COFOG to analyse government finances (European Communities et al., 2009). Under the SNA, social protection benefits are recorded in the secondary distribution of income accounts and categorised as 'social benefits', and defined as 'current transfers received by households intended to provide for the needs that arise from certain events or circumstances, for example, sickness, unemployment, retirement, housing, education or family circumstances', and are provided 'under social insurance schemes or by social assistance'.

While the international community has developed a methodology to measure overall expenditure and financing sources for healthcare in the form of national health accounts that can be seen as an SNA satellite account, no similar attempt has been made in the case of non-health-related social protection expenditures.

Some international organisations – Asian Development Bank (ADB), Eurostat, ILO, OECD, United Nations Children's Fund (UNICEF), Economic Commission for Latin America and the Caribbean (ECLAC), and the World Bank – try to measure the coverage of social protection programmes across a range of dimensions (e.g., functional scope, extent and depth, level, and quality) and collect data on direct and indirect beneficiaries using, in some cases, surveys designed to identify coverage and impact of some specific programmes. However, there is no standardised approach nor commonly accepted guidelines with respect to the use of administrative data or household surveys for that purpose. Rather large time lags exhibited in such studies also limit their use for policy purposes.

The impact of social protection benefits on household/family incomes can potentially be measured through household income and expenditure surveys for different types of households and, at a macro level, through the national accounts framework with respect to measuring the aggregate size of the secondary distribution of income, if the coverage of provision is sufficiently wide, which is not the case in many low-income countries. However, the current SNA framework does not allow the estimation of the impact of specific benefits, as the classification of benefits is too broad.

Similarly, existing recommendations for household surveys do not specifically require collecting data on benefits received from specific social programmes and introduce a rather broad classification of income sources to be covered. The resolution concerning household income and expenditure statistics adopted by the 17th International Conference of Labour Statisticians (2003) categorises incomes from transfers into five categories. A similar classification is adopted in the Canberra Group Handbook on Household Income Statistics (second edition, 2011) prepared by an international task force operating under the auspices of the Conference of European Statisticians and sponsored by the United Nations Economic Commission for Europe (UNECE). It is based on previous work done by experts in household income statistics from national statistical offices, government departments, and research agencies from Europe, North and South America, Asia, Australia, and New Zealand. The Handbook also includes an inventory of practices in measuring household income in different countries.

Previous experience has demonstrated that compiling consistent and detailed data on social protection programming can be done, but isolated efforts do not produce sustainable global coverage. The ongoing, regularly updated (this is part of the challenge), and well-established databases (even if regional) are the European Union's Eurostat ESSPROS (European Integrated System of Social Protection Statistics), OECD Social Expenditure Database (SOCX), IMF Government Finance Statistics (GFS), ILO Social Security Inquiry (SSI), and ADB Social Protection Index (SPI) databases.

The ILO SSI is an online database that includes data on social protection expenditure and financing. Its coverage comes mainly from administrative records and it has reached a stage of completeness that enables global and regional estimates. It also contains qualitative statutory information available from the International Social Security Association (ISSA) on institutional parameters and coverage and other sources. At the same time, the World Bank also monitors pension systems, partly relying on ISSA and ILO data and partly adding to it differently defined indicators. Help Age is producing a full comprehensive inventory of social pensions.

The ASPIRE database of the World Bank in its current form relies mainly on household-level data from more than 100 countries on access to social protection programmes to produce coverage indicators. In addition, for most of these countries, it also provides certain context information on country demographic, labour market, and social context. It further provides information on public expenditure on – mainly – social assistance programmes (as percentage of GDP). At the same time, the social protection platform developed by the ILO lists a number of household surveys and detailed descriptions of their social protection modules. Under the auspices of its SPI work, ADB has developed a large and comprehensive SPI database on social protection programming in 35 countries in Asia and the Pacific that includes coverage, expenditure, and estimates regarding poverty, and gender dimensions of social protection provision. For Latin America and the Caribbean, and a subset of programmes (conditional cash transfers and social pensions), the Economic Commission for Latin America and Caribbean (CEPAL)/ECLAC, with the help of the United Nations Development Programme (UNDP), is maintaining an up-to-date compendium of administrative data (beneficiaries, benefit levels, budgets). Finally, the Eurostat ESSPROS and OECD SOCX databases on social protection have greatly harmonised data among all member countries. The OECD SOCX, like Eurostat ESSPROS, provides quantitative data on social protection expenditure (SOCX and ESSPROS), revenue (ESSPROS), and limited information on the number of beneficiaries (ESSPROS on pensioners).

There are important lessons to be learned. Evidently, all these data could be used complementarily and eventually provide a non-contradictory view of social protection in the world.

A clear distinction should be made between qualitative and quantitative data sets, and survey-based data. Qualitative data includes descriptions/qualifications of schemes and benefits, which have to be systematised at some point using a set of agreed criteria (important work has already been done in this area by Eurostat, OECD, and ILO – being rather similar or with bridges from one to the other). Quantitative data reports the statutory extent of coverage and effective implementation of social protection provision (assessed through expenditure, coverage, level of benefit, financing, and impact indicators). This is an area with considerable gaps and duplication. Currently, collected data also includes survey data on impacts, which exist as isolated and limited research projects.

4. Sound financial governance of social protection requires forward-looking projections and simulations

> Persons in different generations have duties and obligations to one another just as contemporaries do. The present generations cannot do as it pleases but is bound by the principles that would be chosen in the original position to define justice between persons at different moments of time.
>
> (Rawls, 1999, p. 258)

Forecasts . . . are notoriously unreliable. In fact, they almost always are wrong. . . . Nonetheless, . . . without forecasts, we would be totally at sea. That we have to use forecasts or projections that we know will be wrong, and that usually are wrong raises some difficult questions for policy analysts and policy-making.

(Aaron, 2000, p. 193)

Decision-making is about the future. Making decisions about social protection systems today requires making more or less well-informed 'good guesses' about alternative future developments under different policy scenarios. For example, in responding to concerns that pension entitlements might be a burden for future generations, reliable forecasts are needed if one wants to rebalance social and economic policies early, if necessary.

Article 71 of ILO Convention No. 102 on Minimum Standards in Social Security requires that:

The Member shall accept general responsibility for the due provision of the benefits provided in compliance with this Convention, and shall take all measures required for this purpose; it shall ensure, where appropriate, that the necessary actuarial studies and calculations concerning financial equilibrium are made periodically and, in any event, prior to any change in benefits, the rate of insurance contributions, or the taxes allocated to covering the contingencies in question.

Income Security Recommendation 1944 (No. 67) specifies that contribution rates to social insurance schemes should not exceed the rate necessary to ensure what we can call 'collective financial equivalence'; that is, the rate which would yield contribution income from all the insured persons such that its expected present value would be equal to the expected present value of the benefits due in the future to all those insured and their dependants.

However, Recommendation No. 67 also advises that 'the rates of contribution of insured persons and employers should be kept as stable as possible, and for this purpose, a stabilisation fund should be constituted'.

One should note here that although the relative stability of the contribution rates is seen as an important objective, in the end the contribution rate is the variable which should be adjusted so that the present value of the future revenue stream matches the present value of the expenditure necessary to provide benefits at desired adequate levels, levels which at least meet the ILO minimum standards. Sustainability and adequacy of benefits are closely linked. Inadequate benefits will not find enough contributors and taxpayers willing to finance them, and sooner or later the scheme or system will become unsustainable. On the other hand, when generous benefit promises are not matched with sufficient and sustainable financing, these promises will not be actually delivered.

The ILO has for decades stressed that it is important to look at the future finances and balances of the overall social protection system as its components – social protection schemes – are closely interlinked. One of the earliest examples of such comprehensive approach is the reform proposal prepared for the United Kingdom by Lord Beveridge close to the end of World War II. The proposal, presented in the famous 'Beveridge Report', was accompanied by detailed long-term projections of social security expenditure for the period 1945–1965. This good practice is successfully continued by many countries. The European Commission, in cooperation with all the member countries of the European Union, prepares long-term (recently until 2060) projections of all age-related social protection expenditure every three years (Directorate-General for Economic and Financial Affairs of the European Commission, 2014 and 2015).

Projecting the future development of social protection finances requires models that allow projecting future streams of revenues and expenditures with a reasonable degree of reliability. Good models should have high explanatory power in forecasting social expenditure and revenue. They do not only provide insights into the possible future development of social protection finances, but also establish scenarios with different assumptions concerning socio-demographic and economic conditions, and assess the effects of different policies under these circumstances.

Policy decisions taken today obviously have an impact on future generations also. For example, decisions concerning the design and financing of the pension systems and all other fiscal decisions may impact future generations if they involve borrowing.

The intergenerational impact of today's policies has attracted the special attention of researchers and policymakers over the last few decades, particularly in the

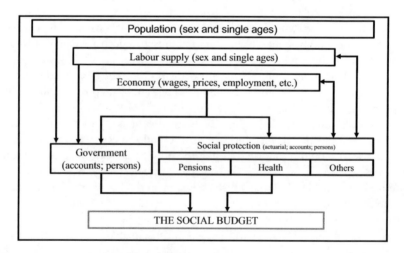

Figure 2.3 Structure of the social budget model

Source: based on Scholz et al., 2000

context of analysing future pension and healthcare expenditures in ageing societies. One of the main concerns was (and is) how to incorporate the long-term liabilities of the government (and thus societies) in government accounting frameworks so that the government's balance sheets, net worth, debt estimates, and other indicators of fiscal sustainability reflect the size of these liabilities. Laurence Kotlikoff (Kotlikoff, 1999) developed the concept of intergenerational accounting, proposing comparisons of estimates of 'net burden' (taxes minus benefits) on currently living and unborn generations. It is an interesting concept and methodology, and many researchers now estimate 'generational accounts' for their countries. However, as the author of the concept believes, social security is an 'immoral Ponzi scheme' (Kotlikoff, 2014); behind a methodological concept are also clear policy intentions to enhance the move away from the public Pay As You Go (PAYG) financed schemes to fully funded and possibly privately managed ones.

A similar intention of 'scaring the public' away from the PAYG pensions was the concept of implicit pension debt introduced and popularised by the World Bank. The main problem with this concept is not the intention to show long-term pension liabilities but how it is being done. Instead of calculating net liabilities as the result of the difference between the present values of the future stream of social security benefits and contributions, implicit pension debts are usually calculated simply as the present value of future projected benefit payments (thus abstracting from the fact that governments and social security schemes run by them are equally committed to pay legislated benefits to entitled beneficiaries as well as collect similarly legislated contributions from those who are obliged to contribute). 'Net' liabilities, however, do not seem to give big enough figures to mobilise the media and scare the public.

At the same time, however, we can see the process of changing accounting standards to incorporate long-term, 'implicit' liabilities. Since 2001, new international accounting standards for corporations, the International Financial Reporting Standards, require corporations to actuarially assess liabilities of benefit schemes provided by employers. The 2001 and 2014 revisions of the IMF Government Finance Statistics (GFS) methodology similarly require the government to estimate such a liability resulting from the pension scheme for government employees and include it in the government balance sheet. The same approach was followed by the 2008 revision of the SNA. With respect to social security liabilities, both the IMF GFS 2001 and the SNA 2008 recommend estimating long-term liability with respect to social security schemes only as memorandum items and not as part of the core accounts.

5. ILO social budgeting methodology and its implementation to assess the sustainability and affordability of the social protection floor

Traditionally, and in many countries still, actuarial projections of social protection revenue and expenditure were made mainly for individual social protection schemes or a group of closely related schemes administered by a single institution.

Annual actuarial reports on US old-age, disability, and survivor's schemes are good practice examples, as these projections also include public components of the US healthcare system – Medicare and Medicaid. The social budgeting approach, which establishes income and expenditure accounts for all existing social protection schemes in the country and then projects those accounts into the future using actuarial methods, started to be developed by the Social Security Department of the ILO in the mid-1990s. The first countries where such social budgets were estimated and projections and simulation models were developed were the countries in central and Eastern Europe undertaking difficult transitions from centrally planned economies to market economies, and which thus needed to restructure accordingly. These included Ukraine, Slovakia, Bulgaria, and Poland.

The experiences in these countries and the ILO Financial and Actuarial Service, and the knowledge developed by actuarial practices in Canada, Germany, US, and United Kingdom (Plamondon et al., 2002) allowed the development of a consistent methodological approach (Scholz et al., 2000). At the same time, it became obvious that the social budgeting approach requires building in each country a full knowledge of all the components of its social protection system (inventory of social protection schemes); a system of comprehensive social protection statistics allowing one to monitor both social protection expenditure and revenue as well as all dimensions of coverage (scope, extent, and level/quality of coverage); and a set of indicators allowing regular monitoring and evaluation.

Another tool was developed to inherently assist social budgeting – the so-called Social Protection Expenditure and Performance Reviews. This methodology was first described in Chapter 6 of another methodological compendium published soon afterwards (Cichon et al., 2004).

The ILO social budget models are all composed of several building blocks (Scholz et al., 2000) which include 1. a demographic module providing population projections by age and sex; 2. a labour market module providing projections of labour force by age and sex; 3. a macroeconomic module usually providing a consistent set of assumptions and a number of alternative scenarios with respect to future trends in the gross domestic product (GDP), productivity, employment, unemployment, wages and other incomes, prices, and interest rates; 4. social protection modules which are actuarial projection models for each of the existing social protection schemes in the country; and 5. a public finance/fiscal module linking the social budget to the public finance framework and the expected future fiscal envelope.

Applications for social protection expenditure and performance review social budgeting later spread to other continents – Latin America (i.e., Chile, Uruguay); Africa (i.e., South Africa, Namibia, Zambia, Tanzania); and Asia (i.e., Cambodia) (ILO, 2012). Full-fledged social budgeting exercises are, however, very demanding in terms of data requirements, and it takes a relatively long time to implement. In the ILO and other quarters of the global social policy debate, discussions started on the need to radically expand social protection coverage to the developing countries of the south – stimulated by important developments in social protection policies in middle-income countries such as Brazil, China, India, or South Africa. Major donor countries such as the United Kingdom, Germany,

France, and a number of Scandinavian countries requested from the international community studies that would assess the cost, impact, and affordability of building social protection systems in other middle-income and low-income countries.

The newly established UNDP International Poverty Centre in Brasilia published studies assessing the cost and poverty impact of the potential implementation of social pensions and conditional cash transfers in Africa, written by its then-director, Nanak Kakwani (Kakwani and Kalanidhi, 2005; Kakwani, et al., 2005). These two papers were far from enthusiastic regarding their assessment of the affordability of social protection in Sub-Saharan Africa. The first one was very critical towards the idea of universal pension, showing that its potential impact on overall poverty incidence and gap is rather small (taking into account the small share of the elderly in the total population). The second paper showed that the poverty impact of targeted conditional cash transfers would be much higher, but under the unrealistic assumption of perfect targeting. Both papers started with an assumption that the maximum amount that low-income countries in Africa can afford to invest in social protection is equivalent to 0.5 percent of their GDP and then, using household survey data sets and static micro simulation techniques, estimated the impact of the different benefit designs on poverty incidence and poverty gap. The static character of the micro-simulation technique adopted did not allow for any projection of future trends in the cost of analysed schemes.

At the same time, ILO studied what the cost would be of a predefined package of basic social protection schemes in selected middle- and low-income countries in Africa and Asia (Pal et al., 2005; Mizunoya et al., 2006). These two papers looked at the current and future costs of the hypothetical benefit package, composed of universal pension of 30 percent of GDP per capita, universal child benefit of 15 percent of GDP per capita, income support programme targeted to the poorest 10 percent of the population, as well as the cost of universal basic healthcare.

The estimates did not take into account the costs of social protection programmes that already exist in the countries analysed, which led to overestimation of costs, particularly with respect to the parts pertaining to healthcare. The purpose of the exercise was, however, to feed more concrete numbers into the evolving global debate on affordability of social protection in low-income countries and to show to the potential donors how much the countries can potentially afford themselves in the shorter and longer run, and thus allow estimates of the size of donor involvement necessary.

Providing policy advice to the countries was *not* the objective of these studies, as it was obvious to all those involved that policy advice can only be developed in a dialogue with the main stakeholders in the country and can be based only on full-fledged social budgeting and actuarial studies done in the countries themselves, combined with micro-simulation studies allowing assessment of potential poverty reduction impacts.

The revised version summarising both studies (ILO, 2008) modified slightly the benefit package assumed (limiting the child benefit to two children in the family), and modified the assumptions used in estimating the health costs.

The changes reduced the estimated figures in the case of some countries but it was obvious that in many countries, such a basic social protection package (called Social Protection Floor [SPF] later) can only be introduced gradually, and that there is a need for temporary external support to start the process.

Further modelling works were done on social budgeting in the parallel streams. The mainstream consisted as usual of full-fledged actuarial studies made upon the request of the country and associated with national policy debates in the country. At the same time, the methodology for the so-called Rapid Assessment Protocols was developed and implemented in a number of countries (see, for example, the study on Vietnam in Cichon et al., 2012, and on Mozambique in Cunha, et al., 2013, but the approach is being implemented also in Thailand, Indonesia, Benin, Nepal, Jordan, Burundi, and Cameroon). A Mozambique study was done jointly with the IMF, where the ILO focused on actuarial projections while the IMF developed a part projecting the future fiscal envelope and fiscal space.

Rapid Assessment Protocols modelling methodology involves abbreviated social budgeting and actuarial techniques, which allows a shorter time to build a projection and simulation model without compromising the quality of the results. There also exists an enhanced version of the methodology, which looks at the impacts of social protection on income distribution and poverty. However, while it serves as a support to well-informed national policy debates, actual decisions concerning policy design and funding should be based on more detailed social budgeting and actuarial and micro-simulation studies.

The Rapid Assessment Protocols modelling methodology, particularly in Asia, was linked strongly to the national policy debates through the approach called 'Social protection assessment-based national dialogue' (Schmitt and De, 2013; Schmitt and Chadwick, 2014). The number of country studies in this volume refers to the results of the studies undertaken within this type of approach with the support of the ILO.

There were also requests from some bilateral donors (mainly the United Kingdom and Germany) to convert the model used by the ILO for cross-country studies into a user-friendly tool that would allow the user to make quick estimates of the consequences of different policy options. The Social Protection Floor Costing Tool, based on the original 2008 ILO model, was then developed, but it was adequate mostly for education/advocacy purposes, as social protection systems are so different in various countries that adequate models can only be tailor-made. However, the tool was further developed by UNICEF and was recommended for use by UNICEF field offices in a number of countries.

The Social Protection Floor Costing Tool, developed in 2011, allows users to quickly estimate the cost of different social protection measures over a 20-year period. Users can estimate the costs for the following cash transfers: old-age pensions, child benefits, disability benefits, orphan benefits, education stipends, birth lump sum benefits, youth labour market programmes, and unemployment programmes. It is accompanied by a step-by-step manual and an explanatory note, and is available for free download.

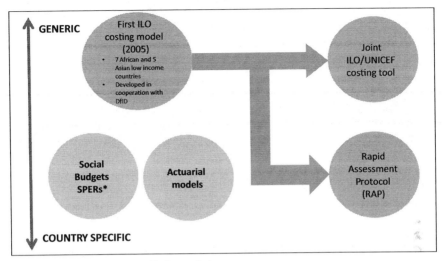

SPER = Social Protection Expenditure and Performance Review.
ILO = International Labour Organization.
UNICEF = United Nations Children's Fund.

Figure 2.4 Generic and country-specific quantitative projection tools developed by the ILO

Notes: SPER = Social Protection Expenditure and Performance Review
ILO = International Labour Organization
UNICEF = United Nations Children's Fund
Source: www.socialprotectionfloor-gateway.org/files/costing_tools_Behrendt.ppt

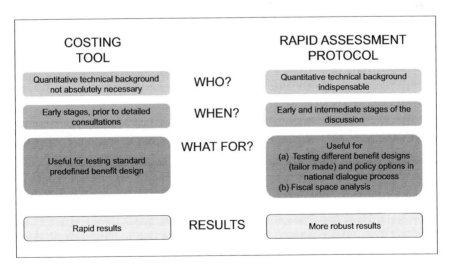

Figure 2.5 Generic vs. country-specific modelling approaches
Source: www.socialprotectionfloor-gateway.org/files/costing_tools_Behrendt.ppt

The different quantitative financial governance tools developed by the ILO, which can be used to support global and national policy debates, are presented in Figure 2.4. Figure 2.5 compares the applicability of generic versus tailor-made, country-specific models.

Concluding, one needs to draw to the attention of the reader that methodological effort described above, aimed at assessing resources needed in different countries to complete their floors of social protection systems. One of the recent examples is the publication by a group of researchers from Maastricht University, led by Michael Cichon (see Bierbaum et al., 2016), former director of the ILO Social Security Department. Methodology proposed estimates – for more than one hundred countries – for the resource gap (expressed as percentage of GDP), which needs to be filled to secure to the population of different countries basic income security and basic security in access to healthcare services. The next step after such estimates will be studies, like the country cases analysed in this volume, which will indicate country-specific ways to create fiscal space necessary to fill the gap – within country-specific policy space for social protection for expanding the available fiscal envelope. The recently published ILO study (Ortiz et al., 2015) discusses various alternative ways of expanding the available fiscal envelope, but the actual feasibility of these different options differs from country to country. Further country studies assessing both resource gap and sources of its financing in the longer time horizon are urgently needed, as achieving sustainable development goals until 2030 requires also important investments in social protection.

Note

1 For an alternative perspective, see Asher's Framework for Generating Fiscal Space in this volume.

References

Aaron, H. (2000). Seeing Through the Fog: Policy Making With Uncertain Forecasts. *Journal of Policy Analysis and Management*, 19(2), 193, quoted after Peter S. Heller, Who Will Pay? IMF, Washington 2003, p. 7.

Bierbaum, M., A. Oppel, S. Tromp, and M. Cichon. (2016). *A Social Protection Floor Index: Monitoring National Social Protection Policy Implementation*, Discussion Paper, Friedrich Ebert Stiftung, Belin. Available at http://library.fes.de/pdf-files/iez/12490.pdf

Cichon, M., F. Bonnet, V. Schmitt, C. Galian, and G. Mazeikaite. (2012). *Analysis of the Viet Nam National Social Protection Strategy (2011–2020) in the Context of Social Protection Floors Objectives. A Rapid Assessment*. Extension of Social Security Series Paper, No. 32. Available at www.ilo.org/gimi/gess/RessShowRessource. do?ressourceId=30497

Cichon, M., W. Scholz, A. van de Meerendonk, K. Hagemejer, F. Bertranou, and P. Plamandon. (2004). *Financing Social Protection*, Geneva, ILO/ISSA. Available at: www.ilo.org/gimi/gess/RessShowRessource.do?ressourceId=8030

Cunha, N., L. Pellerano, J. Mueller, V. Lledo, Y. Xiao, and P. Gitton. (2013). *Towards a Mozambican Social Protection Floor. Consolidating a Comprehensive Social*

Protection System in Mozambique: Analysis Of Policy Alternatives and Costs, Extension of Social Security Series ESS Paper, No. 41. Available at: www.ilo.org/gimi/gess/RessourcePDF.action?ressource.ressourceId=42120

Directorate-General for Economic and Financial Affairs of the European Commission (2014). The 2015 Ageing Report: Underlying Assumptions and Projection Methodologies. *European Economy*, 8|2014. Available at: http://ec.europa.eu/economy_finance/publications/european_economy/2014/ee8_en.htm

Directorate-General for Economic and Financial Affairs of the European Commission (2015). The 2015 Ageing Report: Economic and Budgetary Projections For the 28 EU Member States (2013–2060). *European Economy*, 3. Available at: http://ec.europa.eu/economy_finance/publications/european_economy/2015/ee3_en.htm

European Communities, International Monetary Fund, Organisation for Economic Co-operation and Development, United Nations and World Bank (2009). *System of National Accounts 2008*, Chapters: 2, 4, 7, 8, 13, 17 (part 2), 22, Annex 2, New York. Available at: http://unstats.un.org/unsd/nationalaccount/sna2008.asp

Eurostat (2012). *ESSPROSS Manual*, edition, Statistical Office of the European Communities, Brussels: Luxembourg. Available at: www.bmask.gv.at/cms/site/attachments/2/6/6/CH2292/CMS1314870050196/esspros_manual_and_user_guidelines.pdf

Gassman, F., A. Mideros, and P. Mohnen. (2012). Estimation of Rates of Return of Social Protection Instruments in Cambodia: A Case for Non-Contributory Social Transfers. *Maastricht*. Available at: http://mgsog.merit.unu.edu/publications/external_policy_reports/2012_rates_return_combodia.pdf

International Conference of Labour Statisticians (2003). *Final Report of the 17th International Conference of Labour Statisticians*. Available at: www.ilo.org/global/statistics-and-databases/meetings-and-events/international-conference-of-labour-statisticians/WCMS_087565/lang – en/index.htm?ssSourceSiteId=ifpdial

International Labour Conference (2012). Provisional Record No. 14; 101th Session, Geneva, June 2012, Fourth Item on the Agenda: Elaboration of an Autonomous Recommendation on the Social Protection Floor. *Report of the Committee On the Social Protection Floor*, Geneva: ILO. Available at: www.ilo.org/ilc/ILCSessions/101stSession/reports/provisional-records/WCMS_182950/lang – en/index.htm

International Labour Office (2008). *Can Low-Income Countries Afford Basic Social Security?* International Labour Office, Social Security Department Policy Briefings Paper, No. 3. Available at: www.ilo.org/gimi/gess/RessShowRessource.do?ressourceId=5951

International Labour Organization (2012). *Recommendation No. 202 Concerning National Floors of Social Protection*. Available at: www.ilo.org/dyn/normlex/

Kakwani, N., and S. Kalanidhi. (2005). *Ageing and Poverty in Africa and the Role of Social Pensions*. UNDP International Poverty Centre, Brasilia, Working Paper No. 8.

Kakwani, N., F. Veras Soares, and H. Son. (2005). *Conditional Cash Transfers in African Countries*, UNDP International Poverty Centre, Brasilia, Working Paper No. 9.

Kotlikof, L. (1999). From Deficit Delusion to the Fiscal Balance Rule: Looking For an Economically Meaningful Way to Assess Fiscal Policy, in A. Auearbach, L. Kotlikoff, and W. Leibfritz (eds.) *Generational Accounting Around the World*. Chicago: University of Chicago Press, pp. 9–30.

Kotlikoff, L. (2014). America's Ponzi Scheme: Why Social Security Needs to Retire. *PBS Newshour*. Available at: www.pbs.org/newshour/making-sense/americas-ponzi-scheme-why-social-security-needs-to-retire/

Mizunoya, S., C. Behrendt, K. Pal, and F. Léger. (2006). *Costing of Basic Social Protection Benefits for Selected Asian Countries. First results of a Modelling Exercise.* Issues in Social Protection Series Discussion Paper No. 17, International Labour Office, Social Security Department.

Ortiz, I. et al. (2015). *Fiscal Space for Social Protection: Options to Expand Social Investments in 187 Countries.* ESS Paper no 48 Available at www.social-protection.org/gimi/gess/RessourcePDF.action?ressource.ressourceId=51537

Pal, K., C. Behrendt, F. Leger, M. Cichon, and K. Hagemejer. (2005). *Can Low Income Countries Afford Basic Social Protection? First Results of a Modelling Exercise* Issues in Social Protection Series Discussion Paper No. 13, International Labour Office, Social Security Department.

Plamondon, P., A. Drouin, G. Binet, M. Cichon, W. McGillivray, M. Bédard, and H. Perez Montas. (2002). *Actuarial Practice in Social Security.* Geneva: ILO/ISSA. Available at: www.ilo.org/gimi/gess/RessShowRessource.do?ressourceId=776

Rawls, J. (1999). *A Theory of Justice.* Revised Edition. Oxford: Oxford University Press.

Schmitt, V., and R. Chadwick. (2014). Social Protection Assessment Based National Dialogue Exercises: Cambodia, Indonesia, Thailand, Viet Nam. *International Social Security Review*, 67(1), 95–119.

Schmitt, V., and L. De. (2013). *Social Protection Assessment Based National Dialogue. A Good Practices Guide. Processes and Tools Developed in East and South-East Asia From 2011 to 2013.* ILO Decent Work Technical Support Team for East and South-East Asia and the Pacific, International Labour Office, Social Protection.

Scholz, W., M. Cichon, and K. Hagemejer. (2000). *Social Budgeting.* Geneva: ILO/ISSA. Available at: www.ilo.org/gimi/gess/RessShowRessource.do?ressourceId=8022

World Bank Aspire Database. Available at: http://datatopics.worldbank.org/aspire/ (accessed January 2016).

3 Social protection programs in China

An assessment

Jin Feng

1. Introduction

Social protection as a policy priority has historically lagged behind economic growth in China. During the initial phase of economic reform in the 1980s, social security programs were only made available for a small group of employees, which consisted of urban employees who worked in state-owned enterprises. The development priority at that time was economic growth, and average annual real GDP growth reached 9.6 percent during the period of more than 20 years from 1978 to 2001. In that era of very rapid economic growth, the poverty rate in China decreased sharply. According to the World Bank's criteria, from 1981–2004, the population under poverty in China decreased from 652 million to 135 million. However, income inequality continued to rise after the mid-1990s. The Gini coefficient for income, which measures inequality (ranging between 0 and 1, with lower figure signifying less inequality), reaches 0.37 in 1997 and went up to 0.48 in 2003, and was 0.47 in 2012. Policy makers have increasingly come to recognise the importance of a soundly developed social policy framework for a sustainable economy and an equitable society. In 2004, a strategy seeking to create a "harmonious society" was established.

The new strategy seeks to strike and maintain a balance between economic growth and social development. Social protection is now widely considered as both a social and an economic imperative. The comprehensive social protection system aims to ensure that elderly citizens have basic income security, the ill receive medical care, children enroll in school, workers are paid, families have places to live, and the poor receive assistance. Correspondingly, China has established a social protection system, consisting of social insurance programs, social assistance programs, and labor market policies (Figure 3.1). As China achieves progress in these areas, progress towards several Sustainable Development Goals (SDGs) adopted by the United Nations in September 2015, will also be realised. The Chinese government has continuously and significantly increased its budget allocation to social protection. The percentage of GDP dedicated to social protection expenditures (not including social insurance, education and housing) has increased from less than 2 percent in 2004 to 2.37 percent in 2012 (China fiscal statistics yearbook, 2013).[1] In addition, social insurance expenditures, which are

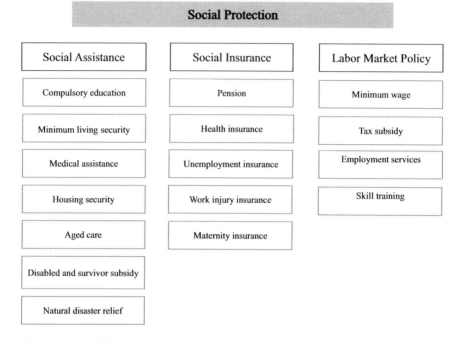

Figure 3.1 A schematic presentation of the social protection system in China
Source: the author

managed separately as social insurance funds, increased from 2.96 percent of GDP in 2007 to 4.76 percent in 2013. According to Asian Development Bank, the social protection index of China was 0.139 in 2009, ranking the twelfth in Asia that year (ADB, 2013). China is among the 62 countries that have achieved the first Millennium Development Goal (MDG), namely halving extreme poverty rates by 2015, and almost met 7 other goals (United Nations, 2014).

An ageing population, however, constitutes one of the major challenges for the development of the Chinese social protection system. The elderly are more economically dependent and socially vulnerable, particularly in health status, so a rapidly aging society calls for more resources to be allocated to social protection. In 1990, the share of the Chinese population aged 65 and above increased from 5.9 percent to 8.2 percent in 2010 (Table 3.1). It will reach 16.5 percent by 2030.[2]

Economic downturn represents another challenge. In 2014, China's GDP grew 7.4 percent, the slowest rate of increase since 1990 (Table 3.1). Though still well above the global average of 3.3 percent, this rate constitutes a significant change from when the Chinese economy regularly produced double-digit growth. At the same time, fiscal revenue grew 8.6 percent to 14.035 trillion yuan (US $2.2 trillion) in 2014. This was the slowest rate of growth since 1991. With

Table 3.1 Select GDP and demographic indicators of China

	1990	1995	2000	2005	2010	2014
GDP per capita (yuan)	1,644	5,046	7,858	14,185	30,015	46,531
GDP growth (%)	3.9	11.0	8.4	11.3	10.6	7.4
Population (million)	1,143	1,211	1,267	1,308	1,341	1,368
Share of 65 and over (%)	5.9	6.4	7.0	7.6	8.2	9.0
# of labor (million)	647	681	721	746	761	773
Urban/rural income ratio	2.20	2.71	2.79	3.22	3.23	3.03

Sources: *China Statistic Yearbooks*

declining growth, long-term government commitment to the social protection system requires reform to become more efficient and effective.

The main contents of the chapter are arranged as follows. Section 2 provides an overview of the social protection system in China from a life-cycle perspective. Section 3 assesses some crucial programs to create a social protection floor, including minimum living security, resident pension, and resident health care. Section 4 discusses future fiscal space as a factor in developing social protection in China. Section 5 concludes the chapter.

2. Social protection system in China: an overview

In the past decade, China has witnessed remarkable progress in its expansion of social protection. The expansion has occurred not only within the urban formal sector but also within the informal sector in both urban and rural areas, a large proportion of which includes poor and low-income families (ILO, 2010; ADB, 2010). Following the World Protection Report 2014/2015 (ILO, 2014), I utilise a life-cycle approach, presenting social protection programs in China for children, working-age people, and elderly people. Table 3.2 summarises all kinds of social protection programs covering risks over a life cycle.

2.1 Compulsory education

In 1986, China issued its compulsory education law. The law aimed to extend universal nine-year compulsory education among the school-aged population and literacy among citizens younger than 20 years old. Many experts have agreed that promoting education represents an approach to alleviate poverty. Ministry of Education (MOE) has formulated a series of policies and organised a number of projects that have been implemented to support and ensure the equal rights to education of many needy groups: children living in poor rural areas, ethnic minority children, disadvantaged girls, disabled children, and rural-urban migrant children. The areas of intervention include the supply of school buildings, the training of teachers and principals, the distribution of free textbooks, and the provision of stipends for students from poor households.

Table 3.2 A summary of social protection programs over lifecycle in China (as of 2016)

Programs	Target groups	Benefits	Financing	Administration
Compulsory education	Children/families Children of 6–15	Extending universal nine-year compulsory education among the school-aged population	Central, provincial and local government budget	Ministry of Education and local branches
Minimum living security (MLSS)				
Urban	Urban household income p.c. below local MLSS level	Cash transfer	Central, provincial and local government budget	Local branch of Ministry of Civil Affairs (MoCA)
Rural	Rural household income p.c. below local MLSS level	Cash transfer		
Social insurance	Working age population in urban sectors			
Basic old age insurance (BOAI)	Urban employees and retirees	Pension after retirement age: male 60, female 50/55	Employer and employee jointly	Under supervision of Ministry of Human Resources and Social Security (MoHRSS)
Basic Medical Insurance (BMI)		Covering part of health care		Managed by local branch
Unemployment		A benefit lasts at most 2 years		
Work injury		Covering medical cost		
Maternity		Covering medical cost and salary during maternity leave		
Labour market policy				
Employment support	Urban employer and employee	Tax subsidy; public training, etc	–	Local branch of MoHRSS
Minimum wage policy	Urban employee Old people	–		

Public pension				
BOAI	Urban retirees	Pension: average replacement rate 59%	Employer and employee jointly	Under supervision of MoHRSS Managed by local branch
Resident pension: Urban	Urban non-employed	Pension benefit after age 60	Individual contribution +central and local government subsidy	Local branch of MoHRSS
Resident pension: Rural	Rural residents	Pension benefit after age 60		
Aged care				
Elder care subsidy	Disabled, or "Three No" elderly Health care for all	Cash subsidy or government procured services	Local government budget	Local branch of MoCA
Health insurance				
Health care (BMI)	Urban employees	Covering part of health care	Employer and employee	Local branch of MoHRSS
Urban (URBMI)	Urban non-employed residents	Covering part of health care	Individual contribution +central and local government subsidy	Local branch of MoHRSS
Rural (NCMS)	Rural residents	Covering part of health care		Local branch of MoH
Medical assistance				
Urban	MLSS beneficiaries; per capita income above MLSS level, but below local minimum wage; or with catastrophic illness	Subsidy for health care	Central, provincial and local government budget	Local branch of MoCA
Rural	MLSS beneficiaries; or with catastrophic illness Housing security			
Housing provident fund	Urban employees	Low interest rate loan	Employer and employee	MoCA and local branch
Economically affordable housing	Urban residents with middle or low income	Low price	Local government budget	
Low-rent housing	Urban MLSS household Social relief	Low rent		
Disabled and survivor subsidy	Pension for Handicapped Bereaved Families; employment support	Cash or in-kind subsidy Job offer	Central and local government budget	MoCA and local branch
Natural disaster relief	Population in disaster-stricken areas	Temporary one-time relief in cash or in-kind transfers	Central and local government budget	MoCA and local branch

Sources: compiled by author

2.2 *Minimum Living Security Scheme*

Children's living security is closely tied to their families' and households' living situations. Minimum Living Security Scheme (MLSS) is the most important social assistance program in China. The program was first introduced in 1999 in urban areas and was extended to rural areas in 2007. The cash grants under MLSS are unconditional transfers by local governments to poor families with per capita income below the minimum living standard. Ministry of Civil Affairs (MoCA) and its local branches are responsible for the program. The cash transfer varies in different regions with different urban-rural situations. In urban areas, cash transfer under MLSS was about 22 percent of per capita consumption and 16 percent of per capital income of the region from 2007 to 2012, while rural eligible households received less than half of the amount received by urban households. In 2013, total beneficiaries reached 74 million people, about 5.5 percent of the population. An estimated 28 percent of total beneficiaries reside in urban areas, while the other 72 percent reside in rural areas. The total fiscal expenditure of MLSS accounted to 1.1 percent of total fiscal expenditures (table 3.3).

2.3 *Social insurance for employees in urban sectors*

For employees in urban sectors, the social insurance system provides a comprehensive social security to defend against the risks of illness, unemployment, workplace injury, and maternity leave. The Ministry of Human Resources and Social Security (MoHRSS) manages social insurance. The current framework was established in mid-1990s. The contribution is paid jointly by the employer and the employee. A document issued by the State Council recommended the contribution rate for each program. The contribution rate for employers is 20 percent of payroll for Basic Old Age Insurance (BOAI), 6 percent for Basic Medical Insurance (BMI), 2 percent for Unemployment Insurance (UI), and 0.5 percent each for Maternity and Industrial Injury Insurance. The contribution rate of employees is 8 percent for BOAI, 2 percent for BMI, and no contribution from employees for the other social insurance programs. The coverage rate of social insurance continues to increase. BOAI is the largest program, covering more than 60 percent of total urban employees in 2013 (Figure 3.2). The total expenditure on social insurance increased to from 2.96 percent of GDP in 2007 to 4.76 percent of GDP in 2013 (Table 3.4).[3]

2.4 *Labor market policies*

Numerous policies target job creation in China. In 2002, the government established active employment policies (AEP) and added more contents in 2005 and 2008. In 2008, it issued the Employment Promotion Law. The government utilises three tactics to encourage enterprises to create more jobs. First, it provides wage subsidies, subsidising small enterprise owners if they hire additional people. Second, it generates jobs through public projects or government procurement,

Table 3.3 Fiscal expenditure on social protection in China (2010–2015)

	2010	2011	2012	2013	2014	2015	Annual growth (%)
Expenditure (billion yuan)							
Total fiscal expenditure	8,987	10,925	12,595	14,021	15,179	17,588	14.4
Social protection expenditure	913	1,111	1,259	1,449	1,597	1,902	15.8
1. Subsidy to social insurance	231	315	383	440	504	660	23.4
2. Public sector pension	235	274	285	321	367	436	13.1
3. Employment subsidy	62	67	74	82	87	87	6.9
4. Urban minimum living security	54	68	67	76	74	75	6.9
5. Rural minimum living security	45	67	70	86	87	91	15.3
6. Natural disaster relief	33	23	27	24	21	20	−10.1
Housing security expenditure	238	382	448	448	504	580	19.5
As a percentage of total fiscal expenditure (%)							
Social protection expenditure	10.16	10.17	9.99	10.33	10.52	10.81	
1. Subsidy to social insurance	2.57	2.89	3.04	3.14	3.32	3.75	
2. Public sector pension	2.62	2.51	2.26	2.29	2.42	2.48	
3. Employment subsidy	0.70	0.61	0.58	0.59	0.57	0.50	
4. Urban minimum living security	0.60	0.62	0.53	0.54	0.49	0.43	
5. Rural minimum living security	0.50	0.61	0.55	0.61	0.57	0.52	
6. Natural disaster relief	0.37	0.21	0.22	0.17	0.14	0.11	
As a percentage of GDP							
Social protection expenditure	2.22	2.29	2.33	2.45	2.48	2.79	
Housing security expenditure	0.58	0.79	0.83	0.76	0.78	0.85	

Source: China Statistical Yearbook, 2016

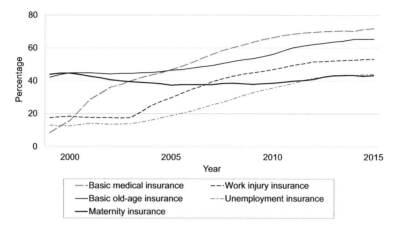

Figure 3.2 Participants/total urban employees in social insurance for urban sectors
Source: *China Statistical Yearbooks, 2016*

Table 3.4 Expenditure on social insurance for urban employees in China (2010–2015)

Billion Yuan	2010	2011	2012	2011	2013	2014	2015
Total expenditure	1,454	1,763	2,151	2,559	2,999	3,509	1,454
Basic old age insurance	1,055	1,276	1,556	1,847	2,175	2,581	1,055
Health insurance	327	401	487	583	670	753	327
Unemployment insurance	42	43	45	53	61	74	42
Injury insurance	19	29	41	48	56	60	19
Maternity insurance	11	14	22	28	37	41	11
Total as a percentage of GDP (%)	3.54	3.64	3.99	4.33	4.65	5.14	3.54

Note: GDP – gross domestic product
Source: *China Statistical Yearbooks, 2008–2016*

such as infrastructure construction and community services. Third, it offers support for business start-ups. Tax incentives and microcredit guarantees have been provided to promote self-employment and entrepreneurship, especially for the laid-off and unemployed.

In July 1994, a labor law that authorised provincial governments to set their own minimum wage standards according to local economic conditions helped formalise a system of guaranteed minimum wages. In March 2004, a new directive established more comprehensive minimum standards and tightened enforcement through threats of tougher punishment for lax enforcement of labor laws. For example, the minimum wage for Shanghai was increased by 155 percent from 2004 to 2013, and increased by 157 percent in Beijing during the same period of time.

2.5 Resident pension

Several kinds of pension exist in China. The most widely implemented pension in urban areas is for retirees who are participants in BOAI in the social insurance system, which has been discussed in section 2.2. Another program concerns resident pension, in which there are two schemes. The New Rural Resident Pension Scheme (NRP) was established in 2009 to cover rural residents, and the Urban Resident Pension Scheme (URP) was established in 2011 to cover urban non-employed residents. NRP and URP are voluntary schemes funded in conjunction with government subsidies. Individual contributions are put into individual accounts. Benefits after participants are 60 years old are composed of two parts: basic pension and individual account pension. The central government in the middle and western provinces provides the basic pension. In the eastern provinces, the central government and each local government pays half of the basic pension. Local governments have the autonomy to raise basic pension benefits according to local priorities, but they are responsible for the resulting financial needs. On a nationwide average, the replacement ratio is at 20 percent of rural per capita net income. At the beginning of 2014, the State Council announced that the two schemes would be merged into a uniform resident pension over time.

2.6 Aged care

In addition to providing pension schemes, local governments also provide social protection for elderly citizens who need aged care. Elderly citizens of so-called "Three No" status (elders who have lost their ability to work, have no income source, and lack a legal guardian) in rural areas have access to free government-owned or -sponsored nursing homes. For example, in 2000, China's Ministry of Civil Affairs created the Star Light (Xing Guang) Program to build community welfare facilities for senior citizens. To increase the affordability of such facilities for the poor or disabled elderly in urban areas, local governments have begun to provide subsidies for them in recent years. Starting in 2008 in Shanghai, for instance, eldercare users who are over 60 and live in households with incomes below the minimum living standard are entitled to a monthly subsidy of 300 yuan. Additional subsidies for nursing services are offered to those with severe disabilities through government purchase, and subsidies are also provided to train eldercare workers.

2.7 Resident health insurance

China is about to reach its target of universal coverage of health insurance. Since the end of the 1990s, public health care has been reformed to favor health insurance programs; the number of participants, therefore, has expanded dramatically. Several forms of health insurance now exist for different population groups. In 1998, the Basic Medical Insurance scheme (BMI) for urban employees was reformed into one of the social insurance programs, as explained in section 2.2.

The New Cooperative Medical System (NCMS) for farmers was introduced in 2003. In 2007, another health insurance program known as the Urban Resident Basic Medical Insurance scheme (URBMI), which covers urban residents not included in the BMI, was introduced. This new scheme covers children, the elderly, the disabled, and other non-working urban residents. Similar to NCMS, there is a government subsidy for the premium payment in the URBMI. By 2012, 805 million people out of a total population of 1.35 billion people were covered by the NCMS, 271 million by the BMI, and 265 million by the URBMI.

Meanwhile, a Medical Financial Assistance program (MFA) was implemented, in order to support poor households and to give them direct support for receiving medical services. MFA provides additional protection over health insurance programs. In addition to the reimbursement from NCMS, eligible households will receive subsidies to cover health care expenditures. Jointly financed by central and local governments, MFA is a highly decentralised program in which local governments have discretion over both policy design and implementation based on local circumstances. As a result, marked variations among localities exist.

2.8 Housing security

Providing decent housing to poor and low-income groups has been a big challenge for governments in China. China introduced a housing-provident fund system in the mid-1990s for urban employees, under which the employer and employee jointly contributed to the system. The participant can enjoy a low interest loan when buying a flat. Besides, there exist two solutions to the housing problem of the poor and low-income families in urban China. First, price-subsidised housing is sold only to low-to-middle-income households. Housing is sold to households qualified as most needy and with incomes below the threshold set by local governments at lower prices than market prices. Second, rent-subsidised public housing is provided only to poor households.

3. Assessing social protection floor components of China

ILO adopted the concept of Social Protection Floors (SPF) in 2012 to recommend that member countries provide basic social security guarantees to all, to ensure effective access to essential health care and a basic level of income security (International Labour Conference, 2012). As a foundation of the whole social protection system, improving SPF is the first step to achieving higher levels of social protection. We assess the three most crucial components in SPF in China, which are MLSS, resident pension schemes, and resident health insurance schemes.

3.1 Achievements and issues in MLSS

3.1.1 Achievements

As one of the largest cash transfer programs in the developing world (Chen et al., 2006), the Minimum Living Standard Scheme (MLSS) has expanded rapidly.

In 1999, 2.6 million persons lived in urban households receiving the minimum living guarantee; the number had increased to 20.64 million in urban areas and 53.9 million in rural areas in 2013 (Figure 3.3). Among people eligible for the MLSS in urban areas, the share of elderly people, working age adults, and children among the total number stabilised at 15 percent, 61 percent and 23 percent respectively. In 2010, among the adult recipients, 5 million were employed, accounting for 21.7 percent of the total, and 9.13 million were unemployed, accounting for 39.5 percent. Unemployed people form the largest category among those living in urban poverty and qualifying for the MLSS. Urban and rural beneficiaries jointly accounted for 5.5 percent of the whole population in 2013.

MLSS had become the dominant social assistance program in urban China, with the poorest 20 percent of the population receiving 55 percent of its transfers in 2001 and more than 80 percent in 2005 (Du and Park, 2007). Compared to the poverty line for rural China measured by the National Bureau of Statistics (NBS), this line is much higher, about 50 percent higher in 2011 (Table 3.5). Recent studies have found that MLSS plays a substantial role in reducing poverty, despite the small benefit amount it offers and the light fiscal expenditure by the government (Chen et al., 2006; Ravallion, 2007; Gustafsson and Deng, 2007). Gustafsson and Deng (2007) find that the poverty rate has been lowered by 16 percent for participants and 5 percent among all urban households during the beginning 2000s. More significantly, the poverty gap was reduced by 29 percent among MLSS participants and by 12 percent among all urban households. Poverty severity has been successfully lessened by 38 percent for MLSS participants and by 20 percent for all urban households. The similar result was concluded

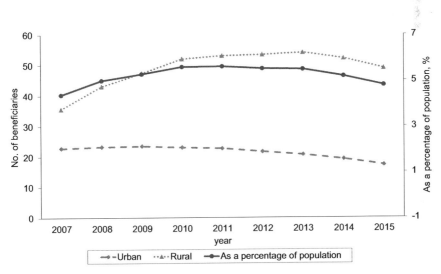

Minimum Living Security Scheme.

Figure 3.3 Number of beneficiaries in MLSS

Note: MLSS = Minimum Living Security Scheme
Source: China Statistical Yearbooks, 2016

Table 3.5 MLSS assistance line and national poverty line in China

Year	MLSS assistance line (Per capita per month)	National poverty line (Per capita per month)
2010	251.2	106.2
2011	287.6	191.7
2012	330.1	191.7
2013	373.3	228
2014	410.5	191.7

Source: *China Civil Affairs Statistical Yearbook, 2016; China Health and Family Planning Yearbook, 2015*

in research by Chen et al. (2006). By using National Bureau of Statistics (NBS) survey data from the 35 largest cities in China, they find that for participants, MLSS narrowed the poverty rate by 20 percent, the poverty gap by 29 percent, and poverty severity by 37 percent. And the reductions of the indicators for all urban households were 6, 10, and 14 percent.[4]

3.1.2 Identification issue

The MLSS is strictly means tested, with rather stigmatising application procedures. The local urban non-agricultural registration is the precondition (a spouse or other family members from rural areas or other provinces without local urban registration would not be counted). In principle, the minimum living standard covers basic food, clothing, housing, gas, and children's education needs, which is based on local average per capita income and basic consumption needs. Eligibility is determined by whether the per capita income of the household is below the local assistance line. MLSS adopts a very inclusive income definition to determine each family's eligibility. Household income is measured as cash income from any sources, including earnings, social benefits, and private transfers. Savings and stocks are also counted as part of income. However, due to difficulties of income measurement, some other indicators, such as financial assets, employment, health status, and housing conditions, are also considered (Chen et al., 2006; Du and Park, 2007).[5]

During identification of the poor, two types of error came out. One is the inclusion of the non-poor, the other is the poor being excluded by MLSS. Incomes of applicants are easily subject to fraud, and hidden incomes from informal employment are prevalent. Typically, the assistance line is set below both the minimum wage and the unemployment insurance benefit in order to create disincentives to welfare dependence by the able-bodied. Even when their incomes are becoming higher than the threshold and the benefit offered by MLSS is getting relatively smaller, the recipients are reluctant to exit the program. The motivation is not to get the limited level of MLSS benefit but to be eligible for other benefits, since the MLSS benefits are often associated with other preferential policies, such as medical assistance and housing security. On the other hand, the program misses a large portion of targeted households. A study shows that only 28 percent of eligible households were actually receiving the assistance (Chen et al., 2006).

3.1.3 Work incentive issue

The MLSS benefit aims to close the gap between a qualifying household's income per capita and the assistance line, providing fewer benefits to households as their income rises. Therefore, for some recipients with less employability, their increase in income could result in a sharp reduction in their household's benefit. When taking the supplementary privilege into account, the marginal tax rate will be raised much higher. Local governments have introduced a range of measures to improve recipients' employability, such as the "work first" idea, training and financial incentives to require MLSS recipients to look for jobs and to improve employability. However, the impact is limited, because few of these services are provided effectively (Peng and Ding, 2012).

3.1.4 Insufficient co-financing

Sub-national governments (at provincial, prefectural, and county levels) have a responsibility to finance the MLSS. The expenditure once relied largely on the county level due to the lack of specific co-financing measurements. Since 2000, the central government has made special transfers to provinces with fiscal difficulties, which stimulated the radical expansion of coverage in the following years. Subsidies by the central government varied across localities, based on the reported number of poor people to be assisted by local governments and local fiscal capacity. Nevertheless, central transfer is not always certain; hence the decentralisation of social expenditure responsibility of local governments without secure arrangements for fiscal transfer has resulted in potential financial issues in the MLSS.

Due to different fiscal capability, assistance lines varied widely among local governments. And there is a conflict between poverty reduction and fiscal capability. The middle and western provinces face more serious poverty rates and poverty gaps, so the coverage rate is much higher than in the coastal provinces, yielding a much heavier financing responsibility. Although the scheme was initially designed to spread the burden of expenditure at different levels of government, in reality, the public transfer from the center or government bodies at upper levels are not based on need but on informal negotiations (Peng and Ding, 2012). Therefore, the local authorities still need to shoulder the final financial responsibility, which requires them to balance the coverage and the benefit level.

3.2 Achievements and issues in the Resident Pension Scheme

3.2.1 Achievements

The Resident Pension Scheme is voluntary and heavily subsidized by government. The rapid increase of resident pensions in both rural and urban areas is largely due to significant government subsidy. Subsidies to benefits and contributions are made from central and local governments to mitigate contribution responsibility while providing a non-contributory basic pension. As discussed in section 2.5, the two programs, NRP and URP, were merged into a uniform resident pension program in 2014. The number of participants in the resident pension scheme keeps increasing; by the end of 2013, the number of insured persons was nearly 500 million, among which 141 million are pensioners (Figure 3.4). The ratio of contributors to pensioners has been stable at around 2:6 since 2010.

Due to rapid ageing, the percentage of population over 65 years old in China will double between 2010 and 2030. The poverty rate has been relatively high by income and consumption measures in elderly households, especially in rural areas. The China Urban and Rural Elderly Survey in 2006, a nationally representative sample of elderly, suggests that 19 percent of the rural elderly had consumption levels below the official poverty line (Dorfman et al., 2013). The scheme provides a universal protection floor to alleviate old age poverty. However, despite the impressive progress in reaching universal coverage, the scheme shows problems in adequacy of the security, incentives for participation, and fiscal sustainability.

3.2.2 Adequacy issue

The benefit level the scheme provides is expected to be sufficient to perform the most basic function of promoting security among the aged. Currently, the benefit is determined by the accumulated amount of individual accounts and basic pensions from government subsidy. The amount of the basic pension varies across

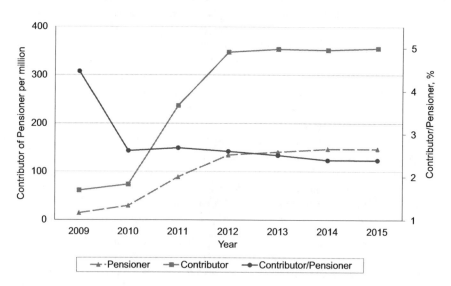

Figure 3.4 Contributors and pensioners in Resident Pension Scheme
Source: China Statistical Yearbooks, 2010–2016

regions. In most provinces, it was 55 yuan a month in first several years after the scheme was introduced and higher in more developed regions; for instance, it was about 300 yuan a month in Shanghai. Participants have several choices of the amount to contribute. The lower level of individual contributions is more in developed regions, so the individual account pension will be more accordingly. However, the higher cost of living in developed regions offsets the higher benefit level to a large extent.

Compared to consumption level, the basic pension is about 10–25 percent of consumption per capita, varying by region. Compared to income level, it is even lower, about 7–20 percent of household income per capita (Table 3.6). Hence, there should be other resources to meet the needs of everyday life. The adult children continue to be the most important source of elderly care and financial support. But NRP has become an important supplement to the traditional elder-care patterns in rural China. Research shows that enrollees were more likely to live independently rather than co-reside with their adult children in rural areas. In addition, enrollees became less dependent on children in terms of financial resources and informal care. There is also research evaluating the effect of resident pension on family transfers. Research indicates a degree of crowding-out effect on family transfers due to resident pensions. (Chen et al., 2013; Chen and Zeng, 2013).

3.2.3 Participation incentive issue

The resident pension scheme has both positive and negative incentives for participation. Obviously, heavy government subsidy provides a positive incentive. Those who were already 60 years old at the time the program starts automatically received a basic pension benefit without paying any premiums. However, the lack of sufficient returns to individual contributions to pension accounts creates negative incentive. This is the most important factor that determines younger people's willingness to participate in the scheme. Currently, the rate of return of the fund is claimed to be the rate of the one-year deposit. Although very secure, such a low rate virtually guarantees a low individual account balance at retirement and thus weakens participation incentives for rural workers (Lei et al., 2014; Dorfman

Table 3.6 Relative level of annual amount of basic pension in China (2014)

	Basic pension (Yuan)	Consumption per capita (Yuan)	Income per capita (Yuan)	Basic pension/ consumption per capita	Basic pension/ income per capita
Shanghai	6,480	14,820	21,191	43.72%	30.58%
Jiangsu	960	11,820	14,958	8.12%	6.42%
Hunan	720	9,024	10,060	7.98%	7.16%
Gansu	660	6,147	6,276	10.74%	10.52%

Source: computed according to Statistic Yearbooks of the region 2015

et al., 2013). As a result, participants tend to choose the lowest premium standard and the shortest contribution period to be eligible to get cash transfers from the basic pension programme.

Empirical investigation using micro data verifies the disincentive phenomena. Lei et al. (2014) employing CHARLS (China Health and Retirement Longitudinal Studies) data of 2011 found that individuals prefer shorter periods of participation and choose the lowest level of premiums.[6] There is an age gradient of enrollment rates, where the enrollment rate is generally low among all age groups, and generally increases with age. Numerous surveys on NRP find similar evidence that the enrollment was observed only from age 45, having 15 years contribution to meet the eligibility standard.

3.2.4 Fiscal sustainability

Since the initial pension benefit, which is less than 20 percent of the household per capita income, is rather low, the scheme has not caused a significant burden of public finance to local governments. China's resident pension relies more on ad hoc governmental support than on sound actuarial principles. The balance between fund revenues and expenditures has not been paid much attention at the current stage.

Simulation results of the future fiscal expenditure for resident pensions are listed in Table 3.7. Population dynamics refer to Feng and Chen (2014). There are several assumptions under the simulations. In scenario 1, the assumptions are the following. First, the urbanisation process is expected to continue in China, with its share reaching 70 percent in 2030. Second, the coverage of BOAI remains stable. Resident pension covers both rural and urban residents elder than 60 outside BOAI. Third, the basic pension of the resident pension scheme will accumulate with the real wage growth rate and inflation rate in the future. Growth rates of wage and GDP are also to be assumed according to the Word Bank projection (World Bank, 2012), where annual growth rate of GDP is 8.6 percent during 2011–2015, 7.0 percent during 2016–2020, 5.9 percent during 2021–2025 and 5 percent during 2026–2030.

In scenario 2, we change the second assumption, that the participation rate of the formal social insurance program BOAI will increase gradually to 80 percent in 2030. The expanding coverage of formal urban social insurance will lead to a slower increase of pensioners.

Each simulation is an estimation of the national average level. In scenario 1, the number of pensioners will increase rapidly, and so will the fiscal expense. In 2030, the annual expenditure of the systems is about 0.38 percent of GDP. In scenario 2, the number of pensioners will increase at first and then eventually decrease, since more people are to be covered by BOAI. Accordingly, the fiscal expense as a percentage of GDP will start to decrease after 2025. Hence expanding coverage of social insurance for urban sectors will lead to a slower increase of pensioners and a declining ratio of fiscal expenditure to GDP.

Table 3.7 Expenditure projections for resident pension in China until 2030

	2012	*2015*	*2020*	*2025*	*2030*
Scenario 1					
Pensioners (million)	156.02	187.77	220.21	249.80	292.15
Fiscal expenditure (billion)	123.88	170.99	259.57	400.70	605.20
Fiscal expenditure /GDP	0.25%	0.28%	0.29%	0.33%	0.38%
Scenario 2					
Pensioners (million)	156.02	169.31	183.01	186.75	180.14
Fiscal expenditure (billion)	123.88	163.29	223.55	299.56	373.20
Fiscal expenditure /GDP	0.25%	0.27%	0.25%	0.25%	0.23%

Sources: simulated by author

3.3 Achievements and issues of resident health insurance

3.3.1 Achievements

As already mentioned in 2.7, the number of participants in various health insurance schemes expanded dramatically (Figure 3.5). There are a number of studies evaluating the effects of resident health insurance. Some find that resident health insurance increases the utilisation of formal medical services. For example, Liu and Zhao (2014) find URBMI has improved medical care utilisation more for the members of the low-income families and for the residents in the poor region, using the 2006 and 2009 waves of the China Health and Nutrition Survey. Chen et al. (2014) use the recent four-wave URBMI Survey (2008–2011) and find that the URBMI has significantly increased the likelihood of receiving inpatient treatment and using outpatient services. Wagstaff et al. (2009) use rural household survey data of 15 counties in 12 provinces from 2003 to 2005 and find that NCMS reduces the health care price and increases the demand for health care of farmers both in outpatient and inpatient care. Other studies also investigate the effect of health insurance on household saving and consumption; a positive effect on consumption has been found (e.g. Cheung and Padieu, 2015; Bai and Wu, 2014).

3.3.2 Limited effect on demand for health care

An important characteristic of China is the large urban and rural disparity: per capita health spending of rural residents has been much lower than the amount of urban residence (Feng et al., 2015). The gap keeps widening. In 2010, per capita health care expenditure of urban residents was 3.47 times as much as that of rural residents. However, China's National Maternal and Child Surveillance reports that rates for maternal, infant, and under-5 mortalities in rural areas were twice as high as those in urban areas in 2007, that is, 0.04 percent, 1.9 percent, and 2.2 percent vs. 0.02 percent, 0.8 percent, and 0.9 percent, respectively.

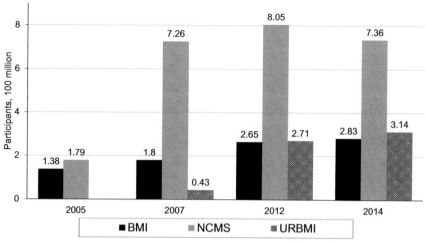

BMI –Basic Medical Insurance; NCMS; New Cooperative Medical System; URBMI – Urban Residents Basic Medical Insurance.

Figure 3.5 Number of participants in health insurance programmes

Notes: BMI – Basic Medical Insurance; NCMS; New Cooperative Medical System; URBMI – Urban Residents Basic Medical Insurance
Source: China Statistical Yearbook, 2012

The disparity is the consequence of insufficient health care supply, poor health care insurance, and low household income in rural areas. According to Shen and Lee (2014), urban residents benefit more from public health care funding than rural residents at all ages, especially after age 60.

3.3.3 Supply-induced demand

Economic theory and international experience suggest that when health insurance is expanded with no appropriate supply-side controls, health care expenditure grows as a result of demand-side moral hazard and, more important, supply-side moral hazard (Yip and Hsiao, 2009). This is what is happening in China. The price increase caused by introducing health insurance offsets the effect of government subsidy. In a study of the effect on price of NCMS empirically, using village- and county-level panel data and employing difference-in-difference method, we find that NCMS has no impact on village clinic price, but will cause county hospital prices to rise. Furthermore, the higher the reimbursement ratio, the higher the price; the percentage of price increase is almost equivalent to reimbursement ratio (Feng et al., 2010). The results are consistent with the theoretical expectation that in a health care market where the provider has market power and is profit-oriented, as in health care programs such as a county hospital, the introduction of health insurance will cause health care price inflation and offset the effect of health insurance. Other studies show that the urban scheme does not seem to have reduced catastrophic medical expenditure and may have increased financial risk from a hospital stay, as hospitals tend to subject insured patients to more procedures (Wagstaff and Lindelow, 2008). Hou et al. (2014) confirm earlier findings of NCMS being effective in increasing access to care but not in increasing financial protection. In addition, they find NCMS enrollees to be sensitive to the price incentives set in the NCMS design when choosing their provider and providers to respond by increasing prices and providing more expensive care.

3.3.4 *Low reimbursement rate*

Benefit packages differ substantially among the three programs. BMI is more generous than the other two programs. For example, the average inpatient reimbursement rate for urban employees was 65 percent in 2008, for urban residents it was 45 percent in 2007, and for NCMS it was only 41 percent in 2009 (Shen and Lee, 2014).[7] In resident health insurance, outpatient services are either very inadequately insured or, in some rural areas, not insured. Inpatient services leave patients with significant costs to bear. Study finds that reimbursement arrangements in NCMS have significant effects on the demand for health care. For farmers in China, the expenditure for outpatient care accounts for a significant fraction of a household's income, so reimbursing outpatient care can also reduce the financial burden to a large extent. The simulation of the outcomes of various arrangements shows that only reimbursing inpatient care cannot reduce the average financial burden, while reimbursing both inpatient and outpatient care is a better choice (Feng and Li, 2009).

4. Generating fiscal space for SPF in China

In the future, China will continue increasing expenditure on social protection. In the twelfth five-year plan, annual growth rate of MLSS has been set at 10 percent; residential elder care coverage for poor and independent rural elderly will increase by 18 percentage points in five years. However, future improvement is entering an unfavorable environment: China's economy is slowing down. Growth of fiscal revenue has declined since 2012 (Figure 3.6). ILO proposes several alternatives to expand fiscal space and generate resources for social investments, including reallocating public expenditures; increasing tax revenues; expanding social security coverage and contributory revenues; lobbying for aid and transfers; eliminating illicit financial flows; using fiscal and foreign exchange reserves; borrowing or restructuring existing debt; and adopting a more accommodating macroeconomic framework (Ortiz et al., 2015).

In the case of China, the overall tax burden has been more than 20 percent of GDP in recent years: for instance, 21.2 percent of GDP in 2013, higher than some of the OECD countries. The social insurance contribution rate is as high as 29 percent and 13 percent for employers and employees respectively, hence the space to increase tax and contributory revenue is limited. We consider the following ways be explored to further develop the social protection system in

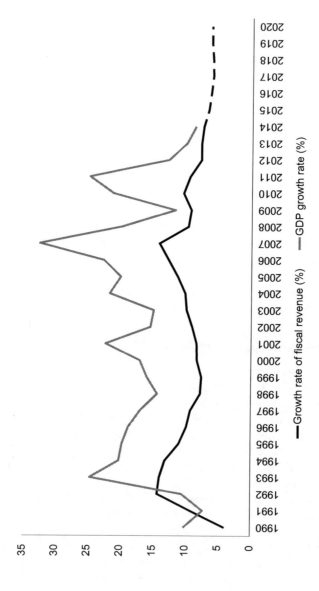

Figure 3.6 Growth rates of fiscal revenue and GDP (2000–2014)

Source: data of 1990–2014 from *China Statistic Yearbooks*; data after 2015 from International Monetary Fund, World Economic Outlook Database, April 2015

China: reprioritising public spending to increase social expenditures, exploring some alternative fiscal sources including dividends of state-owned enterprises (SOE), increasing fiscal capability of local government and improving efficiency in delivery of social protection.

4.1 Reprioritising government spending

During economic transition of China, a large share of government spending has been for "economic activities", while gaps in public services such as health and social protection remains significant.[8] In a five-year period of time of 2007–2012, the share of expenditure on social security and employment changed little, from 10.9 percent to 10.2 percent. The fastest expanding category was in the transportation, whose share grew from 3.85 percent to 6.86 percent (Feng and Chen, 2014). As Table 3.8 shows, China's public spending on social protection and health as a share of GDP is well below OECD and upper-middle income country averages.

As China attains higher income levels and faces larger income inequality, the composition of government spending needs to evolve to reflect China's changing development challenges. As pointed out by Ortiz et al. (2015), there must be strong political will to implement the strategy, since share of some other sectors must be reduced in order to allow for increased social investments. The third plenary session of the 18th Communist Party of China (CPC) central committee in 2013 set out several important reforms to show the intention for reallocation. The government will increase spending on medical services, social security, and

Table 3.8 Composition of public expenditures across countries

Percent of GDP	High income	Middle income		China
	OECD	Upper middle	Lower middle	
Total fiscal expenditure	41.6	33.1	36.1	25.7
General public services	5.6	5.6	5.5	2.9
Defense	1.6	1.5	2.2	1.3
Public order and safety	1.6	2.0	2.6	1.3
Economic affairs	4.2	5.3	6.1	7.9
Environment protection	0.7	0.5	0.3	0.5
Housing and community amenities	0.8	1.2	3.0	1.9
Health	6.3	3.3	3.1	1.0
Recreation, culture and religion	1.2	0.8	1.0	0.5
Education	5.4	3.9	5.4	3.7
Social protection including social insurance	15.2	9.0	6.9	5.3

Notes: Data about all the countries are in 2007 except data about China is in 2008. China's social protection expenditure as a percentage of GDP is from Table 2 and Table 3, the sum of fiscal social protection expenditure and social insurance fund expenditure.
Sources: *China, 2030, World Bank and Table 2 & 3.*

environmental protection while, at the same time, reducing the contribution rate of social insurance.

4.2 Exploring alternative fiscal resources

China has some possible options including dividends from State-owned enterprises (SOE) and investment return on foreign exchange reserves. SOEs were exempted from paying dividends through much of the 1990s and 2000s, which gave these firms an advantage over current and potential competitors by keeping their cost of capital low. At same time, it also reduced the government revenue that could have been spent on pensions, education, and other social services. This changed in 2007 when the State Council mandated central SOEs to begin paying dividends, 10 percent in highly profitable industries, 5 percent in the industries where SOEs were less profitable, and 0 percent for protected firms like military armaments manufacturers. The rates were increased by 5 percent across the board to 15, 10, and 5 percent in 2011. China will moderately increase the ratio of dividends paid out by SOEs to 30 percent by 2020. Further reform also calls for changing of management of SOE dividends. In the past, these funds haven't been included in general budget to pay for public expenditures. It has now been decided that the Ministry of Finance will collect the dividends and place them into a State Capital Management Budget.

Foreign exchange reserves offer another resource to help sustain China's public services. China has recorded over USD 3 trillion in foreign exchange reserve in recent years, accounting for one-third of the world's total and around 50 percent of China's GDP. China has established a sovereign wealth fund (SWF) using foreign exchange reserve to generate higher returns. China Investment Corporation (CIC) is responsible for managing part of China's foreign exchange reserves. Depending on the performance of the fund, it is possible that more foreign exchange reserves will be allocated to the CIC fund and the investment returns can be used to finance social protection expenditure.

4.3 Increasing fiscal capability of local governments

China is among the most decentralised countries in the world when it comes to government expenditures, while government revenues are highly centralised. Local governments are responsible for 80 percent of government expenditure responsibilities, providing public services and social protection, but receive only slightly more than 40 percent of tax revenues. Fiscal transfers to sub-provincial levels remain largely at the discretion of powerful provincial governments and are subject to negotiation, leading to high disparities across sub-provincial local governments. According to the World Bank's suggestion (World Bank, 2012), more fiscal autonomy should be given to local governments to increase the scope to raise their own revenues, such as property taxes, capital gains taxes on agricultural land acquisition, or prudent on-budget borrowing.[9]

In view of the fact that heavy responsibilities for local governments are matched with relative low fiscal capability, it is worth considering raising some expenditure responsibilities to higher levels of government: spending on social assistance, health care, and pensions. Theoretically, pooling finance and spending of redistributive programs at higher levels will be more efficient, since it can pool the risks across regions and encourage labor mobility. Besides, it also helps to narrow regional disparities. In many countries, social security related programs are the responsibility of the central government.

4.4 Improving efficiency in delivery of social protection

With limited budgets, finding ways of delivering social protection more efficiently must always be an option. The efficiency in delivery of social protection is closely linked to cost containment and the extent to which benefits are distributed to the poor. As we have shown in the previous section, one of the problems the Chinese protection system has is ineffective targeting. Means testing targeting is always expensive. During economic downturns, more people would like to apply for social benefits, so the identification of poverty becomes more costly. One means to exclude non-targeted households is to set up self-targeting schemes, in which only those really needing it enroll or take advantage of the program (Ravallion, 2007). Measures proposed in this context concern the way that policy is implemented and ensuring active inclusion of the stakeholders. Policy implementation issues include the complexity of program regulations, the scale of administrative costs and possible fraud and error in benefit claims. Policies to foster active inclusion are concerned more with encouraging labor market participation of beneficiaries (Social Protection Committee, 2011).

In the health sector, as described in the previous section, the monopolistic public hospitals have power and incentive to increase expenditure after insurance has been introduced. To cope with the issue, health insurance administration can play a role as a third-party payer, in changing payment arrangements from fee-for-service to prospective payment. There are already some experiments with prospective payment systems (PPS) in China. A number of challenges exist regarding PPS in China, including lack of sufficient data on costs of medical care, large regional disparities and rural-urban disparities, poor governance in health insurance service, etc. However, a gradual process of developing PPS has been committed to by Chinese leadership.

In pension schemes, making investments in the largely unmanaged pension funds is a viable way to prevent inflation from eroding value and to increase efficiency. There are now more than 3 trillion yuan in pension funds available to be invested. In 2013, the Third Plenum of the Eighteenth Central Committee of the Communist Party of China decided to strengthen the management and supervision of the social insurance fund investment, and facilitate the marketisation and diversification of their operations. There were already experiments that invest pension funds into China's capital markets. A diversified and market-oriented investment guideline has been issued in 2015 by the Ministry of Human Resources and Social Security and the Ministry of Finance jointly.

5. Concluding remarks

Generally speaking, there are eight categories of programs in the Chinese social protection system: 1. Compulsory education for children, 2. Minimum Living Security Scheme (MLSS) for both rural and urban residents, 3. Social insurance for urban employees, 4. Labor market policies for urban employees, 5. Resident pension in rural and urban areas, 6. Aged care for rural and urban residents, 7. Resident health insurance in rural and urban areas, and 8. Housing security for urban residents. Following ILO's concept of social protection floors (SPF), we assess the three most crucial components of SPF in China: MLSS, resident pension schemes. and resident health insurance schemes. Based on literature review, statistical summaries, and simulation, we have the following findings:

1   As one of the largest cash transfer programs in the developing world, MLSS has played a substantial role in reducing poverty. However, targeting performance is always a problem as in many other countries. Recipients are reluctant to exit the program, since obtaining MLSS benefits are often associated with other preferential programs. Decentralisation of social expenditure responsibility of local governments has resulted in potential financial issues in the MLSS.
2   Due to significant government subsidy, resident pensions in both rural and urban areas expanded rapidly. The scheme provides a universal protection floor to alleviate old age poverty. However, despite impressive progress in reaching universal coverage, the scheme shows problems in adequacy of the security, incentives for participation, and fiscal sustainability. The basic pension is about 10–25 percent of consumption per capita, varying across regions. The potential to raise the benefit lies in expanding coverage of formal urban social insurance and a slower increase of pensioners in resident pension system.
3   Resident health insurance schemes involve large amounts of government subsidy. There are a number of studies evaluating the effects of resident health insurance. Some find that resident health insurance increases the utilisation of formal medical services. However, supply-side moral hazard issues and low reimbursement rates provided by the schemes limit the demand for health care, especially the demand from rural residents.

Although China has made outstanding achievements in establishing social protection systems in the last two decades, China faces huge challenges in sustaining and developing the system in future under an unfavorable environment in which China's economy is slowing down. On one hand, necessary measures should be taken to expand fiscal space and generate resources for social investments, including dividends from stated-owned enterprises and foreign exchange reserves.

On the other hand, there is wide potential to improve efficiency in delivery of social protection; for instance, one could set up self-targeting schemes in means test programs, reform payment methods in health insurance programs, and improve the management of individual accounts in pension programs.

Notes

1 The programs of SP in China are listed in Table 3.1. Housing security expenditure is listed in Table 3.2. According to Asian Development Bank, the social protection expenditure as a percentage of GDP was 5 percent in 2009 (ADB, 2013).
2 The figures are from the 1990/2000 Population Census of the People's Republic of China for 1990–2000; The Sixth Population Census of the People's Republic of China in 2010, Population Division of the Department of Economic and Social Affairs of the United Nations Secretariat, World Population Prospects: 2015.
3 China also has a special arrangement for the military. Military personnel do not make any contributions towards their pension benefits. Military members usually receive higher remuneration and pension payments than civil servants of equivalent rank. Both military cadres (including officers, non-ranking officers) and soldiers (excluding volunteers) can retire from the army with entitlement to a monthly military pension as long as certain criteria are met. Military personnel can also transfer to the civil / public sectors or enterprises prior to retirement, receiving a certain amount of compensation (details refer to Leckie, 2011).
4 Poverty rate is the share of population living in poverty, below the poverty line. The poverty gap estimates the depth of poverty by considering how far, on the average, the poor are from that poverty line. Poverty severity is another measure of poverty gap, which is the gap between 'poverty line' and 'the average income of poor people'. The greater the gap the deeper poverty is.
5 Many cities also take into account ownership of durable goods. For example, Beijing has specified that families who own luxury goods such as a vehicle, motorcycle, a cell phone, or who have pets, are ineligible for MLSS benefits.
6 CHARLS is a nationally representative longitudinal survey of the middle-aged and elderly population (45+) in China. It followed strictly random sampling procedures with multistage (counties – villages – households) PPS sampling. All counties in China excluding those in Tibet were included in the sampling frame; 28 provinces are represented in the sampled counties.
7 In 2012, the reimbursement ratio of NCMS increased to 70 percent in township hospitals, 50 percent in county hospitals, and 40 percent in city level hospitals of the medicine and services within the list for inpatient care.
8 A detailed explanation of the financing of local fiscal expenditure is in Feng and Chen (2014).
9 Problems of local-government debt in China have been widely discussed in literature. It has doubled from less than 20 percent of GDP in 2007 to nearly 40 percent at the beginning of 2015. The debt swap is adopted by the Ministry of Finance, aiming to saving interest costs for local governments. Compared to many other counties, total government debt as a percentage of GDP in China is still relatively low.

References

Asian Development Bank (2010). *Toward Universal Social Security Coverage in the People's Republic of China, Observations and Suggestions Series (Manila)*. Available at: www.adb.org/publications/toward-universal-social-security-coverage-prc

Asian Development Bank (2013). *The Social Protection Index: Assessing Results for Asia and the Pacific*. Asian Development Bank. http://hdl.handle.net/11540/79. License: CC BY 3.0 IGO.

Bai, C., and B. Wu. (2014). Health Insurance and Consumption: Evidence from China's New Cooperative Medical Scheme. *Journal of Comparative Economics*, 42(2), 450–469.

Chen H., and Y. Zeng. (2013). Who Benefits More From the New Rural Society Endowment Insurance Program in China: Elderly or Their Adult Children? (in Chinese). *Economic Research Journal*, 8, 55–67.

Chen, G., G. G. Liu, and F. Xu. (2014). The Impact of the Urban Resident Basic Medical Insurance On Health Services Utilization in China. *Pharmaco Economics*, 32(3), 277–292.

Chen, S., M. Ravallion, and Y. Wang. (2006). *Di Bao: A Guaranteed Minimum Income in China's Cities?* World Bank Policy Research Working Paper, No. 3805.

Cheung, D., and Y. Padieu. (2015). Heterogeneity of the Effects of Health Insurance On Household Savings: Evidence From Rural China. *World Development*, 66, 84–103.

Dorfman, M., R. Holzmann, P. O'Keefe, D. Wang, Y. Sin, and R. Hinz. (2013). *China's Pension System: A Vision*. Washington, DC: The World Bank.

Du, Y., and A. Park. (2007). *The Effects of Social Assistance on Poverty Reduction: Evidence from Household Surveys in Urban China*, The International Conference on Policy Perspectives on Growth, Economic Structures and Poverty Reduction, Beijing, China, June.

Feng, J., F. Liu, and Q. Chen. (2010). Impact of New Cooperative Medical System on Health Care Price (in Chinese). *Economic Research Journal*, 11, 127–140.

Feng J., P. Lou, and Y. Yu. (2015). Health Care Expenditure Over Life Cycle in the PRC. *Asian Development Review*, 32(1), 167–195.

Feng, J. and Q. Chen, 2014 "Public Pension System and Fiscal Policy Response in China", in *Pension Reform of China, India and Indonesia*, ERIA working paper.

Feng, J., and Z. Li. (2009). Risk Management for Health Care in Rural China (in Chinese). *Economic Research Journal*, 4, 103–115.

Gustafsson, B., and Q. Deng. (2007). *Social Assistance Receipt and its Importance For Combating Poverty in Urban China*, IZA Discussion Paper No. 2758.

Hou, Z., E. Van de Poel, E. Van Doorslaer, B. Yu, and Q. Meng. (2014). Effects of NCMS on Access to Care and Financial Protection in China. *Health Economics*, 23(8), 917–934.

International Labour Conference (2012). *Provisional Record No. 14; 101th Session, Geneva, June 2012, Fourth Item on the Agenda: Elaboration of an Autonomous Recommendation on the Social Protection Floor*. Report of the Committee on the Social Protection Floor, Geneva: ILO. Available at: www.ilo.org/ilc/ILCSessions/101stSession/reports/provisional-records/WCMS_182950/lang – en/index.htm

International Labor Organization (ILO) (2010). *Social Protection Floor Initiative, SPF Country Brief: China*.

International Labor Organization (ILO) (2014). *World Social Protection Report 2014/15, Building Economic Recovery, Inclusive Development and Social Justice*. Geneva: International Labor Office.

Leckie, S. H. (2011). *Civil Service and Military Service Pensions In China*, Paper provided by Center for Intergenerational Studies, Institute of Economic Research, Hitotsubashi University in its series PIE/CIS Discussion Paper with number 505.

Lei, X., C. Zhang, and Y. Zhao. (2014). Incentive Problems in China's New Rural Pension Program. *Research in Labor Economics*, 37, 181–201.

Liu, H., and Z. Zhao. (2014). Does Health Insurance Matter? Evidence From China's Urban Resident Basic Medical Insurance. *Journal of Comparative Economics*, 42(4), 1007–1020.

Ortiz, I., M. Cummins, and K. Karunanethy. (2015). *Fiscal Space for Social Protection Options to Expand Social Investments in 187 Countries.* International Labor Office, ESS Working Paper No. 48.

Peng, Z., and Y. Ding. (2012). Tackling Urban Poverty in China: The Minimum Living Standard Scheme and its Limitations. *Journal of Poverty and Social Justice*, 20(3), 261–276.

Ravallion, M. (2007). *Di Bao: A Guaranteed Minimum Income in Urban China*, World Bank Policy Research Working Paper No. 4305.

Shen, K., and S-H. Lee. (2014). *Benefit Incidence Of Public Transfers: Evidence From the People's Republic of China.* Asian Development Bank. Manila.

Social Protection Committee (2011). *SPC Assessment of the Social Dimension of the Europe 2020 Strategy – Full report.* Brussels: European Council.

United Nations (2014). *The Millennium Development Goals Report.* New York: Untied Nations.

Wagstaff, A., and M. Lindelow. (2008). Can Insurance Increase Financial Risk? The Curious Case Of Health Insurance in China. *Journal of Health Economics*, 27(4), 990–1005.

Wagstaff, A., M. Lindelow, J. Gao, L. Xu, and J. Qian. (2009). Extending Health Insurance to the Rural Population: An Impact Evaluation of China's New Cooperative Medical Scheme. *Journal of Health Economics*, 28(1), 1–19.

World Bank (2012). *China 2030: Building a Modern, Harmonious, and Creative High-Income Society.*

Yip, W., and W. C. Hsiao. (2009). Non-Evidence-Based Policy: How Effective Is China's New Cooperative Medical Scheme in Reducing Medical Impoverishment. *Social Science and Medicine*, 68(2), 201–209.

4 Social protection system in India

An assessment of the recent initiatives

Mukul Asher[1] *and Yutika Vora*

1. Introduction

India is a low-middle-income federal country, comprising the Union government, 29 states and seven union territories, and has a population of around 1,300 million, ranking it as the second most populated country globally. The role of sub-national governments is quite significant in India. The states account for more than half of the combined Union and state government expenditure; and they have significant responsibilities for implementing various initiatives of the Union government, including those in the area of social protection. This suggests that focusing on social protection programs of the Union government alone, a tendency exhibited by many researchers, including at multilateral institutions, tends to under-report the scope, expenditure, and impact of social protection programs for the country as a whole.

Since independence in 1947, India has gradually evolved a complex system of social protection. But this system is characterised by limited coverage and relatively low benefit levels, fragmentation, lack of coordination among agencies, and insufficient attention to design and professional implementation for obtaining outcomes in terms of improving access to social protection-related public amenities and services to households (Asher and Bali, 2014). These limitations have also constrained India's achievements under the MDGs, especially for stillbirths and neonatal mortality (Table 4.1). While access to old-age income security is not included in Table 4.1, the limitations of the current social protection system have also constrained progress in broadening and deepening of old age income security programs (Asher and Bali, 2014).

India's National Family Health Survey of 2015–2016 suggests significant improvement in health status. In particular, the 2015–2016 total fertility rate (TFR) is estimated to be 2.2, close to the replacement rate of 2.15. In 2015–2016, institutional births accounted for nearly four-fifths of all births. The infant mortality rate was 41 per 1,000 live births in 2015–2016. The Survey however suggests that improvement in the nutritional status of children has been limited, suggesting the need for greater focus and efforts on this aspect. Overall, the Survey suggests that India has laid the foundations for encouraging progress in its social indicators.

Table 4.1 Millennium development goals and performance of India in selected socio-economic indicators

Millennium development goals	Year 1990 (Actual/ Est. value)	MDG Target 2015	Most Recent Data Available
1 Eradicate extreme poverty and hunger			
• Proportion of population below poverty line (%)	47.8	23.7	21.9
• Proportion of under-weight children below 3 years per 1000	52	26	40
2 Achieve universal primary education			
• Net enrolment ratio in primary grade (%)	77	100	99.9
3 Promote gender equality and empower women			
• Ratio of girls to boys in primary school	0.7	1.00	1.0
4 Reduce child mortality: under 5 mortality			
• Under 5 mortality rate (per 1000 live births)	126	42	50*
5 Improve maternal health			
• Maternal Mortality Ratio (per 100,000 live births)	556	109	167
6 Combat HIV/AIDS, malaria and TB			
• HIV prevalence among pregnant women aged 15–24 years	NA	NA	0.4
• Prevalence of TB (including HIV) per 100,000 population	338	NA	249
7 Ensure environmental sustainability			
• Household with sustainable access to an improved water source (Urban/Rural)	87.12 / 58.94	93.56 / 79.47	95.3** / 88.5**
• Households without access to sanitation (Urban/Rural)	24.1 / 87.1	15.84 / 46.64	8.8** / 59.4**

* As per NFHS-4, 2015–16; ** achieved as of 2012.
Sources: Government of India, "Millennium Development Goals: India Country Report 2014". Ministry of Statistics and Programme Implementation www. indiaenvironmentportal.org.in/files/file/mdg_2014%20India%20country%20report.pdf

In May 2014, the BJP government led by Prime Minister Narendra Modi secured a strong national mandate. Since then, India has introduced several social protection initiatives designed to help the country progress towards the goals of the social protection floor (SPF) urged by the ILO in 2012. The SPF focuses on four basic social security areas: access to healthcare; basic amenities for children, particularly provision of nutrition and education; income security for older persons; labour market initiatives to improve employability and livelihood generation; and a lengthened working-age period over a lifetime.

The Agenda for Social Development (ASD) approved by the United Nations (UN) in 2015 also has social protection as an important component. But unlike ILO, its goals reflect the realities of the current and prospective global economic, political, and social environment, and are therefore less ambitious, eschewing strong prescriptive rules and permitting much greater leeway in terms of context-specific initiatives (for details of ASD, see the Overview chapter in this volume).

The current Indian government has accepted in principle the evolving global consensus that social protection programs and schemes should be an integrated part of its economic and social development goals and strategies. It is in the above context that this chapter analyses India's recent context-specific initiatives in social protection. These initiatives are designed to move the current social protection system towards broader and deeper access of households to social protection services in all four components of the SPF; and to enhance professionalism in design and implementation of social protection programs and schemes.

The initiatives recognise that context-specific linkages between a specific initiative on the one hand, and impact on income security, health status improvement, income generation, employability and livelihood generation at both national and sub-national levels on the other, are required. The initiatives also recognise that these are not always attained by simply adopting the social protection programs of high-income countries.

These initiatives represent a marked departure from the past, as they visualise and focus on improving household welfare from the perspective of market and non-market production and consumption activities; and encompass enhancement of income as well as reducing the need for expenditure on social protection services. Thus, both protection and promotion aspects of social sector initiatives are emphasised, though the nature and level of emphasis may vary among the initiatives. The initiatives also focus much more sharply on addressing constraints in their effective implementation, an area where India has traditionally exhibited weakness.

The rest of the chapter is organised as follows. The key characteristics of India's social protection system, reflecting major design, implementation, and assessment challenges are briefly discussed in section 2. This is followed by an analysis of social protection initiatives by the Union government since May 2014, and their implications for enhancing the quality of India's social protection system in section 3. Section 4 discusses issues relating to generating fiscal space in India, which could be potentially available for funding social protection. This section utilises the Generating Fiscal Space framework provided in the Overview chapter of this volume. The final section provides concluding remarks.

2. India's existing social protection system: an overview and reform contours

In analyzing India's social protection system, the relevant characteristics of the country need to be taken into account.

First, under India's federal structure, responsibilities for design, implementation, and evaluation of social protection programs are shared between various levels of government. This poses considerable challenges in policy coherence and organisational coordination. Typically, the Union government designs the social protection programs. Some states support these programs with their own social protection plans. However, the implementation of the social protection initiatives of the Union government is undertaken by the respective state governments. A key requirement for effective implementation, only recently recognised by policymakers, is management information systems that document the flow of funds from the Union government to the state treasuries and implementing agencies in an integrated manner.

The Controller General of Accounts Department (CGA), Ministry of Finance, has been entrusted with the responsibility for managing the PFMS (Public Financial Management System), a single platform for payment, accounting, and reconciliation of government transactions for Union government schemes by integrating existing stand-alone systems. It is not mandatory for states to join, but it is in their interest to do so and all states except for Nagaland have integrated their state treasury IT system with PFMS. By the end 2017, this has resulted in the PFMS being integrated with 135,000 bank branches and 2 million service providers. A senior official in the Ministry of Finance estimated that such coordination could save the Union government INR 100 billion annually by allowing for better cash management.

The emphasis on quality of 'plumbing' (of social protection programs) through measures such as improving management information systems, monitoring the flow of funds from the treasury to the beneficiaries of social protection programs, and making the process less prone to the misdirection of benefits is expected to lead to better expenditure management. This could lead to better outcomes for a given level of expenditure.

Second, India exhibits diverse socio-economic characteristics among different states and regions. As an example, Uttar Pradesh had per capita income of INR 40373[2] in 2014–2015 and poverty ratio of 29 percent.[3] This contrasts with the Uttarakhand with INR 115632 per capita income and poverty ratio of 11 percent. Similar large variations across the country are evident in health, education, livelihood creation, income security, and other social indicators. These variations reflect differing focus of the policymakers, implementation capacity of individual states for these programs, and differing fiscal and human resource capacity of the states.

These variations also suggest that inflexible designs of social protection schemes at the level of the Union government are unlikely to meet the needs of many states. Thus flexibility in individual schemes and considering various schemes with similar broad social protection objectives together could potentially provide better outcomes. Indeed, this is the direction being followed by the recent initiatives.

The third characteristic concerns the nature of the labour force. A large proportion of India's labour force (about three-quarters of the total labour force of about 500 million) is employed in sectors where formal relationships or contracts between employers and employees either do not exist or are weakly enforced. It is reasonable to assume that their participation in social protection schemes which are based on a formal employer-employee contract is extremely limited. This suggests a low coverage of the labour force under such schemes. As an example, the effective contributors to a mandatory provident fund scheme administered by the EPFO covers only around 5 percent of the labour force (www.epfindia.com/site_en/, website accessed on June 15, 2017). Even if all the mandatory and voluntary pension schemes are considered as a group, the coverage is unlikely to exceed a quarter of the labour force. So extending coverage in a manner which takes India's labour force employment-status composition into account is essential. The Indian government is embarking on initiatives to improve the quality and frequency of labour force data.

The fourth aspect concerns the nature of poverty. India does not publish poverty levels based on income. While India's poverty rates based on consumption expenditure have declined over time, the decline is much lower than India's growth performance would suggest. Over the last three decades India has grown at an average rate of 6 percent as measured by real GDP (RBI, 2016); while according to a government-appointed committee's report, the poverty ratio has declined from 39.6 percent in 2009–2010 to 30.9 percent in 2011–2012 in rural India and from 35.1 percent to 26.4 percent in urban India. The decline was thus a uniform 8.7 percentage points over the two years. The all-India poverty ratio fell from 38.2 percent to 29.5 percent (Press Information Bureau, 2014).

As noted, the variation in the poverty rate across India is also high, with the eastern region of the country exhibiting a much higher poverty rate than the rest of the country, even though the natural resource endowments and incomes are well above India's average. Initiatives to narrow the poverty gap between the eastern region and the rest of the country are therefore needed. Moreover, the nature of shocks which lead households into poverty has been changing. Thus, given the low exposure to health insurance and third-party payments, health related shocks could make a household transit from a middle-income to a low-income household. There are also weather-related shocks for farmers and others which require different types of social protection than traditionally employed. Conscientious consideration of the nature of poverty is increasingly being reflected in the recent initiatives of social protection.

2.1 Existing schemes: a brief overview

There are many existing schemes that address the four components of SPF suggested by the ILO. Table 4.2 highlights selected relevant schemes under each

Table 4.2 Selected social protection schemes by the Union government

Social protection component	Existing major schemes	Selected initiatives since May 2014
Universal healthcare	• National Health Policy (NHM) • Rashtriya Swasthya Bina Yojana (RSBY)* • Employees State Insurance Scheme (ESIS)	• Swacch Bharat Mission • Mission Indradhanush • Pradhan Mantri Ujjwala Yojana (PMUY) • Rashtriya Vayoshri Yojna
Pensions and care for older persons	• National Social Assistance Program (NSAP)	• Atal Pension Yojna (APY) • Varishtha Pension Bima Yojana (VPBY)
Social protection for working age people	• Employees' Pension Scheme (EPS) • Employees Provident Fund (EPF) • National Pension Scheme (NPS) • National Livelihood Mission (NLM)	• Pradhan Mantri Suraksha Bima Yojna (PMSBY) • Pradhan Mantri Fasal Bima Yojana (PMFBY) • Pradhan Mantri Jeevan Jyoti Bima Yojna (PMJJBY) • Pradhan Mantri Jan Dhan Yojana (PMJDY)
Social protection for children	• Right to Education Act • Mid-day Meals • Integrated Child Development Scheme (ICDS)	• Beti Bachao, Beti Padhao (Save and Educate the Girl Child) • Intensified Mission Indradhanush (IMI)
Employability and livelihoods	• Mahatma Gandhi National Rural Employment Guarantee Act (MGNREGA)	• Skill India • Make in India • MUDRA (Micro Units Development Refinance Agency) Bank • Start-up India • Deen Dyal Upadhyay Gram Jyoti Yojana (DDUGJY) • Pradhan Mantri Sahaj Bijli Ghar Yojana (Saubhagya)

Notes: *There are indications that the RSBY will be significantly revised, but as the of end of December 2017, details have not been announced.
Source: compiled by authors from official and other sources

component. This section discusses recent reforms in select existing social protection schemes, while new initiatives are discussed in the subsequent section.

Universal healthcare

India has universal healthcare provided by a network of primary, secondary, and tertiary public hospitals run by State governments across India. Any citizen can use services free of cost at these medical centers. However, most of these centers are unable to cope with the level of demand, resulting in inadequate quality of care, long waiting times, and weak infrastructure. They often have very limited access to pharmaceuticals and other essential equipment (Government of India, 2017a). This is illustrated in relatively high out-of-pocket spending on healthcare in India (Government of India, 2015). In responding to these challenges, the Union government introduced the National Rural Health Mission in 2005 (subsequently called the National Health Mission) which consolidates the Union government's health-related funding given to state governments and directs them at targeted programs (focused largely on maternal, child, and preventive health), and emphasises decentralised delivery of services.

In 2008, the Union government introduced the RSBY: a low-cost-low-benefit health insurance program which provides healthcare services at contracted public and private hospitals for INR 30,000 per year to identified families who are living in poverty. Services are portable across India and the program is funded largely by the Union government with some co-contribution required by state governments in the ratio of 75:25. The latter are however responsible for identifying beneficiaries and implementing the program (Amicus Advisory Private Limited, 2011).

The ESIS is implemented by the Ministry of Labour and is a health insurance program for formal sector workers. Its members can receive treatment at ESIS hospitals run throughout the country or at centers the ESIC has contracted with. It faces challenges similar to those of the network of health centers and hospitals run by the state governments.

Pensions and care for older persons

The National Social Assistance Program (NSAP) is a Union government assisted program that provides the finance for the social pensions program that is implemented by the state governments. The Indira Gandhi National Old Age Pension Scheme (IGNOAPS) is one component of the NSAP that provides a minimum annual pension payment of INR 3,600 to persons above the age of 60 who are identified to be below the poverty line. In addition, persons above the age of 80 years are entitled to a pension of INR 6,000 per year. The Union government provides state governments with funding based on the estimates of persons above 60 years of age and considered to be below the poverty line. States are then free to top up the benefit with their own funding or provide the same benefit level but increase coverage based on a higher poverty line estimate. Funding for this program is sourced both by the Union government as well as state governments (KPMG and FICCI, 2015).

In March 2013, the Task Force constituted by the Ministry of Rural Development recommended the universalisation of the NSAP to all older persons above the age of 60. If this is adopted, the fiscal implications as provided by the task force would increase expenditure from the current of INR 45.99 billion with coverage of 16.5 million members to INR 278.61 billion in year five for 42.6 million members (Asher and Vora, 2016).

Social protection for working age people

Social protection for working age people is primarily provided through three programs: the Employees' Provident Fund (EPF), the Employees' Pension Scheme (EPS), and the National Pension Scheme (NPS). The first two are administered by the Employees Provident Fund Organization (EPFO) and the latter by the PFRDA. The EPF and EPS are mandatory programs for formal sector workers. The former is a savings scheme that earns an administered rate of interest, and the latter is a DB pension scheme. Asher and Bali (2014) note that the EPS has large actuarial liabilities as the investment income and contributions are insufficient to cover current and future benefits payable. Traditionally, EPFO assets have been primarily Government of India securities but in recent years, the EPFO has started to access financial and capital markets, and has used technology to improve the quality of its services.

Civil and military personnel have access to both direct contribution (DC) savings schemes as well as relatively generous direct benefit (DB) pension schemes. The National Pension Scheme (NPS), a DC pension scheme, was introduced for all civil service personnel recruited after 2004 in response to the high actuarially projected pension liabilities on Union and State governments for their civil service employees. The NPS is mandatory for civil service personnel and its architecture has been extended on a voluntary basis to private sector workers, including to those employed in the informal sector. The NPS architecture allows accumulated balances to be invested in one of three options, which facilitate varying risk-return preferences. Fund managers are selected on a competitive basis and the scheme is regulated and managed by the PFRDA.

The coverage of the private sector formal and informal workers is indeed very low (Table 4.3).

Social protection for children

Social protection for children is largely provided through the Right to Education Act enacted by Parliament in 2009.[4] The Act recognises free and compulsory

Table 4.3 India's National Pension System, members, and balances (As of June 2017)

Sector	Members Millions (%)		Accumulated Balances INR Billion (%)	
Total	10.4	(100.0)	1,901.5	(100.0)
Central government	1.8	(17)	726.9	(38)
State government	3.4	(32)	943.6	(50)
Corporate	0.6	(6)	166.5	(9)
All citizen model	0.5	(5)	36.2	(2)
NPS lite	4.4	(31)	28.3	(1)

Note: figures in parenthesis are percentage of respective total
Source: adapted from the data provided by the PFRDA, accessed in July 2017

education for all children aged between 6 and 14 years in India. Many public schools introduced mid-day meals through child development schemes funded by Union and State governments to encourage enrollment and attendance in primary schools.

Employability and livelihoods

The MGNREGA was enacted in Parliament in 2005 and provides for employment for between 100 and 150 person days to at least one member of each targeted household. The Union government of India in the 2017 Budget has committed to spending INR 480 billion in the fiscal year on the program (Government of India, 2017b). The program initially emphasised only protections, but since 2014 has focused on creating productive assets, and to using technology and other means to better target the beneficiaries. Thus, a better balance between protection and promotion is being achieved, enhancing its potential sustainability.

The Micro Units Development Refinance Agency (MUDRA Bank) provides priority lending to micro businesses including businesses owned by groups with severe difficulties in accessing finance. The scheme was announced in 2016 and provides three types of loans (based on the principal borrowed which varies for INR 50,000 to INR one million). Of the loans, 92 percent are under INR 50,000, suggesting that micro-enterprises are significant beneficiaries of the MUDRA Bank. The interest rates at which the loans are disbursed are not publicly available but preliminary estimates suggest that they are between 9.7 and 11.7 percent as of March 2017.[5] This augurs well for encouraging a business-oriented culture more widely, with aspirations to become livelihood providers rather than just seeking traditional and, often, government jobs.

2.2 Reforming select existing programs

Recent reforms in existing programs have been characterised by more strategic and outcome-oriented uses of technology, particularly of a biometric identification system called Aadhar (explained below), and digital banking technology, combined with financial inclusion measures. It may be useful to elaborate on these aspects.

The Unique Identification Authority of India (UIDAI), a statutory authority established under the provisions of the Aadhaar (Targeted Delivery of Financial and Other Subsidies, Benefits and Services) Act, 2016, under the Ministry of Electronics and Information Technology, issues all residents with a 12-digit unique identification number based on biometric information of Indian residents. The identification is called the "Aadhaar" card and is increasingly required for accessing social protection services under recent initiatives.

Aadhaar is a central component of a series of recently implemented measures to improve financial inclusion. Key among them is the Pradhan Mantri Jan Dhan Yojana (PMJDY). The core purpose of the PMJDY is to extend modern financial services and financial literacy to all households within India. The Union government recognises that operational bank accounts are essential for overcoming challenges in disbursing subsidies and benefits. Moreover, access to and growth in rural credit has been constrained by the lack of financial services available. It is these impediments that the PMJDY aims to address. For instance, the government has started to transfer benefits including LPG subsidies under the PMUY, and wages earned under the MGNREGA initiative providing up to 100 workdays of employment a year, to individual bank accounts.

The PMJDY allows individuals to open bank accounts at public or private banks, without maintaining a minimum balance. The members are provided with a debit card. It is envisaged that over time current subsidies and cash benefits would ultimately be routed to this Jan Dhan account. Beneficiaries also receive an overdraft facility if they regularly use the account; accidental and life insurance; and other subsidised financial services (transfer of funds, etc.). When PMJDY was announced in 2014, more than 80 percent of bank accounts opened had zero balances. This share has gradually reduced to about a quarter, and is expected to reduce further, while the accumulated balances reached around INR 650 billion in January 2017.

In addition to PMJDY and the use of Aadhar, there has been increasing emphasis on the role of mobile phones. The 2015–2016 economic survey termed the three as 'JAM' and argued that the government would increasingly rely on JAM to improve access in all areas of service delivery. The direct benefit transfer to bank accounts covered around 300 schemes by mid-2017, as compared to only 75 in mid-2016. The eventual goal is to bring 500 schemes under direct benefit transfer programs. In 2016–2017, INR 746 billion was transferred in this manner, for about 360 million beneficiaries. As a given beneficiary can receive multiple transfers, the number of individuals benefitting is less than the number of beneficiaries.

The use of JAM will be further enhanced by the currency-swap (more popularly known as demonetisation) initiative implemented on November 8, 2016, under which INR 500 and INR 1000 notes in circulation were exchanged for a new set of notes. This is likely to facilitate a shift towards a less cash-based and less unaccounted-transactions-based economy.

Table 4.4 Pradhan Mantri Jan Dhan Yojna status (as of January 2017)

	No. of accounts (in million)			Rupay debit cards	Balance in accounts (INR billion)	Percent of zero balance accounts
	Rural	Urban	Total			
Public Sector Bank	12.2	9.9	22.0	17.2	509.9	24.7
Rural Regional Bank	4.0	0.6	4.6	3.4	120.9	20.8
Private Banks	0.5	0.4	0.9	0.8	23.4	35.1
Total	16.7	10.9	27.5	21.4	654.2	24.4

Source: Pradhan Mantri Jan Dhan Yojna Website, www.pmjdy.gov.in/account-statistics-country. aspx, accessed on February 17, 2017

2.3 *Broad contours of social protection reforms*

It is useful to briefly discuss the broad contours of the reforms underway in existing social protection programs. This could help clarify the underlying thinking of the policymakers, and highlight the departure represented by the post-2014 initiatives in social protection.

First, there has been a focused effort to improve coordination and overall policy coherence. Coordination and coherence are terms used to describe the extent to which various government agencies work together to achieve goals, and the latter describes the extent to which goals, objectives, and actions cohere in a given policy area. For instance, until 2015 the RSBY, the principal health insurance program in India, was administered by the Ministry of Labour, which has limited expertise in health policy and management. In 2015, the program was moved to the Ministry of Health so that there could be greater coordination with other health programs including the National Health Mission. The ESIS, a compulsory health insurance program for some section of workers with formal labour contracts, however, continues to be administered by the Ministry of Labour rather than the Ministry of Health. For policy coherence and organisational coordination such a shift merits urgent consideration.

Second, one of the major impediments in social security in India has been the lack of professionalism in performing core agency functions (Asher and Bali, 2014). Post-2014, measures have been taken to improve the professionalism with which EPFO and NPS undertake their core functions. For instance, the EPFO has begun to participate in financial and capital markets more actively, diversifying its investment portfolio. It is also facilitating on-line services for members, and making member accounts portable across the country. This will improve functioning of labour markets by encouraging labour mobility. It has also permitted members to form housing cooperatives to use their EPF balances to finance residential housing.

Similarly, discussions are underway to allow partial withdrawal of accumulated balances in the NPS to be used for housing. The Finance Minister's Budget Speech in March 2016 and in February 2017 highlighted the importance of moving towards a society with accessible pension products. NPS members can now defer their annuity by three years and their lump sum withdrawal by ten years. Members in the voluntary NPS (i.e., not civil servants) are allowed an option of making contributions till age 70, so they can benefit from the power of compound interest for a longer period. This option is however not available to civil service personnel, but should be extended to them as it can potentially increase the replacement rate, as well as provide an avenue to save for those who elect to work beyond the institutional retirement age at 60.

Third, there has been an emphasis on obtaining better outcomes for given outlays. The reforms underway in the MGNREGA help illustrate this point. The program, when judged by its own stated goals of providing employment to those who are not able to find other jobs, has failed to achieve many of its objectives (Samuel and Srinivasan, 2016). Recent reforms to MGNREGA has enabled the program to better reflect differences in State priorities and focus more on creating durable and economically productive assets; and has helped in diversifying liveli-hood opportunities by blending MGNREGA funds with other productive public and private expenditure. As a consequence, its reach among historically disadvan-taged sections of society, including the Dalits and tribal groups, has, arguably, extended considerably.

The program also provides a higher number of days of employment (150 days instead of 100 days) in drought-affected areas. The Economic Survey of 2016–2017 reports that out of 109 million active workers under MGNREGA, 87 mil-lion workers had their job cards linked with Aadhaar. For every 20 workers, 19 workers received wages directly in their bank accounts, reducing the possibility of leakages and corruption, and advancing financial inclusion.

In March 2017, the Union government announced in its National Health Policy (2017) that it aims to improve public health outcomes, and to strengthen primary care (the government plans to allocate about two-thirds of increased spending in primary care), reduce regulatory hurdles to ease manufacturing of drugs and medical devices within India, and to increase spending on preventive care (Government of India, 2017c).[6]

Fourth, there is a tendency to increase choice, contestability and co-contribu-tion in the provision of social protection. With increasing use of technology, par-ticularly information technology, to better target beneficiaries, reduce leakages, and lower transaction costs. For instance, in March 2017, the Union government announced that EPFO members, including of those provident funds regulated by EPFO but who have been managing their own investments, to opt for NPS. This widening of choice to members, and contestability between EPFO and NPS could help spur better governance and greater professionalism. The NPS has not only lowered administrative costs which essentially increase the real rate of return members receive; but has moved towards providing more diversified asset allocation and options with varying risk-return preferences which members can choose from.

We now turn to the post-2014 selected social protection initiatives that have been implemented by the government.

3. Selected social protection initiatives since 2014

Over the last decade, much of the literature on social protection in India has focused on means-tested schemes with funding provided by the Union govern-ment and implemented by the state governments. Those schemes initiated since 2016 are still in the early stages of implementation. However, they show substan-tial potential to provide a social protection net for a much larger population base. This section focuses on the schemes that have been introduced since 2014, and some of the changes that have been undertaken in existing programs in order to respond to the changing context of India. The traditional social protection programs have focused on providing support as populations cope with poverty; this new generation of initiatives also focuses on poverty prevention as well as on mitigating the risks that may cause families to fall into poverty.

The post-2014 social protection initiatives of the Indian government are classified in Table 4.2 using the traditional classification of social protection programs covering healthcare, support for older persons, social protection for working-age persons and for children, and employability and livelihoods. These initiatives are termed innovative because they take into account India's socio-economic context to locate linkages between initiatives and social protection outcomes. As an example, PMUY has provided cleaner cooking fuel (LPG) instead of traditional bio-mass fuel which creates indoor pollution affecting the health of (particularly) women and children. Thus, the health benefits of PMUY are significant. This could positively impact health and economic indicators in India's specific socio-economic context (Sengupta, 2017). A recent launch of one lakh Pradhan Mantri LPG Panchayats is a scheme meant to give an interactive platform to rural LPG users, especially for the beneficiaries of the PMUY. Representatives of oil companies, distributors, ministry, local NGOs, and self-help groups will be involved to discuss issues impacting the realisation of full benefits of PMUY (Desh Gujarat, 2017)

3.1 Atal Pension Yojna

The APY (Atal Pension Yojna) is a pension scheme introduced by the Union government of India in 2015. It is open to all citizens aged between 18 to 40 years. For those eligible (i.e., a member must not be covered by any statutory social security scheme or be an income tax payer), the Union government co-contributes 50 percent of the member's contribution, or INR 1,000 per year, whichever is lower. Such co-contribution is to be provided for five years for those joining between June 1, 2015 and December 31, 2015. The APY is operated through bank accounts, encouraging financial inclusion. There is a provision for exiting from the APY before reaching 60 years, without any penalty.

The APY combines elements of Defined Benefit (DB) and Defined Contribution (DC) methods. This is achieved by the government guaranteeing a specified amount of pension chosen by a member, but whose contribution amount, which varies with age, is also specified. Thus, both contributions and benefits are defined.

This is made feasible as the difference between what is earned on investments from APY balances and the minimum guaranteed amount is borne by the Union government, representing its contingent liability. If investment returns are higher than the minimum guaranteed, the excess is to be provided to the members as benefit, over and above the promised amount. The benefits are not adjusted for inflation.

The investment allocation of APY balances is 85 percent debt and 15 percent equity. It is thus the same as for those government employees who must mandatorily become members of the National Pension System (NPS), administered and regulated by the PFRDA (Pension Fund Regulatory and Development Authority). Thus, the APY members are able to participate in India's financial and capital markets with high degree of confidence using the well-structured, globally compatible NPS architecture.

A member may choose to receive the chosen pension amount as an annuity at age 60 for life, thus addressing the longevity risk (the risk that retirement income resources may be exhausted before death). This feature is particularly attractive to the bottom two income quintiles.

The pension provided has features similar to a joint life policy, with return of purchase price to the nominee. Thus, the APY also addresses survivors' risk. This risk concerns the income security of those who survive the death of the main income earner, usually males. In India, formally recorded labour force participation rate for women is around 30 percent, much lower than the male labour force participation rate of 80 percent. In India, at birth, women as a group live longer than men by around three years in 2017 (and the differential is expected to increase). Women's participation is, however, understated, as they do lot of unpaid family work that is not recorded in official labour and income statistics.

The above suggests that addressing survivors' risk as well as the longevity risk are major positive features of the APY. There is also provision for the return of purchase price in the APY. The APY benefit is not indexed for inflation. It is for these features that the APY cannot be simplistically compared with other retirement products that do not possess the same features.

As of February 4, 2017, less than two years after its implementation, the number of APY members (called subscribers) was 4.27 million,[7] with accumulated balances of INR 16.6 billion, implying a balance of only INR 3,911 per member. The number of members enrolling with the APY in such a short time is moderately impressive, but the mean average balance per member needs to increase to more adequately address old age income security. The mean, however, requires a more nuanced interpretation, as variance around the mean is likely to be large. Moreover, the mean amount is also affected by the choice made by the member concerning the pension option, which varies from INR 1,000 to INR 5,000 per month. Most have chosen the lowest option, and this aspect needs to be addressed.

3.1.1 Suggested reforms to Atal Pension Yojana

There are several refinements, relatively straightforward to implement, which have the potential to significantly improve the APY outcomes. First, there is a need to attempt to minimise frequent changes in the APY, which adversely impact fairness among members, and constrain long-term savings commitments requiring confidence and trust in the pension organisations. It will also help APY intermediaries, including banks and other financial intermediaries, to minimise their costs of managing APY accounts. According to the data provided by the PFRDA, the share of persistent or active contributors varies across the country for 1.6 million APY members registered with 31 major banks in the country, with active contributors averaging around 70 percent of the total members. This record needs to be improved if all members are to earn the full benefits under the APY, and the coverage extended. It will also lead to better utilisation of PFRDA's resources, and help in policy coherence and organisational coordination. A better mechanism to link incentives provided to banks to enrol and service members so there is continuation of APY contributions by current members, and the attraction of new members could be considered.

The PFRDA needs to facilitate public access to regular data (at least on an annual basis) on the APY members by age group, gender, accumulated balances, average balance, and density of contribution (called persistent or active members by the PFRDA). The annual rate of return obtained on APY investments also needs to be stated.

Without available robust databases of the type suggested above, transparency, accountability, and corrective measures needed would be severely constrained. Such data will also enable researchers to undertake rigorous studies, an advantage that can no longer be foregone. Indeed, such data robustness should also be required for other similar schemes, including the VPBY (discussed subsequently) announced in the 2017 budget. The VPBY is administered by the Life Insurance Corporation (LIC) of India. It should be asked to report the VPBY data separately.

For APY and other similar schemes, including the Employees' Pension Scheme (EPS) of the EPFO (Employees Provident Fund Organization), and the NPS for government employees, periodical rigorous publicly available actuarial studies (with enough information that they can be duplicated by others) should be a requirement. The role of actuarial professionals in sound design and sustainability of all pension and insurance schemes (including health insurance schemes) needs much greater recognition by the policymakers, regulators, and other stakeholders than has been the case so far.

3.2 Align asset allocation guidelines for similar schemes

The VPBY (discussed subsequently) managed by LIC should be permitted asset allocation choices similar to APY to minimise the fiscal contingent liability of the state. Regulatory changes required to accomplish this by the IRDA (Insurance Regulatory and Development Authority) of India merit urgent consideration. Two different investment allocation guidelines for essentially similar products suggest insufficient policy coherence and organisational co-ordination. Indeed, there is a strong case for revisiting asset allocation guidelines for all annuity products, especially given the low international interest rate environment manifested in a downward trend in domestic interest rates on savings products, and challenges in matching assets and liabilities for annuity products.

The design and implementing regulations are currently vested with the Ministry of Finance (MOF), but it is implemented through the PFRDA, which has globally compatible sound pension architecture, including for managing investments of balances in a very cost-effective way, and for record keeping. Any amount saved in these functions translates into improved benefits to the members. Finding ways to minimise costs of asset management and of recordkeeping is a challenge globally, and the PFRDA's pension architecture has handled these issues in a competent manner.

It is suggested that the MOF continue its current role of providing broad guidelines for the APY, with details of implementing regulations and supervision being left with the PFRDA.

Moreover, in the APY the minimum saving period is 20 years, and the benefit period could exceed that, given increased longevity. Data from the UN suggests that in 2015, an average Indian has an expected life expectancy of up to 15 years at 65 years of age. This longevity is expected to begin at age 69 in 2050 (Table 2; Chomik et al., 2016). This has important implications for funding India's ageing population. PFRDA is the only pension organisation currently deserving of such long-term trust, through it will need to make improvements to suit different circumstances to sustain such trust.

3.3 *Varishtha Pension Bima Yojana (VPBY)*

The government of India in the Union Budget 2014–2015 announced the revival of Varishtha Pension Bima Yojana (VPBY). The scheme is implemented by a public-sector-owned, so-far-unlisted entity called the Life Insurance Corporation of India (LIC). VPBY offers a guaranteed nominal rate of 8 percent on pension balances for 10 years. This is a helpful step for those eligible (citizens aged 60 years and above) to cope with interest rate volatility. Under the scheme a total number of 0.32 million annuitants are being benefited.

The difference between what the LIC obtains in investment returns on pension balances and the 8 percent guaranteed return will be borne by the Union government. So contingent liabilities (the difference between LIC's rate of return and 8 percent) will arise, and must be appropriately estimated and accounted for in the Union government's budget statements. It would be useful to periodically review the extent of such liabilities and report them to the stakeholders.

The indications are that a maximum of INR 0.75 million (0.75 million) could be invested in VPBY per family. The option to receive pensions on monthly, quarterly, half yearly, and annual basis is provided.

The scheme duration of 10 years is reasonable and indeed a good design, because macroeconomic environments may change over time, and sunset clauses are needed in all such schemes in order for a fresh view to be taken at the time of sunset. Indeed, such sunset clauses merit consideration in all types of subsidy schemes.

The income from VPBY is expected to be subject to income tax, but section 80 C benefits under the Income Tax Act are likely to be available. A feature adding to the attractiveness of the VPBY 2017 is that on the death of the policyholder, the premium is to be returned to the nominee, though in real terms, its value will be low due to the intervening time period.

The above suggests that the VPBY should not be evaluated on the basis that it will provide the only source of income during retirement. With rising longevity (an Indian reaching age 60 in 2015 is projected to have additional life expectancy of around 19 years, with women exhibiting higher than average life expectancy of 20 years), it is essential to obtain retirement income from many different sources. This could include developing marketable skills which may have demand when a person is formally retired. It is the income from all sources in retirement that is a relevant indicator, not whether each scheme meets full retirement needs. Such an arrangement also serves as a sound risk-mitigation strategy, particularly in the Indian context.

The modest impact strongly suggests that in devising any pension scheme, the focus should be on how it fits (in terms of policy coherence and organisational coordination) into the objectives of the pension system as a whole. As this aspect has received insufficient attention, this is an opportune time to consider a national level research think tank (or a Division under Niti Aayog) on retirement income security, and behavior of the aged, and implications for public policies and demand and supply of goods, services, and financial and physical assets. As in other areas, empirical evidence–driven policies in the pension and ageing area are also essential.

3.4 Healthcare: Swachch Bharat Mission (SBM) or Clean India Mission

The Clean India Mission, also known as Swachch Bharat Mission, is among the key post-2014 initiatives. The link between an unhygienic public environment and health status in India has been empirically evidenced by various studies (Desai, 2017). The program could also have a positive impact on the extent to which episodes of ill-health could result in a household falling below the poverty level of income. It includes the construction of household toilets, community public toilets, school toilets, scientific solid waste management, informational and educational communication, and capacity-building of administrative services.

The program encourages private sector companies, civil society, and corporate groups to incorporate SBM objectives in their activities. In urban areas, for three years ending 2017–2018, the target is to build around 10 million individual toilets, around 5 million public and community toilets. The program aims to construct 110 million individual toilets in rural areas by 2019. As of mid-2017, nearly two-thirds of rural households have toilets and the aim is to reach 100 percent by 2019 (Desai, 2017). The program has led to 7 out of 29 states being declared free of open defecation, potentially improving their public health.

The challenge faced by the government in this scheme will be the maintenance and upkeep of this infrastructure once it has been built. The high level political commitment has made sanitation a top priority across the country, but this needs to be sustained over time. However, the total sanitation can only be achieved when communities understand the need for sanitation and demand sanitation services. Behavioural change is therefore essential. There are encouraging signs that such a change is indeed being exhibited in both urban and rural areas.

3.5 Healthcare insurance schemes for the informal sector

The Pradhan Mantri Jeevan Jyoti Bima Yojana (PMJJBY) and Pradhan Mantri Suraksha Bima Yojna (PMSBJ) are two insurance programs that have been developed to encourage informal workers to be covered under social insurance programs. Both these programs are offered at a nominal cost to any person within the eligible age range and who are not member of any other pension program. The PMJJBY and PMSBY were launched in May 2015.

The PMSBY offers a renewable one-year accidental death-cum-disability coverage. The scheme is offered through Public Sector General Insurance Companies (PSGICs) and other general insurance companies willing to offer the product on similar terms, at the choice of the Bank/RRB/Cooperative Bank concerned. As of January 2017, the scheme covered 98 million beneficiaries.

The PMJJBY offers a renewable one-year term life coverage of INR 0.2 million to all subscribing bank account holders in the 18 to 50 years age range, covering death due to any reason, for a premium of INR 330 per annum per subscriber. The scheme is offered/administered through LIC and other life insurance companies willing to offer the product on similar terms, at the choice of the Bank/RRB/Cooperative Bank concerned. According to the Ministry of Finance, 31 million people have been enrolled under PMJJBY and 91 million under PMSBY as on February 2017 (datagov.in accessed on September 6, 2017). India's insurance penetration – the proportion of premiums to GDP – was 3.44 percent in 2015. The budget allocation for both the schemes was INR 200 million for FY 2017–2018.

3.6 Mission Indradhanush

Mission Indradhanush (MI) is a health mission of the government of India launched in December 2014. It aims to immunise pregnant women and all children up to two years in the country protecting them against seven vaccine-preventable childhood diseases. The government has identified 201 high-focus districts across 28 states in the country that have the highest number of partially immunised and unimmunised children. Mission Indradhanush targets these districts through special immunisation drives to improve the routine immunisation coverage in the country. An Intensified Mission Indradhanush[8] (IMI) that aims to reach every child below two years of age and pregnant women who have been left uncovered under the government's routine immunisation programme against preventable diseases was also launched in October 2017. It aims to focus on select districts and cities to ensure full immunisation to more than 90 per cent of children and pregnant women by December 2018. The target is at least 90 per cent coverage by 2020.

3.7 Pradhan Mantri Kaushal Vikas Yojna (PMKVY)

India is currently exhibiting a favorable demographic phase during which the working age population to total population ratio will continue to increase till around 2040, and thereafter decline at a moderate rate (Deloitte, 2017). To translate the favourable demographic phase into higher trend rate of growth requires innovative programs for skilling of the existing and future labour force which results in productive livelihoods.

The PMVYK and its various components are designed to address the above challenge (www.pmkvyofficial.org accessed on October 1, 2017). It is administered by the Ministry of Skill Development and Entrepreneurship (MSDE).

Its target during the 2016–2020 period is to provide employable skills to 10 million people. It gives recognised certificates on the completion of the program as a signal to the potential clients or employers that a certain level of competency has been attained. Prior skills are also recognised under this.

There are various measures under the Skill India initiative to enhance engagement with industry, improve quality assurance, and to set up institutional arrangements for training the trainers. Around 0.3 million people are to be technically trained in Japan as part of bilateral cooperation between Japan and India. There are also plans to set up over 60 international skilling institutes to help Indian workers participate in the global market.

The PMKVY and its components thus are designed to forge an innovative path for vocational and skill training areas which were earlier given insufficient strategic focus. Operationally, this program is connected to the Jan Dhan Yojna. Accordingly, reimbursement for completing the certification is provided directly through the bank account on completion of the training.

3.8 Pradhan Mantri Fasal Bima Yojana (PMFBY)

More than half of India's population is dependent on the agricultural sector for a significant share of its livelihood. Moreover, dependence on adequate monsoon rains continues to be significant. Therefore, the importance of an effective crop insurance system as a social protection instrument cannot be over-emphasised, particularly because of the variability and uncertainty in weather due to climate change.

The underlying rationale and functioning of crop insurance is rooted in certain generally agreed-upon principles. First, the risk of crop failure is transferred from the individual farmer to the insurer, in return for which the farmer pays a designated premium. Second, many participating farmers over a long period of time could enable addressing the vertical spread of risk (over time) and horizontal spread of risk (over a wide area) (Vyas and Singh, 2006).

The inherent limitations of crop insurance, however, are the systemic nature of agricultural risks, constraining operation of the law of large numbers; much wider scope for moral hazard; the difficulty of adverse selection and the trade-off between viability of the program and affordability for farmers (Nair, 2010). These need to be addressed.

The PMFBY, launched in January 2016, with the Ministry of Agriculture and Farmers Welfare (https://www.india.gov.in/spotlight/pradhan-mantri-fasal-bima-yojana#tab=tab-1) as a nodal agency, represents a significant improvement in design, coverage, and implementation processes over the similar schemes existing previously.

The previous schemes were characterised by high premium burdens in relation to compensation; cumbersome claim processes; deficiencies in insurance design;

poor awareness among stakeholders; limited coverage among farmers; and narrow geographic spread (Raju and Chand, 2008).

In 2014–2015, of the gross-cropped area of 194.4 million hectares, 45.3 million hectares (23.3 percent) was insured. The coverage of crops such as sugarcane and fruits was as low as 2.7 percent and 5.6 percent respectively (http://pmksy.gov.in/).

The PMFBY is aimed at all farmers, including sharecroppers and tenant farmers. The participation for those farmers taking loans from financial institutions (loanee farmers) is mandatory. The participation is optional for the non-loanee farmers. The premium paid by the farmer is at the rate of 2 percent and 1.5 percent for Kharif (or monsoon) and Rabi (or winter) crops respectively. For commercial and horticulture crops, the premium paid by the farmer is 5 percent. As these premium rates paid by farmers are not expected to cover the benefits paid, the balance of the premium is shared between the Union government and the states (http://pmksy.gov.in/).

The nodal agency has selected a mix of a public and private insurance agencies to administer the scheme. Each state can select any agency from the lists. The reinsurance is left to the discretion of the states and the insurance companies. This element may be reconsidered, as reinsurance is essential when risks are concentrated and potential liabilities are large.

The PMFBY incorporates localised risk coverage (with the added inclusion of the risk of inundation), post-harvest losses coverage (with the inclusion of unseasonal rain), and prevented sowing coverage.

The PMFBY can be expected to have a positive impact in the following areas. First, the scheme lowers premiums paid by farmers, while providing wider coverage of risks, including for sowing and for post-harvest. It also aims at wider geographical coverage. Second, the use of technology could help in providing to those qualified, and help ensure speedier disbursement of claims to farmers. Third, in times of agricultural distress, it is expected that PMFBY could act as an important endogenous coping mechanism without policy makers having to resort to discretionary initiatives, such as enhancing the Minimum Support Price for crops.

Fourth, by acting partially as collateral for borrowers who approach formal institutions for credit, PMFBY can be expected to help reduce the risk for the lender, aid in recovery of loans, and help maintain the credit eligibility of the borrower (Ghosh and Yadav, 2008). Fifth, PMFBY along with the National Agriculture Market (NAM), an electronic market for selected commodities, could encourage crop diversification by mitigating risks associated with growing high risk–high return crops. It could also encourage some farmers to adopt perhaps riskier but more yield-generating technologies. Finally, the PMFBY could help in increasing the flow of credit to the agricultural sector as the relevant data generated is utilised for better credit assessment.

The policymakers may consider integrating the Weather Based Crop Insurance Scheme (WBICS) with PMFBY, rather than having them as co-existing schemes. This integration can be expected to lead to better insurance protection at lower resource costs.

While PMFBY has a crucial role to play, crop insurance by itself may not be enough to mitigate risks and perform protection and promotion functions. Policies that promote self-insurance such as micro-credit and increasing off-farm employment are also important. In addition, risk mitigation can also be carried out through agricultural practices such as conservation of soil moisture, drainage, use of appropriate irrigation technologies, and more extensive processing of crops and construction of better supply chains. There may in fact be great potential in tying insurance to climate change adaptation and mitigation, by rewarding those who adopt risk-reducing technologies and practices, with lower premiums and deductibles (Swain, 2014).

Effectively addressing the challenge of ensuring good insurance claims processing and monitoring quality of service of insurance companies, to better align their billing with benefits provided, remains among the continuing challenges of PFMBY.

4. Generating fiscal space to fund social protection

This section briefly discusses estimates of fiscal cost of selected social protection initiatives, and suggests broad strategies to generate the requisite fiscal space, using the framework developed in Chapter 1. Given the large number of social protection schemes in India (Table 4.2), it is not feasible to provide an estimate of fiscal space covering all the schemes. Even for the schemes for which fiscal cost estimates are provided, the behavioural aspects of the economic and political agents are not considered. Thus, Asher and Vora (2016) estimate that for pensions alone, India will need to generate between 2 and 4 percent of GDP as additional fiscal space by the year 2030. These estimates are indicative of the magnitude of the fiscal space that India will need to generate. It is also essential that all the elements of the Generating Fiscal Space Framework (Figure 1.2) in the Overview chapter are utilised in a context-specific manner.

4.1 Universal basic income proposal

India's 2016–2017 Economic Survey includes a chapter that analyses the merits and feasibility of introducing Universal Basic Income (UBI) (Government of India, 2017). The UBI is a rights-based minimum income which is budget-financed to all citizens regardless of their income, assets, or other status. The chapter argues that while research on UBI is worth initiating, India is not ready to implement it at this stage. It estimates that the projected costs of the current social protection schemes by the Union government in 2016–2017 would be equivalent to 5.2 percent of GDP. These estimates do not incorporate the social protection expenditure met exclusively from the resources of the states and local governments. Their inclusion will raise the already substantial gross fiscal costs of existing schemes. It would be useful for the Union and state governments to invest in constructing relevant social protection expenditure databases, and to develop relevant analytics capabilities, before ambitions of new initiatives are considered.

In principle, the UBI proposal could substitute for all existing social protection programs of at least the Union government, if not some of the states. The political economy in India, with its federal structure and its populist tendencies, is unlikely to end the existing social protection programs in case UBI is introduced. It will be just an additional program with a high fiscal cost, and substantial incentive effects on labor force participation, saving, and risk taking.

The fiscal costs of UBI are estimated to vary based on the design, level of benefit, and the extent of inclusion errors (those who do not qualify but still receive benefits) and exclusion errors (those who do qualify but do not receive benefits). The Economic Survey estimates that if the benefit level is equal to 10 percent of per capita income of 2015–2016 (INR 105,815), the fiscal cost as percent of GDP in 2016–2017 will be 8.6 percent of GDP. The fiscal costs will decline to 6.4 percent of GDP if a targeted approach is used. These costs when the combined Union and state government fiscal deficits (even on a conservative cash accounting basis) of about 7 percent of GDP are prohibitive.[9]

This proposal, therefore, is designed to initiate discussion on rationalising India's social protection system; it is not a serious proposal to be implemented. The incentives effect on labour supply, saving, investing, risk taking, and others of finding resources to fund the UBI are likely to be very significant. Due cognizance of the incentive effects issue of how social protection programs in general are funded should be taken.

4.2 Projected costs of social pensions

Expanding effective coverage and benefit levels of the existing social pension program, the NSAP, could be more feasible. Asher and Vora (2016) estimate fiscal cost as share of GDP if 70 percent of persons above the age of 60 were to receive a social pension (financed from budgetary sources) equivalent to 10–15 percent of per capita income. Their estimates suggest that by the year 2030, the program would cost between 0.86 to 1.84 percent of GDP (10 percent of per capita income provided to 70 percent of the population above 60 at the lower end, and 15 percent of per capita income provided to the entire population above the age of 60 at the upper end of the estimate; Asher and Vora, 2016).

Asher and Vora (2016) estimate fiscal costs of a hypothetical universal social pension scheme under the following assumptions. First, the scheme is not means-tested, and is universal to all Indian nationals above ages 60, 65, and 80. Second, the GDP is projected to grow in *real* terms at 6 percent per annum. Third, the benefit level for variant A is 20 percent per capita income; and 30 percent per capita income in variant B.[10] Fourth, the projections do not include any administrative or transaction costs. Fifth, the estimates do not take into account differences between rural and urban income levels; and demographic data uses the medium variant of the United Nations Population Forecast.

Table 4.5 Estimated fiscal costs of a hypothetical universal social pension (in percent of GDP)

	Variant A (20%)			Variant B (30%)		
	60+	*65+*	*80+*	*60+*	*65+*	*80+*
2015	1.85	1.15	0.17	2.77	1.73	0.26
2020	2.20	1.40	0.20	3.29	1.40	0.20
2025	2.57	1.68	0.24	3.86	2.52	0.35
2030	2.98	1.98	0.28	4.47	2.97	0.41

Source: Asher and Vora (2016)

The direct fiscal costs vary according to the benefit level and the number of beneficiaries. A targeted or means-tested scheme will be much cheaper as the number of beneficiaries will be smaller; this version may, however, have higher administrative costs. This can be overcome by making the social pension taxable at certain income levels through a 'claw back'. The purpose of this estimation is to meaningfully engage with the debate on extending social protection to the elderly poor, and targeting, a modest level of benefits and improved social pension delivery systems at the state level and help extend social protection coverage.

4.3 Initiatives for generating fiscal space

As with social protection initiatives, the Indian government has also been introducing initiatives encompassing various components of Generating Fiscal Space Framework (Figure 1.2). Implementation of the Goods and Services Tax (GST), replacing several Union and state taxes on domestic goods and services, from July 2017; measures such as requiring swapping certain currency denomination notes in September 2016, helping towards a shift to more recorded and less cash-using economy; renewed emphasis on public infrastructure funding; and improving the business environment, accompanied by social protection initiatives outlined in this chapter, are designed to lay a solid foundation for more broadbased economic growth.

There are also reforms efforts underway that aim to expand the tax base of income tax, sales tax, and property tax; to increase competence in obtaining revenue from such non-conventional sources as more competent auctioning of natural resource rights; to monetise state assets more productively; and to improve expenditure management. The combined impact of these efforts is expected to generate additional fiscal space. This space will have many claimants. The share of fiscal space awarded to social protection expenditure should be based on an empirical assessment on the impact of increased expenditure on improving household welfare. Selective and brief examples of fiscal space–generating measures in India are given below.

The Government of India recently cancelled 16 million duplicate subsidy cards for daily provisions, and is expected to save USD 1.5 billion annually by better targeting. Similarly, 35 million individual subsidy accounts were cancelled as they were receiving a fuel subsidy for which they did not qualify. This is estimated to save USD 2.0 billion annually. Asher and Chaturvedi (2016) note that India's energy reforms, which will replace 770 million incandescent bulbs across India with energy- efficient LED bulbs, will save an estimated 20 gigawatts by 2018. This is enough electricity to reduce annual electricity bills by as much as USD 5.9 billion (Asher and Chaturvedi, 2016).

GeM (Government Electronic Marketplace) is an initiative of the Union Government to enable purchases of goods and services (up to INR 3 million) through the electronic marketplace instead of conventional methods of procurement.[11] It is envisaged that GeM could help improve transparency, efficiency, security, and safety; generate procurement savings (spend less as well); and potentially promote Make in India activities.[12] As of October 3, 2017, the web link suggests that there are around 12,200 buyer organisations, 33,100 sellers, and nearly 180,000 products under GeM.

Asher and Vora (2016) cite an estimate that through competitive procurement practices, the government can save between 0.6 and 1.2 percent of GDP. India's recent initiatives towards direct benefit transfers (DBTs) in bank accounts, combined with the Aadhaar card or similar instruments for identification, and better design of benefit programs could create fiscal space. Thus, official estimates of savings from DBTs for LPG subsidy are around INR 120 billion, a non-trivial amount. The DBTs should be used only where preconditions for its effectiveness are present, however. Speeding up project implementation, such as for road construction, could also generate fiscal space by lowering effective project costs.

The Government of India's Sovereign Gold Bond Scheme is designed to bring part of the privately held gold stock in India (estimated at 20,000 tons, with value of around USD 800 billion) in to financial and capital markets. This could facilitate investment, and as a consequence positively affect growth. Higher growth implies generation of additional fiscal space, available for government initiatives, including in the area of social protection.

The bonds are priced on the market value of gold at the time of issuance and at time of redemption, carrying an interest rate of 2.5 percent per year. They are tradable, thus providing liquidity. The bonds do not attract capital gains tax if held till maturity, a period of eight years.

These bonds have no transaction costs, unlike the substitutes such as gold ETFs (Exchange Traded Funds); they do not incur storage and other costs of physical monetary gold. But the bond holder is able to obtain the monetary benefits of investing in gold.

A recent report in the *Economic Times* (4 March 2017) indicates that Indian Railways will begin to auction branding and advertising rights on 1,000 of its trains to monetise its existing assets and generate a stream of revenue. A commercial circular by the Ministry of Railways on the policy on 'out of home advertising' specifies the advertising rights approach of this policy wherein the Indian Railways shall offer advertising assets at identified sites where existing contracts are operational, at sites where no present contract is operational, and locations which have not been allotted or identified by the Indian Railways (Ministry of Railways, Railroad Board, 2017). This India context-specific initiative is another example of how fiscal space can be generated which potentially could augment resources for social protection.

5. Concluding remarks

India's context-specific social protection initiatives within a federal political structure reflect the acceptance of evolving global consensus that social protection programs and schemes should be an integral part of its development goals and strategies. These initiatives are designed to broaden and deepen access of households to social protection services in healthcare, programs for working age persons, and for the elderly, and employability and livelihood. The initiatives recognise the need for enhancing professionalism in design and implementation of these programs. The need for strategic outcome–oriented use of technology, particularly digital technology, is also recognised (Department of Electronics and Information Technology, Government of India, 2015).

These initiatives represent a marked departure from the past as they visualise and focus on improving household welfare from the perspective of market and non-market production and consumption activities. They encompass enhancement of income as well as the need for reducing expenditure on social protection services by households.

The Indian Government has been utilising the major components of the framework to generate fiscal space discussed in the Overview chapter of this volume. Thus, India has sustained a relatively high growth rate,[13] and has attempted to widen the tax base in terms of the number of taxpayers and the proportion of income reported. It has used government assets such as land and auctioning of mining and spectrum rights to generate revenue, and has focused on expenditure management, including reforming procurement systems to obtain better outcomes from given level of expenditure.

The National Health Policy 2017, income security schemes aimed at the elderly, encouraging small businesses (which number around 55 million) to expand, programs for skilling of the workforce, and other related policy programs and scheme initiatives are designed to help India progress towards better social protection outcomes.

Given the size of India's population, and insufficient emphasis on achieving social protection outcomes in the past, major challenges remain. These include the need for an integrated outcome-oriented view, and a more systemic view, of social protection initiatives of the Union and state governments. Higher investments in constructing social protection databases, better use of data analytics, and encouragement of policy-relevant research in social protection, as well as linking it with public financial management, also merit serious consideration. Establishment of a national center for research on ageing, and linking it with public financial management merits serious consideration. A change in the mindset of stakeholders, particularly policymakers and the beneficiaries of government programs, from mere protection to promotion aspects as well is needed for laying the strong economic and organizational foundations for rapidly progressing towards the social protection goals contained in the SDGs.

Notes

1 The authors thank Devyani Pande, Stuti Rawat, Kwan Chang Yee and participants at ERIA workshops for constructive comments. The usual caveat applies.
2 Source: Per Capita National Income, Ministry of Statistics & Programme Implementation, Press Information Bureau, Government of India (22-July-2015) http://pib.nic.in/newsite/PrintRelease.aspx?relid=123563
3 Source: Uttar Pradesh: Poverty, Growth & Inequality: http://documents. worldbank.org/curated/en/187721467995647501/pdf/105884-BRI-P157572-ADD-SERIES-India-state-briefs-PUBLIC-UttarPradesh-Proverty.pdf
4 Department of School Education and literacy, Ministry of Human Resource Development website, 2017
5 Information from Pradhan Mnatri Jan Dhan Yojana website, 2017
6 Press Information Bureau News Release dated 16th March 2017 on 'National Health Policy, 2017 approved by Cabinet Focus on Preventive and Promotive Health Care and Universal access to good quality healthcare services'. http://pib. nic.in/newsite/PrintRelease.aspx?relid=159376
7 Assuming a family size of 4, this implied 17 million persons could benefit from this scheme. This needs to increase substantially.
8 Press Information Bureau News Release dated 8th October, 2017 on 'Prime Minister launches Intensified Mission Indradhanush (IMI)'. http://pib.nic.in/news-ite/PrintRelease.aspx?relid=171499
9 Chinoy S and T Jain (2017) What is the "state" of India's public finances? Asia Pacific Emerging Markets Research, J.P. Morgan.
10 While this is a simple projection exercise, the benefit level is arbitrarily chosen. As the benefit level is indexed to share of per capita GDP, it aims to mitigate relative and not absolute poverty. Australia's means-tested age pension has similar benefit level, albeit with varying design and institutional features.
11 https://gem.gov.in/
12 http://pib.nic.in/newsite/PrintRelease.aspx?relid=157610
13 India has sustained an annual real GDP growth rate of about 7 percent. Economic Survey (2016–17).

References

Amicus Advisory Private Limited (2011). *Rashtriya Swasthya Bima Yojana : Studying Jaunpur (Uttar Pradesh)*. Available at www.rsby.gov.in/Documents. aspx?ID=14(Accessed on November 12).

Asher, M. G., and A. S. Bali. (2014). Social Security Reform and Economic Development: The Case of India. *Reforming Pensions in Developing and Transition Countries*. London: Palgrave Macmillan, (pp. 158–186).

Asher, M. G., and L. Chaturvedi. (2016). Achieving Energy Efficiency in India: LED Bulb at a Time. *MyIndMakers*, April 29. Available at www.myind.net/Home/viewArticle/achieving-energy-efficiency-india-one-led-bulb-time

Asher, M. G., and Y. Vora (2016). Age Related Pension Expenditure and Fiscal Space in India, in Mukul G. Asher, and F. Zen (ed.) *Age Related Pension Expenditure and Fiscal Space*, New York: Routledge, ch. 4, pp. 72–103.

Chinoy, S., and T. Jain. (2017). *What Is the "State" Of India's Public Finances?* Asia Pacific Emerging Markets Research, J. P. Morgan.

Chomik, R., P. McDonald, and J. Piggott (2016). Population Ageing in Asia and the Pacific: Dependency Metrics for Policy. *The Journal of the Economics of Ageing*, 8, 5–18

Deloitte. (2017). *Voice of Asia*. September. 3rd ed.

Department of Electronics and Information Technology, Government of India (2015). *Digital India: A Program to Transform India Into a Digitally Empowered Society and Knowledge Economy*. Available at http://deity.gov.in/sites/upload_files/dit/files/Digital%20India.pdf

Desai, K. (2017). Swachch Bharat Mission: Making of a Jan Andolan and a Governance Mantra, in B. Debroy, and A. Malik. (eds.) *India @70 Modi @3.5*, New Delhi: Wisdom Tree, pp. 91–108.

Desh Gujarat. (2017). *One Lakh Pradhan Mantri LPG Panchayats to Be Held; Launch in Gujarat Tomorrow*. September 22.

Ghosh, N., and S. S. Yadav (2008). *Problems and Prospects of Crop Insurance: Reviewing Agricultural Risk and NAIS in India*. Delhi: Institute of Economic Growth.

Government of India (2014). *Swachh Bharat Programme for Urban Areas. Press Information Bureau*. September 24. Available at http://pib.nic.in/newsite/PrintRelease.aspx?relid=109990 (accessed on March 26, 2015).

Government of India (2015a). *Economic Survey 2015–16*. Available at http://indiabudget.nic.in/survey.asp (accessed on December 15, 2015)

Government of India (2015b). *Millennium Development Goals: India Country Report 2014*. Social Statistics Division, Ministry of Statistics and Programme Implementation. Available at www.indiaenvironmentportal.org.in/files/file/mdg_2014%20India%20country%20report.pdf (Accessed on 20th April).

Government of India (2015c). *Ministry of Housing and Urban Poverty Alleviation*.

Government of India (2016). *Pension Fund Regulatory and Development Authority (PFRDA)*, Annual Report 2014–15, New Delhi.

Government of India (2017a). *Economic Survey 2016–17*. Available at http://indiabudget.nic.in/survey.asp Accessed on March 7, 2017

Government of India (2017b). *Expenditure Profile 2017–18*. Available at http://indiabudget.nic.in/ub2017-18/eb/stat3b.pdf (Accessed on February 06).

Government of India (2017c). *National Health Policy: Ministry of Health*. Available at http://mohfw.nic.in/showfile.php?lid=4275

Government of India. *About Pradhan Mantri Fasal Bima Yojana*. Available at https://india.gov.in/spotlight/pradhan-mantri-fasal-bima-yojana#tab=tab-1

Government of India. *Universal Basic Income: A Conversation With and Within the Mahatma, Economic Survey 2016–17 – Volume I*. Available at http://indiabudget.nic.in/es2016-17/echap09.pdf

Government of India, Ministry of Railways, Railway Board (2017). *Commercial Circular No. 4 of 2017*. Available at www.indianrailways.gov.in/railwayboard/uploads/directorate/traffic_comm/Comm_Cir_2017/CC_04_2017.PDF

KPMG and FICCI (2015). *Employee Pensions in India – Current practices, Challenges and Prospects*. December. Available at https://home.kpmg.com/in/en/home/insights/2015/12/employee-pensions-in-india.html

Nair, R. (2010). Crop Insurance in India: Changes and Challenges. *Economic and Political Weekly*, 45(6), 19–22.

Press Information Bureau (2014). *Rangarajan Report on Poverty. Government of India. Planning Commission.* Available at http://pib.nic.in/newsite/PrintRelease. aspx?relid=108291

Reserve Bank of India (RBI) (2016). *State Finances: A Survey of Budgets.* Available at www.rbi.org.in/SCRIPTs/AnnualPublications.aspx?head=State%20Finances%20 :%20A%20Study%20of%20Budgets. Accessed March 8, 2017.

Samuel, M., and S. Srinivasan. (2016). Toward Livelihood Security Through the Mahatma Gandhi National Rural Employment Guarantee Act (MGNREGA). *Social Development and Social Work Perspectives on Social Protection,* 175.

Sengupta, H. (2017). Inside India's Cooking Gas and Cashless Transaction Revolution, in B. Debroy, and A. Malik. (eds.) *India @70 Modi@ 3.5.* New Delhi: Wisdom Tree, pp. 91–108.

Swain, M. (2014). *Crop Insurance for Adaptation to Climate Change in India.* Asia Research Centre Working Paper 61. LSE Asia Research Centre.

Vyas, V. S., and S. Singh. (2006). Crop Insurance in India: Scope for Improvement. *Economic and Political Weekly,* 41 (43/44), 4585–4594.

Wansink, B. (2003). Farmers' Preferences for Crop Insurance Attributes. *Review of Agricultural Economics,* 25(2), 415–429.

World Bank (2013). *World Development Indicators 2013.* Washington, DC: World Bank. doi: 10.1596/978-0-8213-9824-1. License: Creative Commons Attribution CC BY 3.0

5 Social protection system in Indonesia: an assessment

Fauziah Zen[1] and Astrid Dita

1. Introduction

Indonesia's social protection system has evolved dramatically in recent decades. Social protection was long ignored – especially during Soeharto's New Order regime (1970s-1990s) when the government was swayed by the robust growth and development being exhibited. At that time, Indonesia's social protection system had been largely anchored to ad hoc and limited measures for social assistance. In 1997, the sudden onset of the financial crisis sent many Indonesians into poverty and unemployment, and caused upheaval that ended the Soeharto regime. The crisis had revealed the severe fragility of the economy and the inadequacy of the social protection system. The government was left with no option but to overhaul its social protection policy framework to address the issues of vulnerability and poverty. Initially, reform and expansion of social assistance as safety net for the poor was implemented. In the following years, a new regime managed to improve the situation, as indicated by lower levels of poverty,[2] improvement in employment levels, and increase in per capita GDP, which doubled in the span of a decade.

The next progress made was the introduction of the National Social Security (Sistem Jaminan Sosial Nasional or SJSN) Law in 2004, which adopted social insurance as the primary method of social protection for the whole population. This represented a fundamental reorientation of thinking about social protection, paving the way for a more comprehensive social security system. A holistic framework for social protection became more relevant as Indonesia raised its ambitions to pursue the attainment of Millennium Development Goals (MDGs). The country has made significant progress towards these goals; especially in the areas of poverty, education, and health. For example, poverty has declined steadily, though it is still relatively high in rural areas[3] where infrastructure is limited, and access to facilities is still difficult. Extreme poverty has been effectively eradicated, with less than 2 percent of the population living under extreme poverty in 2014. Universal education (12 years of cumulative primary and secondary education) became mandatory for all Indonesian citizens in 2015. Child mortality and transmittable diseases have largely been curbed, although maternal health – particularly maternal mortality – remains a challenge.

While the welfare indicators in Indonesia have improved in the last decades, the policy-directed measures could not really be suggested as the deciding factors, due to the low baselines adopted for measurement, especially in the case of poverty. With the low poverty baseline, only a small increment in welfare is needed to eliminate an individual from being defined as poor. Testing on the sensitivity of the assumed poverty line suggests that Indonesia still faces significant vulnerability, as around half of its population is standing on the brink of poverty.[4] On the other hand, inequality has arisen as a debilitating side effect of post-crisis growth, with the Gini coefficient increasing from 0.33 in 2002 to 0.41 in 2012, and only slightly reduced to 0.40 in 2016.

The growing inequality between the haves and the have-nots appears to have affected political and social cohesion on a range of recent public policy issues (such as minimum wage). Further, lower consumption growth of the poorest may also adversely impact the national economy. If 40 percent of the Indonesian households belonging to the low-income group fail to move into the middle class, it could weaken economic growth, which otherwise can be maintained by growing consumption. Such a growth pattern is likely to be domestic-led and therefore less volatile.

It is, however, a matter of concern that in the post-Soeharto era Indonesia is missing comprehensive growth strategies[5] to address those challenges, despite the fact that there is a relatively strong and large domestic demand base. But the window of opportunity is open only for a relatively short period. Between 2010 and 2030, Indonesia will exhibit a vibrant youth population, potentially providing a demographic dividend. Usually this represents a period of above-trend growth. It will be subsequently followed by ageing phase, during which social protection programs to support the old-age population will be even more essential. Since the lead time for social protection programs is long, an early beginning sustained over time is required.

An initiative called the Social Protection Floor (SPF) is one among the policy initiatives advocated by international agencies such as the ILO to policymakers worldwide. The SPF suggests taking a view of social protection risks faced by all groups over a life-cycle. Within the SPF framework, a citizen will be rightfully entitled to state-provided healthcare and income securities throughout the whole life-cycle. When Indonesia ratified the Sustainable Development Goals in September 2015, it also inadvertently signed up for SPF, mentioned as one of the goals related to social protection.

Given the goals already set, it is important to start the discussion regarding the existing systems and commitments, how SPF might fit in, and how much it would cost. This chapter analyses Indonesia's recent policy initiatives, and suggests measures (including those for generating fiscal space) to meet Indonesia's social protection goals. The chapter is organised as follows. A brief discussion of the evolution of Indonesia's social protection system is provided in Section 2. The following section (3) provides an assessment of the social protection system. Future social protection strategies and initiatives are discussed in Section 4. The final section provides the concluding remarks on Indonesia's social protection vis-a-vis SPF.[6]

2. Evolution of the social protection system in Indonesia

In this section we will briefly discuss the evolution of the social protection system in Indonesia, before the birth of SJSN Law in 2004 (pre-SJSN era) and after (post-SJSN era). The timeline of this evolution can be found in Figure 5.1.

2.1 Pre-SJSN era

For decades prior to the 1997 AFC shock, Indonesia had not recognised the need for establishing a social protection system. In the original National Constitution declared in 1945 – which is the basis for all derivative law products to the present day – the social protection aspect was only brought up twice, and that indirectly.[7] As a recently independent country with no means and capacities to develop a social protection system, in the early years of the Old Order (1940s up to the 1960s), Indonesia was more preoccupied with domestic political turbulence, until the military took over and established the New Order. By the time Indonesia started to develop around mid-1960s, it was in dire need, and so the country heavily pursued supply-driven growth and gave little attention to the social protection aspect. The pragmatic New Order regime opted to distort the market and rolled out universal commodity subsidies – mainly for fuel – to stabilise prices.

In this military-led New Order Era, which lasted for 32 years, the government only slowly developed limited social assistance and – to even more limited extent – social insurance programs. The social assistance programs involved simple targeting mechanisms, particularly to *desa* (rural areas), and were mostly given in the form of block grants to build rural infrastructures termed Inpres Desa Tertinggal (IDT). There were also credit programs for farmers, also with limited targeting. These social assistance programs nevertheless had helped improve rural welfare.

As for the public social insurance, there were mandatory programs initiated by the New Order which would later fall under the administration of 4 main operators: ASKES, TASPEN, ASABRI, and JAMSOSTEK. ASKES was the public health insurance operator, whose program was mandatory for civil servants, complimenting the tiny private health insurance industry. TASPEN managed a mandatory old-age security program through a defined benefit (DB) pay-as-you-go (PAYG) scheme for the civil servants, while similar program for armed forces fell under the management of ASABRI. Meanwhile, the private sector – comprising companies of State-Owned Enterprises (SOE) and non-SOE companies – was obliged to participate in mandatory schemes of retirement, work-accident, and death benefits under JAMSOSTEK management. Additionally, private workers could top up their mandatory old-age security programs with other voluntary programs. The voluntary (private) pension funds are either managed by the employer through Dana Pensiun Pemberi Kerja (DPPK), or by the financial institutions through Dana Pensiun Lembaga Keuangan (DPLK) – the latter also accessible for subscription by informal workers (Handra and Dita, 2016).

It was evident that the social insurance programs were mainly organised for civil servants and military personnel (Suryahadi et al., 2014). Further, the social

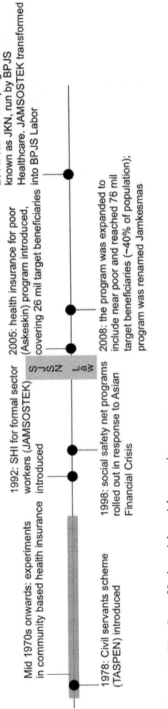

Figure 5.1 Timeline of Indonesia's social protection system

Source: modified from Wagstaff et al. (2015)

insurance funds were opaque and plagued with mismanagement. For example, the PAYG public pension system for the civil servants has not been operating according to the intended design. It was supposed to be a fully funded system with contributions coming from both government and the civil servants. However, TASPEN as the management body had been known to collect and grow the contributions from the civil servants, but not use the returns to pay pensioners' benefits. TASPEN had cited a mismatch between returns and liabilities, as well as government's failure to contribute to the system, as reasons to obtain a periodical bailout from government. TASPEN kept the contributions and returns intact, while monthly pension payments were fully borne by the government out of the state budget. Such a convenient arrangement – though noncompliant with international financial and budgeting practice standards – existed and went unnoticed, while the protection for other parts of society continued to remain very limited.

The event of financial crisis in 1997 revealed the vulnerability of the Indonesian economy to external shocks and the importance of robust social protection for the whole population. In the event of the crisis, mass lay-offs, high inflation, as well as other economic challenges, sent a quarter of the non-poor Indonesian population into poverty. As response, the government launched the first nationwide social safety net program, Jaminan Pengaman Sosial (JPS), in 1998 as depicted in Table 5.1. The program was based on four strategies (Sumarto et al., 2002): 1. guaranteeing that food is made available at affordable prices; 2. safeguarding public purchasing power by creating job opportunities through labour-intensive public works projects; 3. preparing access to basic services, in particular education and health; and 4. making credit available for small-scale enterprises. However, Sumarto et al. found out that many of these programs hardly achieved

Table 5.1 Post-AFC JPS programs

Safety Net Area	Programs
Food security	Sale of subsidised rice to targeted households.
Employment creation	*Padat karya*: a loose, uncoordinated, collection of several "labour-intensive" programs in a variety of government departments.
	PDM-DKE (*Program Pemberdayaan Daerah dalam Mengatasi Dampak Krisis Ekonomi*): a "community fund" program that provides block grants directly to villages for either public works or revolving fund for credit.
Education	Scholarships and block grants: Scholarships directly to elementary up to high-school students; Block grants to selected schools.
Health	JPS-BK (*Jaring Pengaman Sosial Bidang Kesehatan*): a program providing subsidies for medical services, operational support for health centers, medicine and imported medical equipment, family planning services, nutrition (supplemental food), midwife services.

Source: modified from Sumarto et al. (2002)

their goals due to mistargeting and low coverage, and that many of the benefits were enjoyed by non-poor groups.

The programs continued for quite some time, as the policymakers developed a more elaborate and comprehensive framework for social protection. In 2004, a bill on Sistem Jaminan Sosial Nasional (SJSN) or National Social Security System was passed. While it was awaiting implementation by 2014, the ad hoc social safety net programs were formalised and extended (Cook and Pincus, 2014).

2.2 Current SJSN era

Today, Indonesia has improved and formalised its social assistance programs beyond safety nets. There were significant improvements in terms of targeting, satisfaction, and outreach. The improved database contributes to better targeting and monitoring. The programs have been undergoing incremental improvements over the years, although challenges still arise on the targeting and the political economy nature of several programs. The current social assistance programs to protect the poor in Indonesia may be classified in three groups (Asian Development Bank, 2011b):

1. *Programs that focus on handling structural poverty problems.* One example is the National Community Empowerment Program (Program Nasional Pemberdayaan Masyarakat – PNPM) in 2007–2014. The PNPM involved local members of the community in determining solutions for local problems.
2. *Programs aimed at dealing with the poverty trap or the chain of intergenerational poverty.* Examples of this type of program are the School Operations Assistance (BOS), Community Health Guarantee (Jaminan Kesehatan Masyarakat – Jamkesmas), and Family Hope Program (Program Keluarga Harapan – PKH). These programs emphasise a long-term human resources investment.
3. *Programs to overcome shocks.* An example is the Direct Cash Transfer (Bantuan Tunai Langsung – BLT), which is a form of unconditional cash transfer (UCT).

On the other hand, Indonesia is significantly reforming its social insurance programs to implement Law No. 40/2004 on Sistem Jaminan Sosial Nasional (SJSN) or National Social Security System. The SJSN framework covers five areas for the whole population: healthcare, work accident, old-age savings, pension, and death. SJSN follows a staircase approach with non-contributory schemes for the poorest, contributory schemes (with nominal contributions) for the self-employed and informal economy workers, and statutory social security schemes (with contributions set as a percentage of wages) for formal sector workers. Some of the necessary supporting regulations, including the Law No. 24/2011 on National Agency for Social Security (Badan Pengelola Jaminan Sosial – BPJS[8]), have been enacted while other regulations are in the formulation stage.

This reform was deemed necessary as pre-SJSN schemes had been inadequate in providing social security benefits to the population because of a low coverage ratio, limited benefits, low investment returns, together with issues of poor governance and management. Before the SJSN reform, the system was heavily fragmented, with individual schemes operated by separate operators (ASKES, TASPEN, ASABRI, JAMSOSTEK), and with scattered coverage. Today, only half of Indonesian citizens are covered by some form of social protection – the workers in the informal sector suffering the worst exclusion.

In contrast, the SJSN framework aims to cover all the population and is undertaken by an overarching institution, the BPJS, who bears the responsibility for specific areas of coverage as mandated by the new legislation. There are two management bodies: BPJS Healthcare that delivers a reformed healthcare insurance system, and BPJS Labour that delivers the systems of labour safety, old-age savings, pension, and death benefits. Institutionally, BPJS Healthcare will be established by transforming the current operator of national insurance policy, ASKES, while BPJS Labour will arise from a merger of state-owned pension operators (JAMSOSTEK, TASPEN, and ASABRI).[9] This transformation is as depicted in Figure 5.2. Roadmap documents have been issued for the two BPJS operators, which outline the future directions of Indonesia's social insurance programs (BPJS Healthcare, 2012; BPJS Labour, 2015). The performance of the two BPJS operators is subject to oversight of the National Social Security Board (Dewan Jaminan Sosial Nasional, DJSN).

The two BPJS are working towards universal coverage of social protection by merging current social insurance programs, including those already run by the local governments.

On healthcare, the BPJS Healthcare is committed to introducing universal health coverage (UHC) under National Health Insurance (Jaminan Kesehatan Nasional, JKN) by 2019 to cover a projected population of 257.5 million. The

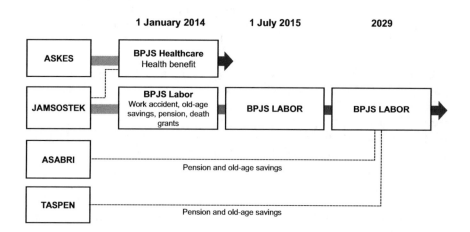

Figure 5.2 Transformation of BPJS

universal coverage for the JKN healthcare program cannot be achieved over-night. Instead, it will happen in sequence, as various schemes and participants will be enrolled into the program (see Figure 5.3). The migration had started in 2012 with the older healthcare insurance programs previously managed by ASKES (ASKES Sosial and Jamkesmas), JAMSOSTEK (mandatory health insurance for private sector workers), ASABRI (health insurance for armed force personnel), and local governments (regional health insurance scheme or Jamkesda). Gradu-ally, additional memberships will be sought from big enterprises, down to the micro-enterprises. Finally, inclusion of all non-salaried workers will complete the

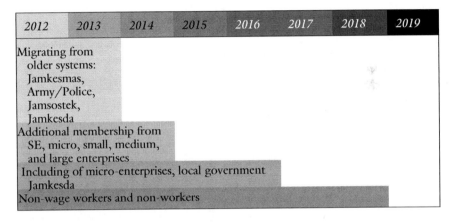

Figure 5.3 Membership roadmap towards universal coverage
Source: TNP2K, 2014

Table 5.2 JKN membership: at time of migration from old systems and after

Scheme	Members on Dec 2014	Members on Dec 2016
PBI (Subsidised members)	**95,167,229**	**106,514,567**
• *PBI-APBN:* **Subsidised by central government** (*Jamkesmas*)	86,400,000	91,099,279
• *PBI-APBD:* **Subsidised by local government** (*Jamkesda*)	8,767,229	15,415,288
PPU (Salaried worker members)	**29,168,507**	**41,027,229**
• *PPU-Pemerintah:* **Public sector (civil servants, police, armed forces, and family members)**	19,091,099	N/A
• *PPU-BU:* **Private sector** (*JAMSOSTEK*)	10,077,408	N/A
PBPU & BP (Voluntary self-contributing members)	**9,087,917**	**24,397,458**
Total	133,423,653	171,939,254

Source: unpublished, Ministry of Finance 2014 and BPJS Healthcare monthly report 2016 universal coverage in 2019. National UHC will cover a basic benefit, and those who wish to extend their benefits may do so by topping up their health insurance with private insurances through a coordination of benefits (CoB) scheme.

As of January 2017, around 170 million Indonesians are already covered by various schemes affiliated in the JKN, such as the scheme for poor citizens subsidized by both central government and local governments, who have integrated their regional health insurance schemes, covering salaried workers in both public and private sectors, and using a self-contribution scheme for non-salaried workers and non-workers (see Table 5.2). The trend of coverage increase compared to the early JKN system is thus indeed promising; 28.9 percent membership increase in the span of two years.

The BPJS Labour is also working towards universal provision of social security. Before the SJSN, Indonesia's mandatory social security system – particularly for old-age security – was carried out by JAMSOSTEK for private sector workers, TASPEN for civil servants, and ASABRI for armed forces personnel. Thus, under the old-age security programs, informal workers and non-workers suffered the most from exclusion. The formal workers in public and private sectors were guaranteed by law to be at least covered in a mandatory old-age security program (either under JAMSOSTEK, TASPEN, or ASABRI) – with contributions coming from both the workers and their employer – workers in the informal sector and non-workers were not covered. Until recently, their option for obtaining old-age security is to participate in the private voluntary system – which may not be affordable for many. Social pension or subsidised pension schemes are not yet in place. JAMSOSTEK had a particular voluntary old-age savings program targeted towards workers in the informal sector, but membership and compliance remain low even after the transformation to BPJS Labour. In contrast, under the SJSN framework, BPJS Labour is tasked to deliver a pension program for all called Jaminan Pensiun (JP) – a form of a social pension.

3. Social protection system in Indonesia: an assessment

As is evident from the previous section, there are now several national and local level social protection programs in place providing health and income security to various groups in Indonesia. These can be classified into social insurance programs (which are occupation-based), social assistance programs (which are prioritised on poverty alleviation), and private out-of-pocket insurance programs. By the end of 2014, these programs cater to a large population of 250 million with average per capita income of USD 3,500, 11 million of them are poor, and 6 percent of them unemployed. Excluding the private out-of-pocket spending, most of the programs are large, state-funded, nation-wide programs. The social insurance programs are managed by BPJS Healthcare & BPJS Labour, and social assistance programs are carried out by several relevant government agencies, such as the Ministry of Social Welfare and Ministry of Education.

Several studies – using different tools – have assessed these programs. For example, ADB (2011, 2016) used the Social Protection Index and Social Protection Indicator to assess the social protection system adequacy, and there are

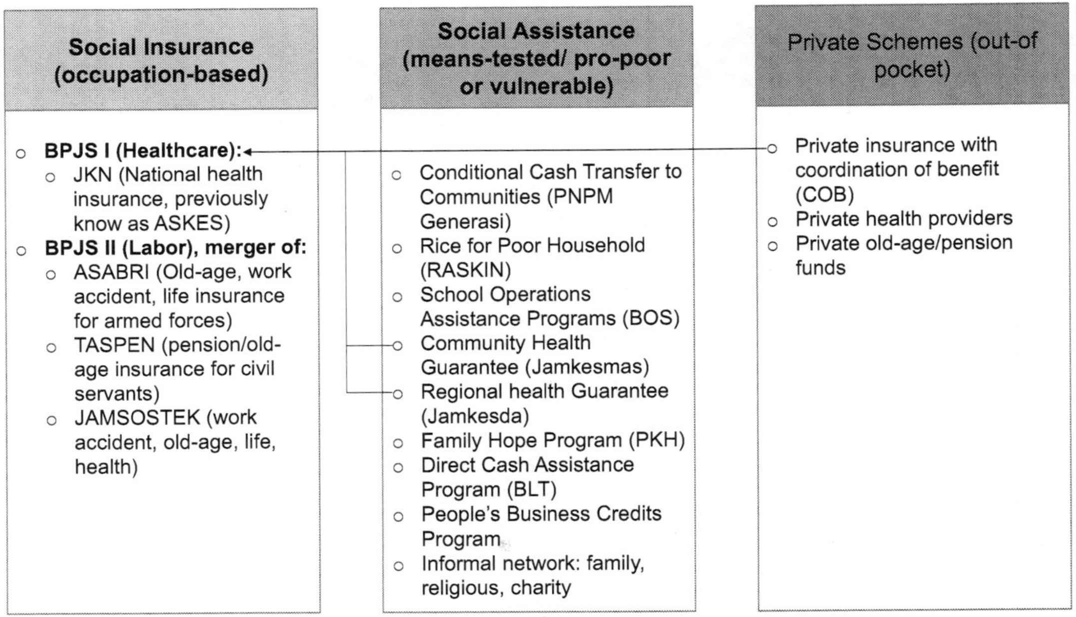

Social Insurance (occupation-based)

o **BPJS I (Healthcare):**
  - o JKN (National health insurance, previously know as ASKES)
- **BPJS II (Labor), merger of:**
  - o ASABRI (Old-age, work accident, life insurance for armed forces)
  - o TASPEN (pension/old-age insurance for civil servants)
  - o JAMSOSTEK (work accident, old-age, life, health)

Social Assistance (means-tested/ pro-poor or vulnerable)

- o Conditional Cash Transfer to Communities (PNPM Generasi)
- o Rice for Poor Household (RASKIN)
- o School Operations Assistance Programs (BOS)
- o Community Health Guarantee (Jamkesmas)
- o Regional health Guarantee (Jamkesda)
- o Family Hope Program (PKH)
- o Direct Cash Assistance Program (BLT)
- o People's Business Credits Program
- o Informal network: family, religious, charity

Private Schemes (out-of pocket)

- o Private insurance with coordination of benefit (COB)
- o Private health providers
- o Private old-age/pension funds

Figure 5.4 Indonesia's social protection in late 2014

numerous impact studies on the social assistance programs (Widjaja, 2013; Syukri et al., 2010; Olken et al., 2011). In this chapter, we will assess each program on the outputs/outcomes, efficiency and effectiveness, and demand/supply gap. We will do this by first presenting the profile of each social insurance and social assistance programs, and then discuss the main issues facing each program. Figure 5.4 provides a reference in classification of various social protection programs in Indonesia.

3.1 Social insurance programs

3.1.1 Healthcare programs: Jaminan Kesehatan Nasional (JKN)

Indonesia's National Health Insurance – the Jaminan Kesehatan Nasional (JKN) of BPJS Healthcare – began in 2014 with the goal of delivering universal healthcare in Indonesia. There are several membership segments under the JKN umbrella, which can be classified by who pays for the premium contribution, namely:

1. PBI (Penerima Bantuan Iuran) or those whose contributions are fully subsidised, either by the Central Government through the State Budget (APBN) (also known as Jamkesmas scheme previously managed by ASKES) or local government through Local Budget (APBD) (also known as the Jamkesda scheme that is channeled through BPJS Healthcare);
2. PPU (Pekerja Penerima Upah), or salaried workers who may transitioned from under the management of ASKES (for public sector workers) or JAMSOSTEK (for private sector workers); and
3. PBPU (Pekerja Bukan Penerima Upah or non-salaried workers) and BP (Bukan Pekerja or non-workers) who voluntarily enrol themselves into the system and thus are self-contributing members.

There are three tiers of membership depending on service class chosen, from lowest to highest: 3, 2, or 1. For most of the members, service class is predetermined: for example PBI (subsidised) members can only enrol in the lowest service class, while for PPU (salaried worker) members, it will correspond with their rank in their institution for public sector workers, or the salary level for private sector workers. Only voluntary members may freely choose to enrol in any service class. The contribution amount varies for each membership segment. PBI members' single contribution rate to be paid by the Central Government is determined by DJSN. PPU members' contributions come from both the workers and the employers, as a percentage of their salaries – for the members and their family. In 2015, for voluntary members (PBPU and BP), the monthly contribution rates were IDR 25,500; 42,500; and 59,500 (approximately USD 2, 3.26, and 4.6) for service class 3, 3, and 1, respectively – where each family member should enroll individually.

In 2016, the government revised the regulation: Presidential Regulation No. 19/2016 and Presidential Regulation No. 28/2016; where contribution rates were slightly revised: IDR 25,500 (USD 2) for service class 3 (unchanged), IDR 51,000 (USD 4) for service class 2, and IDR 80,000 (USD 6.2). Unlike private insurance, JKN members do not have to provide any co-payment for any service claimed, which could induce moral hazard.[10] Before, there was no waiting time for the members to claim their benefits. Since 2015, the management has set 14 days of waiting period after the first premium payment, and imposes suspension of services if membership goes inactive due to failure to pay the premium on time.

Standard costs formulated by Ministry of Health's INA-CBG's (Indonesia Case Base Groups) scheme are used to determine the tariffs of healthcare services. INA-CBGs system sets a 'one-size-fits all' costing system for all healthcare service providers throughout Indonesia, which consists of 'package tariff' and 'fee-for-service tariff'. What INA-CBG's means by 'package tariff' is that it assumed that for a particular case, the patient will only be entitled to a set of healthcare services amounting to certain ceiling based on average of national records of such cases. The 'package tariff' is applied for a set of healthcare services comprising consultation, accommodation, health equipment, and drugs, as well as the operative and non-operative medical procedure. The 'package tariff' differs by hospital type, class of inpatient room, and severity level. On the other hand, the 'fee-for-service tariff' is applied for cancer drugs, medical aid devices, drugs for unstable chronic diseases, ambulance, and CAPD.

After criticisms from healthcare service providers who protested the unrealistic low ceilings set by INA-CBG's, the system faces a huge deficit, necessitating contributions from the state budget. In 2014, BPJS Healthcare suffered IDR 3.1 trillion (USD 235 million) deficit, which ballooned to IDR 5.8 trillion (USD 440 million) in 2015, and IDR 6.8 trillion (USD 515 million), approximately 0.1 percent GDP, in 2016. A snapshot on the JKN benefits and contributions from all membership segments suggest that the two segments causing deficit are actually the members migrated from the Jamkesda (PBI-APBD) and self-contributing members (PBPU & BP). The self-enrolled members had average claim ratio of 645 percent in 2014. This is clearly not sustainable.

To address the above, the stakeholders have set up regional INA-CBG tariffs to reflect the regional price disparities better, and Coordination of Benefits (CoB) between the JKN and private health insurance, for which the private health insurance will act as top-up to JKN benefits.

JAMKESDA

The Jamkesda (Jaminan Kesehatan Daerah or local government insurance scheme) membership segments that are now recorded in the JKN are only some that have been integrated into JKN, where the local governments (LGs) follow the scheme by paying the premium for their poor people to BPJS Healthcare, instead of providing their own services as in the past. As of January 2017, there were still 81 Jamkesda programs yet to be integrated into the scheme. For some LGs, they continue to different Jamkesda programs even after the integration, where they manage their own financing and service delivery. Some programs

Table 5.3 Indonesia National Health Insurance snapshot in 2014 (in nominal IDR bn)

Membership Segment	Benefit claim	Premium contribution	Contribution – benefit	Claim ratio
PBI-APBN (Subsidised by Central Government (Jamkesmas)	13,962	19,933	5,971	70.1%
PBI-APBD Subsidised by Local Government (Jamkesda)	3,365	1,352	(–2,013)	248.9%
PPU-Pemerintah Public sector (civil servants, police, armed forces, and family members)	13,752	14,005	253	98.2%
PPU-BU Private sector (JAMSOSTEK)	2,738	3,545	807	77.2%
PBPU & BP Voluntary self-contributing members	12,849	1,885	(–10,963)	681.5%
Total	**46,666**	**40,720**	**(–5,946)**	**114.6%**

Source: Ministry of Finance, 2015

even involve shared financing between province and districts, which may pool the risk in the respective province and strengthen the referral system within the province.

There could be several motivations for LGs to persist in managing their own Jamkesda. The first is the legal aspect. In contrast to the JKN, which only has a single legal reference for all levels of regulation, Jamkesda in the regions could be endorsed by different levels of regulation – one may be rectified in Municipal Enabling Act or simply a Decision Letter of District Health Office. Thus, the integration of the remaining Jamkesda programs into JKN will be complex as it deals with different kinds of legal challenges in each region.

The second is the fiscal flexibility and sustainability issue. Regions that are more advanced in managing their healthcare programs will be less motivated to integrate to JKN because it will leave less flexibility in their budget. On the contrary, regions with weak management practices often find themselves in deficit because of imprudent healthcare programs. These regions will be keener to join JKN by paying premium to BPJS Healthcare. This is exacerbated by the provisioning portion made in the Central Government budget to BPJS Healthcare, which intends to provide funds for those LGs contributions which remain uncollected.

Additionally, the Law on Local Government mandates that basic healthcare belongs to local governments' obligatory task, but there is no clear explanation in the law on LGs' role in JKN. Therefore typically during local election campaign, candidates put forward local healthcare programs rather than highlighting the JKN.

There are private health insurance schemes based on Law No. 2 year 1992, catering to smaller yet growing portion of the population. Meanwhile, out-of-pocket (OOP) expenditures remain high (40 percent to 60 percent of total health expenditure) in Indonesia, this despite the gradual roll-out of the JKN and increasing number of voluntary JKN members. The most plausible explanation for this might be on the aspect of access. Even though there is now affordable insurance for all with zero co-payment, not everyone can access the healthcare facility easily, especially those who live in hard-to-reach and remote regions. They prefer or have no option but to get nearest help (which may not be affiliated with JKN scheme) and do not utilise the insurance. Even if they do opt to utilise the insurance services, the transaction cost incurred will be high, especially for transport between their residences and the healthcare facilities, as well as for privately buying unavailable medicines in the healthcare facilities. A comprehensive cross-sector planning will be needed to minimise this problem.

Since the introduction of JKN started with low-income groups and those already covered by previous governmental insurance, the coverage now mainly consists of the lower income level (the poor) and the higher income level (the haves) – missing a large portion of middle-income people working in the informal sector or self-employed. Dartanto et al. (2015) used the data analysis from 400 households of the informal sector, and showed that the main factors that prevent them from joining JKN are: 1. the availability of hospitals at district level, 2. having treatment experience, and 3. having knowledge about insurance and/or the JKN program. Thus, dissemination and education on JKN program is urgently needed.

3.1.2 Pension programs

The recently introduced BPJS pension program (*Jaminan Pensiun*, JP) is governed by SJSN Law (Article 39–42) which stipulates that the JP program shall be delivered by BPJS Labour as social insurance, with defined benefits, based on a predetermined formula and paid upon retirement age as a lump sum (for those whose contribution period is less than 15 years) or as an annuity (for contribution period is greater than 15 years). This program will include the following benefits: old-age pension, disability pension, widow pension (50 percent of benefit), child pension (50 percent of benefit), and parent pension (20 percent of benefit). The benefit is defined as weighted average of the member's salary during the contribution period. Contribution is borne by both the worker and employer, with rates as stipulated in regulations (1 percent by worker and 2 percent by employer; this will be reviewed every three years until it reaches the total of 8 percent contribution). Individuals who voluntarily enroll as non-salaried workers will have to bear a 3 percent contribution by themselves. The benefit received by pensioners is 40 percent of average wage. The members will thus benefit from the future wage growth.

Since universal JP has not officially started, only limited comments can be made, though it has stirred the private pension industry, fearing that it may create a crowding-out effect. There is also a question of sustainability, as the program offers generous benefits (it basically covers the whole family, including the contributor's parent, for one person paying contributions) which are hard to project and match in over the long term.

TASPEN AND ASABRI

There are 2 mandatory public pension programs yet to be absorbed into BPJS Labour: pension civil servants (managed by TASPEN), and pension for armed forces (managed by ASABRI). Their future position with regard to BPJS Labour's JP program is unclear, as both institutions resisted merger with the system, citing the difference of the pension programs as their main argument. Meanwhile, TASPEN's PAYG-DB pension payment liabilities have grown to become a burden to the state budget. This burden is unsustainable unless the program undergoes radical change to a fully-funded arrangement (for further discussion, see Handra and Dita, 2016).

PRIVATE PENSION

There are two voluntary private pension schemes: the Dana Pensiun Lembaga Keuangan (DPLK), private pensions managed by a financial institution, which companies and individuals can subscribe to; and Dana Pensiun Pemberi Kerja (DPPK), private pensions managed by an employer that is only open for its employees. The size of the private pension industry is miniscule when compared to the public system (see Handra and Dita, 2016), moreover it faces further uncertainty upon impending introduction of BPJS Labour's universal pension program (JP).

3.1.3 Old-age savings program

The old-age savings program (JHT or Jaminan Hari Tua) is delivered by BPJS Labour and under the SJSN Law. Membership is mandatory for all, including informal workers. If the worker is registered in more than one company, then he/she should have a separate account for each company. Contribution rate for formal workers is at 5.7 percent of salary, with 2 percent contribution coming from the worker, and 3.7 percent contribution from the employer. For informal workers, the contribution rate follows government regulation. Upon retirement (minimum age 56 years), members will receive their accumulated contribution and their investment returns, paid as a lump sum. The investment return is guaranteed at the minimum of average time deposits rate of state-owned banks. One-time partial withdrawal before retirement is possible when minimum contribution period reaches 10 years.

This program was managed by JAMSOSTEK as its main program before it was transformed into BPJS Labour. In December 2014, BPJS Labour was managing IDR 166 trillion (approximately USD 12.8 billion or ~2 percent of GDP) assets to meet Old-Age Savings Program' liabilities. The chosen instrument of investment is mainly government bonds, followed by time deposits and equity. The JHT program has suffered from low compliance rates under JAMSOSTEK management.

For civil servants and armed forces, TASPEN and ASABRI manage their old-age savings programs separately, which altogether with their pension programs were supposed to be integrated into BPJS Labour. However, as with the pension programs, TASPEN and ASABRI are currently reluctant to comply with the BPJS roadmap which sees them to merge into BPJS Labour by 2029.

3.1.4 Death grants program

Death grants program (JKM or Jaminan Kematian) grants a lump sum benefit to legal inheritors of a member when he/she dies from non-work causes. The premium rate depends on the membership type. Formal workers pay 0.3 percent of their monthly salary, while informal workers pay a fixed rate of IDR 6,800 (approximately USD 0.5) per month.[11] Besides the lump sum benefit, JKM program benefits also include a funeral service fee, and a one-time scholarship grant for the member's dependent if the contribution period was more than 5 years. For civil servants and armed forces, TASPEN and ASABRI manage this program separately.

3.1.5 Work accident program

The work accident program (JKK or Jaminan Kecelakaan Kerja) gives protection for accident risks within the scope of work, including disease and accidents that may happen during the commute. The contributions are paid by the employers and differ based on the risk group. The low-level risk group pays 0.24 percent of monthly salary; high-level risk group pays up to 1.74 percent.[12] The program benefits package includes a lump sum benefit, temporary monthly allowance, payment for medical services with unlimited ceiling, and return to work assistance. For members who die because of the accident, the program will pay for the funeral service and a scholarship for the member's dependent. For civil servants and armed forces, TASPEN and ASABRI manage this program separately.

3.2 Social Assistance Programs

As of 2014, there are numerous social assistance programs administered by different agencies (as depicted in Figure 5.4). For health, the government's social assistance is disbursed in the form of a health insurance premium subsidy to the poor and near-poor through the JKN program. The non-contributory health insurance scheme, Jamkesmas (or PBI membership scheme) covers approximately 32 per cent of the population. This program is administered by the Ministry of Health; the state-funded premium is paid to BPJS Healthcare, and this still continues.

The school assistance program, Bantuan Operasional Sekolah (BOS), provides block grants to schools with the aim of guaranteeing free basic education until grade 9 (since 2016, this has been be extended until grade 12 – the completion of high school). The BOS program is mostly administered by the Ministry of Education, except for religious schools which fall under the responsibility of the Ministry of Religion. In 2016, the program was also supplemented with Smart Indonesia Program (Program Indonesia Pintar) which through disburses through an electronic card a monthly allowance to poor students.

There are conditional and unconditional cash transfer programs. The Family Hope Program (or Program Keluarga Harapan, PKH) conditional cash transfer and scholarship programs for the poor families further facilitate access to education, nutrition, and healthcare for poor children. Unconditional Cash Transfer (UCT) is disbursed mainly to respond to economic shocks, which happen especially when the government reduces subsidies – particularly the fuel and electricity subsidies. Both unconditional and conditional cash transfer programs are administered by Ministry of Social Affairs, which also disburses the in-kind transfer, particularly in the form of subsidised rice (Raskin or Rice for Poor Households, now called Rastra). There are also other programs targeted for disabled and elderly persons.

Indonesia's UCT program is designed to support poor or near-poor households coping with economic shocks, in particular coping with reductions in the fuel price subsidy. Thus, the UCT is not meant as a way to shift the poorest into a higher percentile of income. It is understood that the UCT program usually only lasts for several months. In 2014 and 2015, 15.5 million households were beneficiaries of this program. There are various program names under UCT classification with only minor technical differences between them (BLT, BLSM, KKS, KSKS).

The now-defunct community empowerment program, Program Nasional Pemberdayaan Masyarakat (PNPM), supported both rural and urban communities in the design and implementation of their own community-level development plans, which may include income-generating activities, small-scale infrastructure development, and social services for their populations. There were numerous PNPM sub-programs, which concerned different central government stakeholders. This program, however, only lasted up to late 2014.

Additionally, there are also micro-credit programs (Kredit Usaha Rakyat or KUR), which provide some micro-entrepreneurs access to credit, administered by the Ministry of Small and Medium Enterprise. In addition to the large-scale national programs, there are also several smaller-scale programs targeting people with disabilities, abandoned children, and vulnerable elderly – under the responsibility of Ministry of Social Affairs.

In 2008–2011, the Unconditional Cash Transfer, Rice for Poor Households (Raskin, now Rastra), and Jamkesmas (now JKN) competed for the largest share of government expenditures on social protection (Alatas, Purnamasari and Wai-Poi in Sumarto and Bazzi, 2011). In 2016, however, the trend changed, with spending on education assistance for poor students (Program Indonesia Pintar) now in the top 3 programs with an IDR 14 trillion (~USD 1 billion) budget allocation alongside premium payments for poor subsidised members under PBI-APBN membership segments of JKN at IDR 25.5 trillion (~USD 1.9 billion), and Rice for Poor Households (Rastra) at IDR 22.5 trillion (~USD 1.7 billion) (World Bank, forthcoming).

3.3 Public spending on social protection

Indonesian public budget nomenclature suffers from ambiguity of definitions, making it difficult to pinpoint spending items by category. There is also fragmentation of spending among different ministries and agencies. The main stakeholder of social protection is the Ministry of Social Affairs, which oversees most of the social assistance programs, but large spending items are also posted by the Ministry of Health for JKN bailouts, and the Ministry of Finance for civil servant pension payments. Formally, these large items of social protection spending are not captured in the Government of Indonesia's definition of social protection, as the definition is rather different from the more widely accepted one.

For instance, what would be accepted as 'social protection' spending is called 'social assistance' spending by the Central Government. This is made up of several components: social rehabilitation, social security, social empowerment, 'social protection', poverty alleviation, and disaster response. In relation to GDP, the Central Government social protection spending using this definition has been relatively steady over the last years, recorded at an average of 5 percent of the Central Government budget, or 0.9 percent of GDP in 2012–2015 (see Table 5.4).

Table 5.4 Government spending on social protection* (nominal IDR bn)

Classification	2012	2013	2014	2015
Social rehabilitation	461	578	379	849
Social security	24,660	33,451	38,385	32,736
Social empowerment	35,773	41,650	35,317	40,023
'Social protection'	1,992	3,406	10,576	16,359
Poverty alleviation	11,685	11,162	11,918	4,619
Disaster response	1,050	1,889	1,351	1,353
Total	**75,621**	**92,136**	**97,925**	**95,941**
Total (% of Central Government budget)	**5.1%**	**5.6%**	**5.5%**	**5.3%**
Total (% of GDP)	**0.9%**	**1.0%**	**0.9%**	**0.8%**

Dubbed "social assistance" (bantuan sosial) *spending in Government of Indonesia reporting*
Source: Central Government audited financial statements 2012–2015, does not include contribution by Local Government

If the official government definition of social protection is to be used, the Central Government's social protection spending would appear to be severely underestimated, as can be seen in Figure 5.5. Consolidated data on public spending (at central, provincial, and district levels), on the other hand, shows that 2014 public spending for the social protection function (by government definition)[13] stands at 0.3 percent of GDP, and health 1.0 percent of GDP,[14] while subsidies (mainly for price subsidies of electricity and fuel) stands at 3.9 percent of GDP. Thus, public social protection spending – in the broader definition – can be approximated at 5.2 percent of GDP in 2014.

This wide discrepancy shows that there is much to be done to standardise the definition of social protection in Indonesian public expenditures for better control and monitoring of its effectiveness.

3.4 Main issues of Indonesia's social protection

The purpose of Law No. 40/2004 on the National Social Security System is to ensure that every citizen can fulfil their basic needs sufficiently. The principles of humanity, benefits, and social equity shall be translated into an adequate level and scope of benefits received by all citizens. The current programs of BPJS Labour (social labour protection), JKN (universal healthcare program), and various social assistances have not covered all citizens and provided adequate levels and scope of benefits. The challenges of covering all citizens mainly come from limited fiscal capacity, implementation capacity, and insufficient database, while lack of benefits' adequacy and scope is also related to supply adequacy and capacity of social security fund managers to invest in better portfolios.

The inequality issues arise in part because the country has an uneven distribution of population (60 percent in Java Island, whose area is less than 10 percent

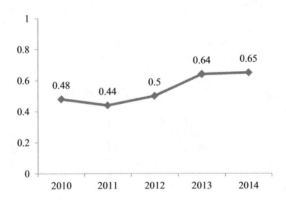

Figure 5.5 Central government-defined social protection* spending as percent of Central Government budget

Source: unpublished from Ministry of Finance Republic of Indonesia, 2014, does not include: civil servant pension payments, subsidies, bailout to JKN

of Indonesia); geographical challenges (approximately 13 thousand islands); lack of connectivity; and diverse knowledge, education, and income levels across and within regions. The uniform JKN premium for the voluntary members, for example, is too low for the majority of individuals in Java but far from affordable for many in the eastern part of Indonesia. Access to healthcare facilities is also far easier for members in well-connected Java compared to other regions – making members in Java the main beneficiaries of the supposedly national program.

The social protection programs can also benefit more from design improvements – particularly for the social insurance programs, where incentives can be better aligned. Before 2015, there was no waiting time for a new member to claim healthcare benefits, and there was no entry-exit barrier. This has led to a huge deficit in 2014 for BPJS Healthcare. The no co-payment system for healthcare services also induced moral hazard, since the risks were fully born by BPJS. Such classic problems of adverse selection and moral hazard are more limited in private insurance schemes due to proper safeguarding.

As the membership for JKN expands, and the referral system strengthens, there is a question of supply-side readiness and the big gap between urban and rural. The challenges occur both in terms of quantity and quality of healthcare services. In 2014, there were only 350 sub-districts with a minimum of one accredited Puskemas (Pusat Kesehatan Masyarakat or Community Health Centre), in contrast to the 5,600 which Ministry of Health targets in 2019. There were also only 233 districts with a minimum of one accredited public general hospital, in contrast to 477 targeted in 2019. On the aspect of quality, in 2014 only 6,751 units (69.4 percent) of the Puskesmas are in good condition, only 80.3 percent have access to 24-hour electricity, and only 69.6 percent have tap water access.

Those structural issues – low coverage, inequality, and flawed design – need structural and comprehensive solutions. Increasing legal and effective coverage must confront and address the problems of inequality, and at the same time both subjects shall be linked with fiscal policy adjustment and improvement of the design of pension and healthcare schemes. Some examples and related issues regarding design and operation of the system are provided in Table 5.5.

In pursuing the efforts to increase coverage, many challenges remain. In healthcare, major challenges are the strategies to match the increasing members with a currently unfavourable high claim ratio, and to reach more equal distribution of supplies and benefits of health services. The sustainability of the BPJS Healthcare is of huge concern to the stakeholders. In its first year of operation, 2014, the claims ratio was 104 percent (as the premiums received was 41.06 trillion IDR, while benefits paid was 42.60 trillion IDR). The claims ratio increased slightly to 105 percent in 2015 and until November 2016, the claims ratio was 100.14 percent. To be sustainable, the ratio has to be brought down below 100 percent to allow for some space in case of contingencies. A claims ratio of 90 percent could be a workable goal.

The equity concern is also a huge challenge for social protection programs in Indonesia, as the better-off groups are often the biggest receivers of the benefits. For example, informal workers have to pay more for their health insurance

Table 5.5 List of issues in Indonesian social protection

BPJS Labour	*Programs: JP, JHT, JKm, JKK*

Issues:
- Vulnerable to political intervention. Example: after receiving hard political pressure from the workers, old-age savings of JHT can be withdrawn at any time despite that accumulation of contribution does not meet the minimum threshold stated in the regulation.
- There is no unemployment benefit, while a rigid labour market makes it hard for the unemployed to get a new job.
- JP is now applying an annuity scheme that is extended to the family of pensioners (spouse, children, and parents), make it more difficult to estimate future liabilities.
- Problems in integrating former programs due to resistance from the existing management (afraid of reduced benefit if it is integrated with SJSN). Fragmented programs make the management and policymaking process inefficient.
- Confusing design: TASPEN applies to both DB and DC at the same time. The Government is thinking about migrating the system into a fully funded scheme, but to the date there is no comprehensive cost and benefits assessment over the migration schemes provided.
- Potential crowding out of private social security schemes.

BPJS Healthcare	**Program: JKN** **Subprograms:** • **National: Jamkesmas** • **Local: Jamkesda**

Issues:
- Uneven distribution of healthcare facilities, where the pool of capable health workers and facilities are concentrated in urban areas, making it overwhelmed with difficult cases; while it is insufficient, and also costly for the users in rural areas to access the healthcare facilities. This situation resulted in very low utilisation rate from the subsidised group of the poor and near-poor, contrast with very high utilisation rate of self-enrolled group.
- High out-of-pocket payment.
- JKN suffers significant deficit contributed by self-enrolled (non subsidised) member group.
- Since JKN is mandatory for every resident in Indonesia (regardless nationality) with low premium, thus it creates incentives for private companies to shift from currently joining private insurance to JKN for their employees. Additionally, since coordination of benefits between JKN and private insurance is yet to be determined and agreed, JKN potentially crowds out private insurance, especially for middle-size companies.
- Many Jamkesda runs parallel with JKN because of the complexities in regulation (or local political economy factor) and flexibilities in managing local governments' budget.

Social Assistance	**Programs:** • **In-kind** • **School assistance programs** • **UCT** • **Empowerment**

Issues:
- Outdated and insufficient database is prone to inconsistent implementation. Some households may receive various types of social assistances while others may get less than their eligibilities.
- The usage of UCT is mostly uncontrolled and some reports indicated the money is used for non-primary consumption spending (paying for motorcycle instalments, buying new mobile phones, etc.). It is also related to inaccuracy in defining the targeted recipients.

premiums – in terms of percentage of their per capita expenditure – to get the same level of benefit compared to formal workers. Affirmative policies are still needed to ensure that equity can be met by addressing affordability and access for the poorest of the group.

In labour schemes, besides fixing the pension scheme to be sustainable, another major challenge is to expand the coverage to the informal sector. In 2014, BPJS Labour active membership – meaning members that are contributing to the system – only covered 34 percent of national salaried workers and 0.97 percent of non-salaried workers (see Table 5.6).

The current pension system may be characterised as unfair, discriminatory, and limited. It lacks intergenerational equity in the case of the PAYG public sector pension, where the government uses the present tax revenue to finance the gap between the inadequate contributions made by the retirees in the past and the amount of pensions they receive in the present. It is discriminatory in the sense that only the civil servants are entitled to guaranteed pension and retirement funds, while private sector employees' retirement welfare and needs depend on the policy and ability of their employer. It is limited, as only the workers in the formal sectors (approximately a quarter of the workers in the formal sector) are insured in TASPEN, ASABRI, and BPJS Labour schemes, with informal workers typically omitted.

Performance of the public sector in managing its social protection assets is lagging compared to the private sector. There are also the issues of early retirement age (50 years for early retirement and 56 years typically for civil servants), and benefits inadequacy, especially for public sector pensions. The reporting of public social security schemes is also problematic: accurate and transparent data on assets, liabilities, fund management, and accumulated contributions and benefits

Table 5.6 Contributing members in BPJS Labour, 2014

Actively contributing companies				
2014			*2015*	
216,593			296,791	
Actively contributing members				
Program	*Salaried workers*		*Non-salaried workers*	
	2014	*2015*	*2014*	*2015*
Work-accident program (JKK)	13,012,856	14,042,592	683,532	286,065
Death benefit program (JKm)	13,012,856	14,042,592	690,436	286,065
Old-age savings program (JHT)	12,675,917	13,112,283	48,331	42,503
Pension program (JP)		6,481,983		
Construction worker program	3,088,105	4,946,404		

Source: BPJS Labour performance report, 2014 and 2015

are not easily accessible. This is possibly due to lack of governance, as only the private social security operators are under detailed scrutiny by OJK (Muliati, 2013).

4. Future strategies and initiatives

In terms of social development, Indonesia has achieved most of the MDGs targets by 2015. Now the MDGs is succeeded by the Sustainable Development Goals (SDGs) – which serve as the direction for global development post-2015. As a middle-income country aiming to graduate to a higher status, higher development goals are relevant for Indonesia to reach. One of the subjects covered in the SDGs is social protection, with Social Protection Floor (SPF) as on the agenda.

Conceptually, the rights-based SPF is in line with the spirit of Indonesia's constitution, which guarantees the rights of all citizens to protection. Indonesia has also been working towards the same objectives as does SPF. Hence, progressing towards broad goals of SPF can be deemed as relevant for Indonesia.

The SJSN Law was made to guarantee rights to healthcare and to secure income for children and older people. Even though formally there is no unemployment insurance for "working-age population unable to earn sufficient income" as stipulated in ILO's SPF, various social assistance programs are in place to support the poor to meet basic needs in income, education, and healthcare. The question to be asked is thus not about how Indonesia adopts SPF, but how to improve and strengthen the current system to achieve the goals of social protection in a sustainable and equitable way, without adversely affecting other national goals and priorities.

4.1 Future direction for Indonesia's social protection

We now outline the initiatives for better social protection in Indonesia, mostly systematic improvements that will become prerequisite for efficient planning, budgeting, and implementation before a universal framework such as SPF can take place.

4.1.1 Unified Database

By and large, the future direction of Indonesia's social protection system – particularly for the social insurance programs – is foreseeable, due to the mandate of the SJSN Law, which unifies Indonesia's social security systems. The unification is one of the most challenging tasks, given diverse schemes of current social assistance, which leave loopholes for inclusion and exclusion errors in various programs. Government is looking for ways to improve the beneficiary database (such as utilising a single national registry) to be resistant to such errors (Brodjonegoro et al., 2016).

Government – through its TNP2K task force – had set up the Unified Database (Basis Data Terpadu) of social assistance with the following rationale: 1. to identify the poorest households in Indonesia based on scientific methods and unified technical criteria; 2. to minimise targeting errors in order to improve the

Table 5.7 Unified database as single data source for social assistance programs

Program	Total			Implementer	Notes
	Families	Individuals	Groups		
Social Assistance Card (KPS)	15.5 mil	65.6 mil	25% lowest	Ministry of Social Affairs	Given to families as indicator of poverty
Family Welfare Card (KKS) Family Welfare Deposits (SKS)	15.5 mil	65.6 mil	25% lowest	Ministry of Social Affairs	Given to heads of families.
Raskin	15.5 mil	65.6 mil	25% lowest	Ministry of Social Affairs	Given to heads of families.
Family Hope Program (PKH)	2.8 mil	11.2 mil	8% lowest	Ministry of Social Affairs	Given to families.
Cash Transfers for Poor Students (BSM)/Smart Indonesia Card (KIP)	15.5 mil	11.1 mil students	25% lowest	Ministry of Education & Culture and Ministry of Religious Affairs	Given to school-aged children from KPS/ KKS recipient families.
Premium Assistance Beneficiaries (PBI) for National Health Insurance/Healthy Indonesia Card (KIS)	21.8 mil	86.4 mil	35% lowest	Ministry of Health via BPJS Health	Given to each family member in the bottom 35%
Regional Program	65 requests from 31 provinces, and 513 requests from 308 districts/cities to use unified database data in the implementation of social assistance programs, funded by regional budgets.				
Ministry/Institution Programs	56 requests from 21 Ministries/Institutions to use unified database data in the implementation of social assistance programs.				

Source: TNP2K, 2014

effectiveness of Indonesia's social protection programs; and 3. to facilitate the coordinated use of a high-quality database of poor households by social protection program stakeholders. The database utilises 2011 survey data covering 40 percent of families with the lowest socio-economic status, which contains information on 25 million households or 96 million individuals. The database is then used as single data source to determine the recipients of social assistance programs (see Table 5.7). There is a caveat for this database, as it is based on the PPLS survey last conducted in 2011, where it only sampled populations with physical addresses. This means that those who are extremely poor and homeless – who were under the administrative radar – were likely not included.

4.1.2 Streamlining the programs

Streamlining existing fragmented programs is crucial to improving their efficiency and effectiveness. In doing so, Central Government is set to redesign the overlapped programs, disbursement mechanisms, shared responsibilities between the stakeholders, as well as total benefits received by eligible recipients. Extra efforts should be made to review impacts of the existing programs and design least-distortive transitions.

Legal context is crucial in the streamlining efforts. This is particularly true for the most visible social protection program, the JKN, which aims to integrate various schemes – particularly the Jamkesda or local public health insurance schemes – under its umbrella. Many of the existing fragmented Jamkesda programs have legally binding local regulations as their legal basis, which the transition arrangements will be required to be overuled. Additionally, the Law No 23/2014 on Local Government states that healthcare is also part of concurrent obligatory tasks for both central and local governments. As a matter of fact, the integration of Jamkesda into JKN (targeted in the BPJS Healthcare roadmap) was not completed in 2016. To overturn this situation, the central government will need to issue clear guidance on this integration, particularly to provide legal certainty for the transition.

Devereux et al. (2015) has argued that globally there is a drive towards strengthening social protection program linkages with labour markets, first by enhancing access to employment opportunities through social protection, second by extending social insurance to the informal sector, third by replicating 'graduation' programmes that deliver packages of social protection plus livelihood support to move people out of poverty. The same is true for Indonesia. These particular components of social protection – strengthening the base, protecting the vulnerable ones, and empowering community-based economies – has shaped Indonesia's Social Protection Programs, as we can see in Figure 5.6.

Establishment of SJSN actually fulfils the idea of an SPF for Indonesian people, albeit with different contributory and statutory provisions. In the basic floor, there are provisions of basic healthcare and income securities for most during the life cycle. This is complemented with social assistance provisions in the form of unconditional cash transfers and in-kind transfers (such as RASKIN or rice-for-the-poor program).

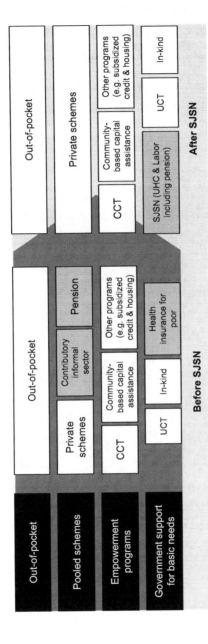

Figure 5.6 Indonesia's social protection programs: objectives context

Source: authors

One layer at the top of it is the public support for empowerment, through which one's potential can be maximised. Such programs include conditional cash transfers (such as the Family Hope Program or Program Keluarga Harapan, PKH), community-based assistance, and other subsidies directed towards leveraging society's capital (such as affordable productive loans and affordable housing).

Private contributions come next, whether in the form of contributions in pooled-risk schemes or out-of-pocket expenditures. Figure 5.6 also illustrates the difference between these steps before and after SJSN.

It is to be noted that although SJSN has covered universal healthcare as well as income security for the elderly, the disabled, and unfit-to-work persons of productive age, it does not cover income security for the productive age (such as unemployment benefits) and children. While the former is strategically omitted by the government, the latter is actually indirectly covered by other schemes. For example, in-kind transfer of Bantuan Operasional Sekolah (School Operational Assistance) covers textbook provision for all children of school age, while rice-for-poor also benefits children in poor families. Meanwhile, the PKH program disburses cash to families, intending to improve nutrition for children. In some regions, the local governments provide additional cash and in-kind support for students to cover school uniforms, transportation costs, and school supplies.

At the subnational level, an example can be made out of DKI Jakarta Province's Kartu Jakarta Pintar (Smart Jakarta Card) which is designed to fulfil children's income security and whose implementation has been improved and might see some success when replicated in other regions.

Box 5.1   Smart Jakarta Card *(Kartu Jakarta Pintar)*

Smart Jakarta Card *(Kartu Jakarta Pintar)*

Kartu Jakarta Pintar (KJP) is a local conditional cash transfer program of DKI Jakarta Province which started in 2013. It hands out subsidies for school operational fees to eligible local students studying in elementary school, middle school, and high school. In 2015, students are given monthly allowances of IDR 210,000–390,000 (USD 15.6–28.9) – depending on their level of study – in the form of a debit card which can be used to shop for school-related needs such as reading glasses, stationery, and uniforms. Students can also withdraw the allowance in cash. In a later phase of the program, the KJP card can also be used to pay for public bus rides within the TransJakarta service network. The program has met with some success, albeit it faced difficulties in its first year of implementation.

In its first year, local government of DKI Jakarta used TNP2K's unified database (based on a 2011 survey) to target eligible beneficiaries. In that year, IDR 455 billion (USD 33.7 million) was spent for 403,808 beneficiaries. There were issues of mistargeting: many poor students were left out due to outdated data, while some received duplicate benefits. Misuse of funds was widely reported, as it was hard to track the use of cash. There was also rent-seeking in several schools, where eligible students were forced to hand over a sum of money in return for their KJP cards.

In a later phase of the program, the list of beneficiaries is obtained through staged nominations by the school principal, school committee, and a district education official before approval by a provincial education official. Excluded students may opt in by proving their eligibility through certain documentation. Data for the nominee list is collected twice each year, the first collection commencing in the beginning of the academic year. The problematic schools from the previous period of the implementation were cut off from the program. The benefit delivery was changed into a debit card with limited use; it can only be used for assigned merchants for intended goods and services. To allow for some flexibility, students can still withdraw benefits in cash not exceeding IDR 50,000 (USD 3.7). The provincial budget for the KJP program in FY2014 and FY2015 amounted to IDR 668 billion (USD 49.5 million) and IDR 2.3 trillion (USD 170.4 million), serving 573,000 and 489,000 students, respectively.

It is apparent that provision of social protection in the Indonesian context is a shared responsibility between the central and local governments. Further research is needed to explore the optimal task division and financing arrangements between the levels of the government.

For the long-term strategy, Indonesia may be able to reduce the estimated cost for expanding social protection by pursuing industrialisation so as to shift workers from informal to formal jobs, create more employment, and reduce poverty – which purposes are in line with the goals of the national development plan.

4.1.3 Creation of fiscal space

The basic challenge is to explore fiscal space: to use a country's financial capabilities to raise money from various sources to achieve risk sharing and adequate health protection for all citizens. This will be more effective if approached as part of an integrated framework for generating fiscal space. As illustrated in the Overview chapter, there are 1. long-term effort and strategy to enhance growth rate and broaden its base, 2. ways to improve revenue performance, and 3. ways better manage expenditure. Specifically, social protection spending is also influenced by relevant variables, including demographic structure, distribution of population, natural challenges, economic structures, socio-economic status, etc.

Fiscal space may also be generated through reduction of costs, through synergy effects, and by improved efficiency that increases the cost effectiveness of care as well as reducing management costs. Increasing cost effectiveness includes measures such as focusing on generic drugs, negotiating prices and quality with providers, utilising economies of scale, getting discounts for bundling orders, strengthening referral systems, and so on. If BPJS Healthcare and BPJS Labour can be run in compliance with good corporate governance principles that include transparency and accountability, as well as regularly releasing significant data, then the public can participate in monitoring the system, reporting misconduct, giving relevant information, etc. All of these efforts may free up some fiscal space, which can be used to extend coverage, cover risks, and increase the amount of benefits.

Another way to generate fiscal space is by having a better expenditure management – particularly through optimal spending allocation. Government can review the current social spending using a comprehensive framework, and the design can be improved through: 1. eliminating overlapping, inefficient, or ineffective programs, 2. strengthening or scaling up good programs, 3. shifting or merging programs to enhance the results (including reshaping the coordination mechanism, changing the authorities, or changing the execution bodies).

On the revenue side, the issue of Indonesia's suboptimal tax revenues as the conventional source of fiscal space warrants a mention. Indonesia has faced challenges in meeting annual tax targets, as indicated by the 20 percent shortfall from the target for 2015. Such a shortfall has been a recurring feature recently. A major contributing factor to this is structural: only approximately 30 percent of total workers are registered as taxpayers, and the compliance with income reporting is only around 60 percent.

Central government has tried to improve tax revenue and to widen the tax base by rolling out a Tax Amnesty Program in July 2016, to be effective for nine months. For the first phase (the first 3 months) the penalty rate for nonpayment was only a 2 percent tariff on unreported domestic assets and 4 percent for unreported overseas assets. This gradually increased to 5 percent and 10 percent, respectively, in the third phase, which ends in March 2017. The official Tax Amnesty targets are IDR 165 trillion (USD12 billion) from the penalty payments – or about 13 percent of total tax revenue in 2015 – and IDR 4 quadrillion (USD 300 billion) for the amount of asset declaration, or about 35 percent of total GDP in 2015. By the end of 2016 (the end of the second phase) the government received about IDR 100 trillion from penalty payments (60 percent of the target), while asset declaration reached about 25 percent of the target. However, the amount of asset repatriation by the end of 2016 was only about 62 percent of the declared assets. Relatively modest compliance, even during the amnesty program, suggests that tax administration and compliance processes still need strengthening.

In terms of the nominal amount of penalty payments, Indonesia compares very favourably when compared with other countries that have launched tax amnesty programs. However, as long experience with tax amnesties globally suggests, it may only provide immediate and short-run additional revenue, but no (or very little) effect in the long term if it is not supported by appropriate tax policy and administration reform, and by the efforts to alter taxpayer mindset towards compliance (Alm et al., 1990; Alm et al., 2007). Therefore, the government of Indonesia must take necessary steps to align tax reform policies with the tax amnesty program ending in March 2017.

Finally, an innovative approach that might be considered is cooperation with the private sector. Let the programs utilise the benefits of having competent, innovative, efficient, and effective mechanisms augmented by the private sector in selected areas of public services delivery. Some examples are: 1. subcontracting the distribution of UCT through the banking system, which also supports the financial inclusion program, 2. more privately run facilities participating in JKN, 3. professional fund managers to manage portfolio investments, 4. subcontracting the collection of premiums, and so on.

4.2 Towards SPF attainment

The discourses on introducing SPF in Indonesia have been brought forward mainly by ILO. In its study, ILO has calculated that *additional* costs of implementing selected SPF measures (access to healthcare and income security for children, the working age, people with disabilities, and the elderly) for Indonesia over the 2012–2020 period would cost between 0.74 percent and 2.45 percent of GDP annually by 2020. If we exclude the component of 'income security for working age population', the total *additional* fiscal space needed will be somewhere from 0.28 percent to 1.98 percent of GDP (Satriana et al., 2012).

It has to be noted that historically, the size of the central government budget has been around 20 percent of GDP, with maximum deficit capped at 3 percent of GDP. In FY2015, the central government deficit was estimated at about 2.7 percent of GDP – much higher than the originally planned 1.9 percent of GDP – mainly due to the shortfall of projected tax revenue. In FY2016, the deficit only slightly improved, to 2.5 percent of GDP. This suggests that there is only very slim fiscal space in a business-as-usual trend, and affording SPF measures – even for the projected low scenario – will require extraordinary efforts to generate fiscal space.

ILO's methodology also has some strong limitations. Unit cost assumptions used in the projection were far too low (e.g., third-class insurance was assumed to cost IDR 16,560 or approx. USD 1.2 per person/month) (see Table 5.8). Furthermore, the study was done before the implementation of the SJSN has been undertaken. Thus, the numbers will not be immediately applicable without updating the assumptions to post-SJSN implementation. If the assumptions were to be updated to match existing conditions, the additional fiscal space required to afford SPF measures as defined by ILO will no doubt be much higher.

While it is important to insure that citizens have income security, the government should be careful in its choice of which policies to focus on. Successful delivery of policy instruments relevant for active labour market policies which focus on boosting productivity will be more desirable for the entire economy than the passive ones, since the issues of social security cannot be separated from the dynamics of demographic trends and labour markets. At this stage, given its constraints, Indonesia is in no position to afford unemployment insurance – a component integral to ILO's SPF concept.

Table 5.8 ILO's assumptions

Aspect	Cost (% of GDP)	Note
Health	0.17–0.98	Low scenario: extension of third-class health insurance benefit for 40% poorest. High scenario: extension of first-class health insurance benefit for all population.
Income security for children	0.03–0.18	Low scenario: expansion of PKH (Program Keluarga Harapan) to all poor households. High scenario: plus universal child allowance.
Income security for working age population	0.47	Public work program and vocational training
Income security for elderly and people with severe disabilities	0.08–0.82	Low scenario: extension of existing non-contributory pension scheme for all persons with severe disabilities and vulnerable elderly. High scenario: extension of existing non-contributory pension scheme for all persons with severe disabilities and the establishment of a universal pension for old age covering 55 years of age (the legal retirement in the formal sector) and older.

Source: ILO (2012)

Government needs to have a comprehensive strategy to optimise its resources. Public budget and resources are limited, and SPF programs are competing with other equally important and good programs to be financed. Optimal resource allocation can be achieved through a thorough inter-linked program among related sectors and subsectors. Shifting inefficient social protection programs, particularly inefficient subsidies, into empowerment programs, for example, can improve the output and eliminate structural poverty. The programs should be designed to avoid moral hazard or inducing excessive demand.

For the public pension reform, Handra and Dita (2016) have proposed: 1. increasing tax revenue, 2. regularly increasing contributions from civil servants, as well as from the private sectors, including the informal one, 3. maximising the return on investment of the accumulated pension fund, 4. burden-sharing between the central and local governments for the local civil servants.

5. Concluding remarks

Arising from the analyses in this chapter are several conclusions. The first is the very pertinent observation that the social protection system in Indonesia has gone through much improvement in the span of two decades since the 1997 financial crisis. The SJSN Law serves as a legal framework in shaping the modern social security system in Indonesia. Its universal characteristics still face several challenges but when it is achieved, it will be the second largest universal health-care system in a single country.[15]

Second, Indonesia is currently still underinvesting in social protection, especially in non-fiscal aspects, such as: straightening out current policies to reduce moral hazard and to improve equal distribution and accessibility of healthcare facilities across the country, as well as to have a clear strategy to achieve universality. Regarding fiscal issues, spending policy should be prioritised to determine optimum allocation of resources. It is also equally important to ensure that relevant cross-cutting programs – including the policies in labour market, education, health, small and medium enterprises, finance/banking, and basic infrastructure – are coherent. There is opportunity to gain long-term increasing tax revenue by using tax amnesty momentum as a transition period to move towards stronger enforcement and a tougher tax regime in the future.

Third, the development of social protection policy should be coherent with other linked policies, especially labour market, health, education, and inter-governmental relations. Indonesia's rigid labour market can be relaxed and harmonised with employment protection from the social security system. Social protection dynamics can be anchored to the roadmap for the health and education development plan. Concurrent tasks in providing social protection across governmental tiers should be made clear and linked with an appropriate incentive system.

Fourth, database resources should be a focal point for minimising mistargeting and inclusion/exclusion error. Government should move faster in updating and improving population databases, and should create a system that can be updated periodically without any complications. Again, this is a cross-cutting issue, mainly under the authority of the Ministry of Home Affairs and Bureau of Statistics, while several institutions, especially the Ministry of Finance, Ministry of Social Welfare, Ministry of Education, Ministry of Health, National Development Planning Agency, and sub-national governments are the main users of the output.

Indonesia has approached progress towards the SPF, and towards those SDGs goals consistent with its priorities, in a manner which is specific to its economic, social, and political contexts. Considerable progress has also been made. If challenges identified in the chapter are addressed, Indonesia is likely to emerge as an 'over-achiever' in effective provision of social protection among the middle-income countries.

Notes

1 Authors can be contacted at fauziah.zen@eria.org.
2 Poverty in Indonesia is calculated using the 'cost of basic needs' approach. A person in poverty is defined as an individual whose expenditure is below a certain threshold ('poverty line') required to purchase a basket of food and non-food commodities considered as the minimum standard of living.
3 Using national baseline, in 2013, 17.13 million poor people live in rural area and 10.75 million live in urban.

4 In 2013, the poor – measured by national poverty line – make up 11.47 percent of the population, with Poverty Depth Index (PDI) of 1.89. Doubling the poverty line to around 36 USD (423,452 IDR) per month will categorize 58.00 percent of the population as poor (TNP2K, 2013).
5 Indonesia's economic policies (G20, 2014) have been criticized as being myopic with weak implementation.
6 For the purpose of simplification, in this paper USD 1 is assumed to be equivalent to IDR 13,500.
7 The two closest related articles were Article 27, Subsection 2, which stated that: 'Every citizen has the right to work and to live in human dignity'; and Article 34, which stated that 'The poor and destitute children shall be cared for by the State'.
8 Despite the five-year preparation period granted by the SJSN Law, Indonesia only managed to establish the SJSN implementing agencies in 2011, by way of Law no. 24/2011 on BPJS.
9 Although BPJS Labour will start its operation in early 2015, full implementation of the new system – where institutional transformation will have been completed – will not take place until 2029 with the eventual inclusion of TASPEN and ASA-BRI into the system. Unlike ASKES immediate transformation into BPJS Health-care, members of TASPEN and ASABRI will not be joining the BPJS Labour scheme until 2029, and even until then, the two institutions had insisted – as indicated in their respective roadmap documents – that they will not be absorbed into BPJS Labour, only the pension and old-age programs will be 'synchronized' with BPJS Labour. There is huge resistance from TASPEN and ASABRI to giving up their portions.
10 This refers to demanding of healthcare beyond equalization of marginal benefit and marginal costs. The extent of moral hazard in each needs to be empirically estimated, however, for nuanced policy design decisions.
11 The premium rate and benefit packages are periodically reviewed every 2 years.
12 The risk grouping is periodically reviewed every 2 years.
13 Social protection, according to Law 11/2009 on Social Welfare, is defined as all efforts directed to avoid and address the risk coming from shocks and social vulnerabilities so that individual, family, group and/or community may meet their minimum basic needs. The efforts may be conducted through social assistance, social advocacy, and legal help.
14 For fiscal year 2016, the central government will implement the mandate of Health Law which mentions that a minimum of 5 percent of the state budget must be earmarked for health spending.

References

Alm, J., J. Martinez-Vazquez, and S. Wallace. (2007). *Do Tax Amnesties Work? The Revenue Effects of Tax Amnesties During the Transition in the Russian Federation.* Working Paper. International Studies Program, Andrew Young School of Policy Studies, Georgia State University.

Alm, J., M. McKee, and W. Beck. (1990). Amazing Grace: Tax Amnesties and Compliance. *National Tax Journal,* 43(1), 23–37.

Asian Development Bank. (2011a). *The Revised Social Protection Index: Methodology and Handbook.* Mandaluyong City: Asian Development Bank.

Asian Development Bank. (2011b). *Enhancing Social Protection in Asia and The Pacific: The Proceedings of The Regional Workshop.* 21–22 April 2010. Manila: Asian Development Bank.

Asian Development Bank. (2016). *The Social Protection Indicator: Assessing Results for Asia*. Mandaluyong City: ADB.

BPJS Healthcare. (2012). *Peta Jalan Menuju Jaminan Kesehatan Nasional 2012–2019 (Roadmap of BPJS Healthcare 2012–2019)*. Jakarta.

BPJS Labour. (2015). *Peta Jalan Penyelenggaraan Jaminan Sosial Bidang Ketenagakerjaan 2013–2019 (Roadmap of BPJS Labour 2013–2019)*. Jakarta.

Brodjonegoro, B., S. Nazara, and F. Zen. (2016). Policy Challenges in Indonesian Social Security, in M. G. Asher, and F. Zen. (eds.) *Age Related Pension Expenditure and Fiscal Space: Modelling Techniques and Case Studies from East Asia*. Routledge.

Cook, S., and Pincus, J. (2014). Poverty, Inequality and Social Protection in Southeast Asia: An Introduction. *Journal of Southeast Asian Economies*, 31(1), 1–17.

Dartanto, T., J. F. Rezki, Usman, C. H. Siregar, H. Bintara, and W. Pramono. (2015). *Expanding Universal Health Coverage in the Presence of Informality in Indonesia: Challenges and Policy Implications*. LPEM-FEUI Working Paper 004, November 2015. ISSN 2356-4008.

Devereux, S., K. Roelen, and M. Ulrichs. (2015). *Where Next for Social Protection?*. Institute for Development Studies. UK.

G20. (2014). *Comprehensive Growth Strategy: Indonesia. G20 Australia Meeting 2014.* Available at www.g20australia.org/sites/default/files/g20_resources/library/g20_comprehensive_growth_strategy_indonesia.pdf assessed on

Handra, H., and A. Dita. (2016). Pension System and Its Fiscal Implications in Indonesia, in M. G. Asher, and F. Zen. (eds.) *Age Related Pension Expenditure and Fiscal Space: Modelling Techniques and Case Studies from East Asia*, p. 104.

Muliati, I. (2013). *Pension Reform Experience in Indonesia*. IMF Conference for Designing Equitable and Sustainable Pension Post Crisis World, Tokyo, January 9–10.

Olken, B. A., J. Onishi, and S. Wong. (2011). *Indonesia's PNPM Generasi Program: Final Impact Evaluation Report*. World Bank.

Satriana, S., V. Schmitt, and T. Muhamad. (2012). *Social Protection Assessment Based National Dialogue: Towards a Nationally Defined Social Protection Floor in Indonesia*. International Labour Organization. Jakarta, Indonesia.

Scheil Adlung, X., and Bonnet, F. (2011). Beyond Legal Coverage: Assessing the Performance Of Social Health Protection. *International Social Security Review*, 64(3), 21–38.

Sumarto, S., A. Suryahadi, and W. Widyanti. (2002). Designs and Implementation of Indonesian Social Safety Net Programs. *The Developing Economies, XL-1*, March 3–31.

Sumarto, S., and S. Bazzi. (2011). *Social Protection in Indonesia: Past Experiences and Lessons for the Future*. MPRA Paper No. 57893. 18 March 2011. Available at http://mpra.ub.uni-muenchen.de/57893/1/MPRA_paper_57893.pdf

Suryahadi, A., V. Febriany, and A. Yumna. (2014). *Expanding Social Security in Indonesia: The Processes and Challenges*. UNRISD Working Paper 2014–14, November.

Syukri, M., S. Arif, M. Rosfadhila, and W. Isdijoso. (2010). Making the Best of all Resources: How Indonesian Household Recipients Use the CCT Allowance. *IDS Bulletin*, 41, 84–94. doi: 10.1111/j.1759–5436.2010.00155.x

TNP2K. (2014). Perjalanan Menuju Jaminan Kesehatan Nasional. (JKN). Jakarta. Available at http://www.tnp2k.go.id/images/uploads/downloads/Final_JKN_Perjalanan%20Menuju%20Jaminan%20Kesehatan%20Nasional%20-%20Copy.pdf

Wagstaff, A., D. Cotlear, P. H. Eozenou, and L. R. Buisman. (2015). *Measuring Progress Towards Universal Health Coverage: With An Application to 24 Developing Countries.* World Bank Policy Research Working Paper 7470.

Widjaja, M. (2013). *An Economic and Social Review on Indonesias Direct Cash Transfer Program to Poor Families in 2005 (No. 201304).* Faculty of Economics, University of Indonesia.

World Bank. (Forthcoming). *Indonesia Social Assistance Public Expenditure Review.*

6 Social protection system in the Philippines

An assessment

Aniceto C. Orbeta, Jr.[1]

1. Introduction

This chapter provides an assessment of the social protection system of the Philippines. The focus is on the extent of its compatibility with international norms, in particular with the ILO's Social Protection Floor (SPF); searching for gaps in the system; and discussing current proposals for addressing them. The paper also discusses the merits and implied cost of the current proposals.

The Philippines GDP annually grew at a respectable average of 6.4 percent during the 2010 to 2014 period. The high growth in GDP has not been accompanied by a commensurate growth in employment. This has lead analysts to describe the phenomenon as "jobless growth" (Figure 6.1). Paqueo et al. (2014), however, argue that this popular notion requires qualification. They have pointed out that it should not be taken to mean that high growth did not generate additional jobs, but that the additional jobs created were not enough to make a dent on the unemployment and underemployment.

The progress in poverty reduction has also been modest. Thus, between 2009 and 2014, only 2.8 percentage point reduction in poverty incidence was observed, while the corresponding reductions were 1.2 percentage point in poverty gap, and 0.7 percentage point in poverty severity.[1] These outcomes pushed inclusive growth high on the agenda of the government. The inequality as indicated by the income Gini coefficients also hardly changed (Figure 6.2).

The government has taken major initiatives to accelerate social development. It has embarked on a data-based identification of poor households through proxy means testing based on household characteristics. It has invested in building the database that became the basis for identifying poor households, called the National Household Targeting System for Poverty Reduction (NHTS-PR). The first survey, done in 2008, covered 10 million households and 50 million individuals. Early in 2010, updating of this database was undertaken, promising to cover more households. This became the basis for identifying the beneficiaries of the Philippine version of the Conditional Cash Transfer – the Pantawid Pamilyang Pilipino Program (Pantawid). From about six thousand households in 2007, the program covered 4.4 million households in December 2014. Pantawid became the third largest CCT program in the world in terms of households covered, next

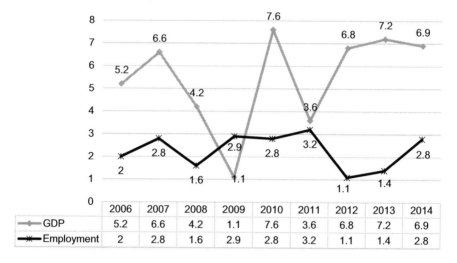

Figure 6.1 Philippines' annual growth rates (percent) in GDP and employment

Source: National Income Accounts, Philippine Statistics Authority (various years)

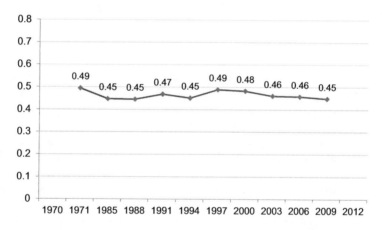

Figure 6.2 Inequality trends (Gini coefficient)

Source: Philippine Statistics Authority – National Statistical Coordination Board (Obtained from NSCB; obtained from Paqueo et al. (2014))

only to Brazil (8.8 million households) and Mexico (6.5 million households) (World Bank, 2014). Another important development has been the mandatory coverage of all Pantawid beneficiaries by the PhilHealth program, with premiums paid through the proceeds from the taxes on "vice good" (or "sin taxes").

The latest update on the attainment of MDG is presented in NEDA (2014). Table 6.1 summarizes the assessment as of 2014. This suggests that the country is

Table 6.1 Philippines' poverty incidence, gap and severity, first semester, 2009–2014

	2009	2012	2013	2014
Incidence	28.6	27.9	24.6	25.8
Gap	6.6	6.5	5.1	5.4
Severity	2.8	2.7	2.0	2.1

Source: Philippine Statistics Authority – National Statistical Coordination Board

on track in terms of achieving targets for 1. providing universal access to primary education, 2. providing education opportunities for girls, 3. reducing infant and under-five mortality, 4. reversing the incidence of malaria, 5. increasing tuberculosis detection and cure rates, 6. increasing the proportion of households with access to safe water supply, and 7. achieving the targets in access to basic sanitation. The country, however, appears to be lagging behind achieving objectives in 1. completion rates for elementary education, 2. maternal mortality, 3. access to reproductive health, and 4. HIV/AIDS.

The succeeding sections will provide an overview and assessment of the country's social protection system. Based on this, the paper then presents options identified, specific initiatives planned, and measures suggested to improve the current social protection system, with due recognition of the costs of the proposed measures.

2. Social protection system in the Philippines: an overview

Social protection in the Philippines is defined as "policies and programs that seek to reduce poverty and vulnerability to risks and enhance the social status and rights of the marginalized by promoting and protecting livelihood and employment, protecting against hazards and sudden loss of income, and improving people's capacity to manage risks" (NEDA-SDC Resolution No. 1, s. 2007). Social protection has four core components, namely, social insurance, social welfare, social safety nets, and labor market interventions.[2] Figure 6.3 shows the country's Social Protection Operational Framework.

The succeeding discussion presents the existing social protection programs under each component according to the ILO Recommendation 2012 (No. 202) concerning the establishment of social protection floors (SPF). The social security guarantees proposed in the SPFs include universal health care, social protection for children, social protection for the working age, and social protection for the elderly or older persons.

2.1 Universal health care

PhilHealth[3] implements the National Health Insurance Program. It aims to achieve total universal health care coverage and provide financial protection for

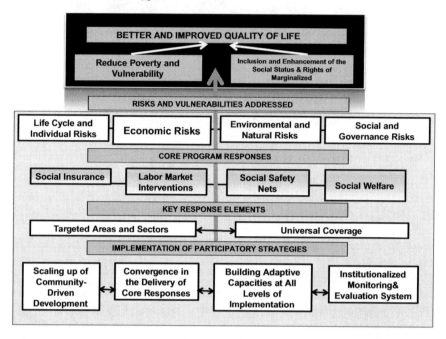

Figure 6.3 Social Protection Operational Framework and strategy of social protection
in the Philippines

Source: Villar (2013)

the poor. It is mandated to extend universal coverage to the following: 1. the
formal sector, including all government and private sector employees, household help/*kasambahay,* and enterprise owners and family drivers; 2. the informal
economy, including migrant workers/OFWs, self-earning individuals, and organized groups and others; 3. indigents; 4. members sponsored by local government
units; and 5. lifetime members. Coverage is also extended to their dependents.

The PhilHealth Senior Citizens Program, a non-contributory health insurance
(RA 10645), expanded coverage to all senior citizens instead of only the indigent
senior citizens under the National Health Insurance Program of PhilHealth. It
is financed by proceeds from the 'sin taxes' (RA 10351), mainly alcohol and
tobacco taxes.[4]

The PhilHealth also extends coverage to beneficiaries of special government
programs for areas in conflict, such as the Payapa at Masaganang Pamayanan
(PAMANA) Program and the Sajahatra Bangsamoro Program.

To advance social health insurance, PhilHealth prioritizes those included in the
National Household Targeting System for Poverty Reduction (NHTS-PR) of
the Department of Social Welfare and Development (DSWD), namely, the poor,
vulnerable non-poor, and DSWD-identified poor, and the displaced. Those who
are not yet included in the NHTS-PR list are covered through Point of Care.

PhilHealth benefits include in-patient hospital coverage, out-patient coverage, and other health care services as may be specified by the PHIC (PhilHealth, 2015). In-patient hospital coverage includes all case rates,[5] type Z benefits,[6] maternity care benefits, newborn care benefits, malaria package, out-patient HIV treatment package, and TB-DOTS package. Out-patient coverage includes minor surgical procedures / day surgeries, ambulatory surgical procedures, hemodialysis, chemotherapy, radiotherapy, and primary care benefits – the Tamang Serbisyo Para sa Kalusugan ng Pamilya (TseKap) package.[7] It also provides information and services through ALAGA KA – Alamin at Gamitin.

PhilHealth provides increased financial risk protection for the poor through its Case Rates System and Type Z-Benefits. The No-Balance Billing policy of Philhealth assures indigent, *kasambahay*, and sponsored members and their beneficiaries that they will not incur any additional expenses over and above the fixed rates whenever staying in government facilities under ward-type accommodation.

The SSS also provides sickness benefits[8] to members who are unable to work due to sickness or injury and who are confined in a hospital or at home for at least 4 days. Sickness benefit is also extended to members who have been separated from employment, a voluntary or self-employed member, and members who have used up all company sick leaves with pay for the current year.

The Employees Compensation Commission (ECC) also extends medical benefits[9] to all employees in the public and private sectors including member overseas Filipino workers (OFWs) below 60 years old who are experiencing work-related injury or illness, subject to specified conditions.

For veterans and their dependents, the Philippine Veterans Affairs Office (PVAO) – Veterans Memorial Medical Center (VMMC), under the Veterans Hospitalization Program (VHP) – provides free hospitalization and medical services. The VHP is also being implemented in 599 government hospitals all over the country. Benefits range from PhP 16,000 to PhP 200,000 (PVAO, 2015).[10]

2.2 Social protection for children

For children, social protection consists of social welfare and social safety net programs. Social welfare programs provide direct assistance mainly through the Pantawid Pamilyang Pilipino Program or Pantawid, a conditional cash transfer program, as well as social services like family and community support, and alternative care services implemented by the DSWD.

Since its inception in 2007, the Pantawid provides qualified poor households with cash grants to improve health, nutrition, and education of children aged 0–14. In 2014, the program was expanded to include children up to 18 years old, to cover secondary education. The cash grants consist of a PhP500 per month per household subsidy for health and nutrition expenses and a subsidy for educational expenses for a maximum of three children amounting to PhP300 per child in pre-elementary or elementary and PhP500 per child in high school per month for a period of 10 months or one school year. Total subsidy per household beneficiary with three qualified children is P1,600 per month for one school year.

Cash grants are transmitted to the household heads through the government's Land Bank cash card. The Pantawid is financed from government appropriations.

The Pantawid targets the poorest of the poor. Household beneficiaries are identified using the Listahanan or NHTS-PR, a comprehensive socio-economic database of poor households nationwide which government agencies use as a basis in identifying beneficiaries for social protection programs. Qualified household beneficiaries meet the following criteria: an economic status within or below the provincial poverty threshold based on the proxy means test; with children 0–18 years old; with pregnant woman during the time of assessment; and meet the conditions specified in the program.[11]

The DSWD also provides alternative care and services to children through the Intergenerational Program for children, six months to six years, and older persons 60 years and above. It also implements on a pilot scale community-based alternative care and social services programs for child victims or witnesses of abuse, street children, disadvantaged youth, out-of-school youth, and children in conflict with the law.

There are two existing safety net programs for children being implemented by TESDA and the DPWH. TESDA, in coordination with LGUs, NGOs, POs and other agencies, provides scholarships for unemployed and disadvantaged children for institution-based, enterprise-based, or community-based technical-vocational education and training programs. The DPWH, in coordination with the PNP, provides marginalized OSY emergency employment in their roadside maintenance, education, and skills training and sports development under the Out-of-School Youth Servicing Towards Economic Recovery (OYSTER) Program.

2.3 Social protection for the working age population

For the working age population, social protection is provided mainly through work-related or contributory social insurance. Social insurance includes pension or retirement benefits (discussed in section 2.4 below), health insurance (discussed in section 2.1 above), and other social insurance for contingencies such as work-related injury, disability, separation/unemployment, maternity, and death. For the unemployed, displaced/distressed workers, the government provides social protection through social safety nets and labor market programs. Social safety nets include emergency employment for displaced/distressed workers and cash/food for work program. Labor market programs include skills training, reintegration assistance, and employment facilitation.

Eight major institutions are engaged in the provision of social security in the Philippines. Table 6.2 summarizes the type of risks/contingencies addressed and the sectors or type of workers covered by each of these institutions.

Maternity benefits

The GSIS[12] grants married women, in case of pregnancy, a 60 days maternity leave with or without pay depending on their status of employment and years of

Table 6.2 Social security institutions and risks/contingencies covered in the Philippines

Risks/ Contingencies	Formal sector workers				Unemployed, housewives, dependent children
	Government		Private (domestic)	OFW	
	Civilian	Military			
Old age/ Retirement	GSIS	AFP-RSBS	SSS	SSS	
Maternity	GSIS		SSS		
Disability	GSIS, ECC	AFP-RSBS	SSS, ECC	SSS, ECC OWWA	
Death/Survivorship	GSIS, ECC, HDMF (Pag-IBIG)	AFP-RSBS	SSS, ECC	SSS, ECC OWWA	
Separation/ Unemployment	GSIS	AFP-RSBS			
Sickness /Health	PhilHealth	PhilHealth	PhilHealth, SSS, ECC	PhilHealth, SSS, ECC OWWA	PhilHealth Private insurers (voluntary)
Funeral	GSIS, ECC	PVOA	SSS, ECC	SSS, ECC OWWA	
Life insurance	GSIS (compulsory plus optional), Private insurers (voluntary)	Private insurers (voluntary)	Private insurers (voluntary)	SSS, OWWA, Private insurers (voluntary)	Private insurers (voluntary)
Mutual Fund/ Provident Fund	GSIS(optional), institution-based, HDMF (Pag-IBIG)	AFP-RSBS, HDMF (Pag-IBIG)	HDMF(Pag-IBIG), institution-based	SSS, HDMF (Pag-IBIG)	HDMF (Pag-IBIG) (voluntary)
Lending program	GSIS (salary, emergency, policy, housing), HDMF(Pag-IBIG)		SSS (salary, emergency, housing), HDMF (Pag-IBIG)	SSS, OWWA	

Source: Orbeta (2010, modified Table 6, p. 227)

service. Those with permanent and regular status are granted half pay with less than two years, and full pay with more than two years, of continuous service. Those with temporary status are entitled only to a maternity leave with an assurance of readmission to the service.

The SSS also grants a 60 day maternity leave but with full pay to all female members who are unable to work due to childbirth or miscarriage, regardless of marital or employment status. The only requirement is payment of at least three monthly contributions within the 12-month period preceding childbirth or miscarriage (RA 8282). A longer maternity leave (78 days) is granted for caesarean section delivery. The maternity benefit is limited to the first four deliveries or miscarriages only.

Disability benefits

The GSIS and SSS grant disability benefits[13] to members who suffer work-related disability. The benefits include a lump sum, a basic monthly pension, or a combination of both depending on the length of service or number of monthly contributions and type of disability. For SSS, payment of at least one monthly contribution prior to the semester of disability entitles a member to a disability benefit. For GSIS, the requirement is at least three years of service at the time of disability, or if separated, has paid at least a total of 180 monthly contributions prior to disability. The ECC, in addition, provides cash income benefit and rehabilitation services. For OFWs, the OWWA provides a cash benefit ranging from PhP2,000 to PhP100,000 for work-related disability (EO 126). The disability benefit is terminated upon recovery, re-employment, or refusal to take an annual exam.

Separation/unemployment or involuntary separation benefit

The GSIS provides members separated from government service a cash benefit or a cash benefit plus old age pension, depending on the length of service (RA 8291, Sec. 11 and 12).[14] Permanent employees separated involuntarily due to abolition of office or position are entitled to monthly cash payments for a period of two to six months.[15]

Death/survivorship benefits

The GSIS and SSS grant primary beneficiaries and dependents[16] of a pensioner or an active member who dies a survivorship benefit in lump sum or monthly pension or both.[17] The ECC, in addition, provides a monthly income benefit of not less than Php15,000 to primary beneficiaries and dependents. For beneficiaries of veterans who died in the line of duty or a disability pensioner who died from a service-related disability or sickness, the PVOA grants a monthly pension of PhP1,000 each for the surviving spouse, unmarried children, and parents. For single parents, the monthly pension is PhP2,000, with accretion.

Funeral/burial benefit

The GSIS and OWWA each grant a funeral benefit of PhP20,000 to whoever paid the burial expenses of the deceased member. The SSS increased its burial benefit from PhP20,000 to a variable amount ranging from PhP20,000 to a maximum of PhP40,000 starting August 2015. The ECC also grants a funeral benefit of PhP3,000 to beneficiaries of the deceased member or PTD pensioner. For veterans, the PVOA grants PhP10,000 for burial expenses and the Philippine flag to adorn the veteran's casket.

Life insurance

Unlike SSS, the GSIS provides compulsory life insurance coverage to all government employees except for members of the AFP and PNP. They are either covered by a Life Endowment Policy (LEP) or an Enhanced Life Policy (ELP).[18] Optional insurance is also offered to GSIS members (e.g., pre-need coverage for life, health, hospitalization, education, memorial plans, and other plans). For OFWs, OWWA provides life insurance coverage for the duration of their employment contract, valued at PhP100,000 for natural death and PhP200,000 for accidental death.

Mutual/provident fund

The GSIS Kinabukasan Fund, a balance fund managed by the Philam Asset Management Inc. (PAMI) since 1998, provides affordable investment options for government employees for a minimum of PhP1,000 for members and PhP5,000 for non-members.

Lending program

The GSIS provides service loans to members and pension loans for retirees. The SSS provides members' salary and housing and business loans. The OWWA provides members with collateral loans.[19]

Portability of benefits

Under RA7699, members of the GSIS or SSS who transfer employment from one sector to another can combine their government service or contributions with their SSS creditable years of service or contributions to qualify for retirement benefits and other social security benefits under either PD 1146 or PD 8291. The process is called 'totalization'. The benefits that will be received from GSIS or SSS will be in proportion to the contributions remitted to each System.

For OFWs or migrant workers, the POEA has entered into bilateral social security agreements (SSAs) with other countries to guarantee their social security benefits. SSAs have four salient features: mutual assistance, equality of treatment, export of social security, and 'totalization' of membership period (Matula, 2007). As of 2014, the Philippines had existing bilateral agreements with nine European countries: Austria, Belgium, France, Germany, Norway, Spain, Switzerland, the United Kingdom, and Northern Ireland and Canada (Quebec) (CMA, 2012).

Social safety nets

The DOLE and the DSWD provide emergency employment for displaced/distressed workers. The DOLE, in coordination with LGUs, implements the Tulong Panghanapbuhay sa Ating Disadvantaged Workers (TUPAD) for displaced workers, long-term unemployed poor, out of school youths (OSYs), workers in flood-prone areas, and victims of natural calamities. TUPAD provides employment in various community work projects such as infrastructure works for a period of one month to one year at minimum wage. Other program benefits include PhilHealth premiums for one year, SSS premiums, and livelihood assistance including capacity building, provision of raw material inputs, tools and equipment.

The DSWD, through its cash / food-for-work program, provides distressed/ displaced individuals 18 years and above with temporary employment in community projects and activities for a minimum of 10 days to a maximum of three months at wage rates equal to 75 percent of prevailing daily wage rate.

Labor market programs

The DSWD implements the Sustainable Livelihood Program (SLP) / Self-Employment Assistance – Kaunlaran (SEA-K) Project for unemployed and underemployed poor families nationwide. The program provides entrepreneurial skills training through an organization of community-based associations, and loans[20] to finance small businesses.

The DOLE implements a reintegration and employment facilitation program for returning OFWs and the unemployed. The DSWD, in partnership with LGUs, also provides livelihood assistance to distressed returning OFWs through its reintegration program under the SLP/SEA-K. Livelihood assistance includes transportation allowance, basic business management training, skills upgrading, house repair, livelihood skills training, provision of school supplies and uniforms for children, medical assistance, and burial assistance.

2.4 Social protection for older persons

For the elderly, social protection consists of social insurance in the form of pension or retirement benefits for eligible members of contributory social security schemes, social pension for those who are not covered, health insurance, and social assistance guaranteed by the government through the Expanded Senior Citizens Act of 2010 (RA 9994).

Workers from the formal sector are covered by either the SSS or the GSIS retirement schemes. Those in the military are covered by the AFP-RSBS scheme.

To be eligible for retirement benefits, members have to be at least 60 (optional) or 65 (compulsory) and have contributed at least 10 years (in SSS) or 15 years (in GSIS).

GSIS members have five retirement options[21] to choose from depending on the length of service, age, and date of entry into the service. Retirement benefits are in the form of a lump sum payment, a monthly pension, or a combination of both, computed based on the contributions paid. For SSS, retirement benefits also come as a lump sum equal to the amount of contributions paid plus 6 percent interest for members with less than 10 credited years of service (CYS); a basic monthly pension of PhP1,200 for those with at least 10 CYS and PhP2,400 plus dependents' pension and thirteenth month pension to those with at least 20 CYS.

The SSS and the GSIS differ in their computation of basic monthly pension (BMP). For the GSIS, BMP is based on the retiree's average monthly compensation (AMC) and years of service (YOS) and is computed as follows: 37.5 percent of the re-valued AMC for the last three years plus 2.5 percent of the AMC in the last three years for each year of service in excess of 15 years. For the SSS, BMP is based on the average monthly salary credit (AMSC) and credited years of service (CYS) and is estimated using this formula: BMP = 300 + 0.2* AMSC +0.02 *(CYS-10) * AMSC.

For the AFP-RSBS, officers and enlisted personnel who have reached 56 years of age or a minimum of 20 years of service (optional) or 30 years of service (compulsory) are eligible for retirement (PD 1638). The benefits include a gratuity equivalent to one month of base pay and longevity pay of the grade next higher than the permanent grade last held for every year of service, payable in lump sum or as a monthly pension. For those in the active service of the AFP who have been separated from the service through no fault of their own fault, the benefit includes a lump sum refund of the retiree's personal contribution with 4 percent interest (PD 1656).

For veterans, the PVAO under the Department of National Defense pays old age monthly pensions amounting to PhP5,000 for life to war veterans[22] 65 years old and above and the surviving spouses of deceased war veterans unless they are receiving a similar pension[23] from other government funds, such as from the United States of America (RA 7696, Sec. 3 and 4). Monthly pension for the surviving spouse is revoked when he/she remarries or dies.

For indigent senior citizens,[24] a social pension program by virtue of RA 9994 was implemented by the DSWD in coordination with the Office of the Senior Citizens Affairs (OSCA) and the LGUs. At present, a monthly pension of PhP500 is provided to support their daily subsistence and medical needs.

Health insurance

The PhilHealth provides lifetime coverage to members who have reached 60 years old (55 for underground miners, 56 for uniformed personnel) and have paid at least 120 monthly contributions with PhilHealth and the former Medicare Programs of SSS and GSIS.

Under the PhilHealth Senior Citizens Program, a non-contributory health insurance (RA 10645), coverage has been extended to all senior citizens (and not only the indigent senior citizens) under the National Health Insurance Program. It is financed by proceeds from the sin tax (RA 10351).[25]

Social assistance

Under the Expanded Senior Citizens Act of 2010 (RA 9994),[26] senior citizens are entitled to privileges, social safety nets, and social welfare assistance intended to provide social security for them.

The privileges include: 1. a 20 percent discount and exemption from the value-added tax on the sale of goods and services from all establishments; 2. exemption from payment of income taxes for minimum wage earners; 3. a minimum of 5 percent discount on monthly utilization of water and electricity supplied by the public utilities; 4. free medical and dental services, diagnostic and laboratory fees in all government facilities; 5. free vaccination against influenza virus and pneumococcal disease for indigent senior citizens to be administered by DOH; 6. continuance of GSIS, SSS, and PAG-IBIG benefits and privileges to the extent practicable and feasible; 7. upgraded retirement benefits from both the SSS and GSIS at par with the current scale, to the extent practicable and feasible; 8. special discounts on purchase of basic commodities; 9. express lanes or priority in all commercial and government establishments; and 10. death benefit assistance of a minimum of Php2,000, adjusted for inflation.

Government assistance includes: 1. employment-related assistance to senior citizens who want to work (e.g., training programs that will provide skills and welfare or livelihood support of senior citizens; 2. access to formal or non-formal education; 3. a health program for senior citizens which includes the establishment of a senior citizens or geriatric ward in every government hospital; 4. provision of 50 percent discount on the consumption of electricity, water, and telephone by facilities operated for the well-being of abandoned, neglected, unattached, or homeless senior citizens; 5. a national shelter program that incorporates the special housing needs of senior citizens; 6. full access to public transport facilities; 7. incentives for individuals or nongovernmental institutions providing foster care (e.g., realty tax holiday).

To cushion the effects of economic shocks, disasters, and calamities, senior citizens are also provided assistance such as food, medicines, and financial assistance for house repairs. Funds utilized for this purpose are sourced from the disaster/calamity funds of the LGU where the senior citizens reside.

Social welfare assistance

Assistance in the form of alternative care and services has also been designed for older persons who are poor, without family members, abandoned, neglected, and homeless. The DSWD is currently implementing pilot-scale programs such as group home, foster home, and sheltered workshop.

3. Social protection system: an assessment

The framework used in the assessment is presented in Figure 6.4. It comprehensively covers the three dimensions of coverage: 1. width – covered population; 2. breadth – risks or contingencies covered; and 3. depth – amount of direct cost supported. The assessment is done at two levels. One uses the Social Protection Index that uses numerical values to summarize the characteristics of the social protection system of the country. The other does the assessment at the subcomponent level, covering the four basic pillars of the social protection floor, namely, 1. universal health care, 2. social protection for children, 3. social protection for working age population, and 4. social protection for older persons.

3.1 Overall assessment using Social Protection Index

The overall assessment will use the Social Protection Index (SPI). Based on ADB's assessment (ADB, 2013), the country's overall SPI[27] is 0.085, signifying that expenditure on social protection per intended beneficiary represents 8.5 percent of the poverty line expenditure. The country is among 19 countries in Asia and the Pacific with an SPI that is lower than 0.100. It was noted that in order to have a suitable SPI, these countries will have to substantially increase SP expenditures, with Korea's SPI of 0.200 as a realistic medium-term objective (that is, 20 percent of the poverty line expenditure).

By component,[28] social insurance is the predominant form of social protection in the country, as it is in Asia and the Pacific and in Southeast Asia (Table 6.3). The country's SPI for social insurance is 0.068, lower than the average for Asia

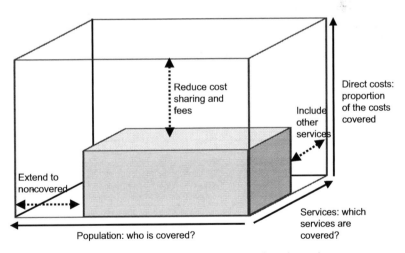

Three dimensions to consider when moving towards universal coverage

Figure 6.4 The assessment framework

Source: www.who.int/health_financing/strategy/dimensions/en/

Table 6.3 Social Protection Index and depth and breadth of social protection: Asia and the Pacific, Southeast Asia, and the Philippines, 2009

Item	Asia & the Pacific	Southeast Asia	Philippines
Social Protection Index			
Overall	0.110	0.095	0.085
By Components			
Social Insurance	0.075	0.077	0.068
Social Assistance	0.032	0.015	0.011
Labor Market Programs	0.003	0.003	0.005
Depth[1]		0.284	0.368
Social Insurance		0.798	1.056
Social Assistance		0.071	0.082
Labor Market Programs		0.228	0.190
Breadth (unweighted)[2]		0.474	0.231
Social Insurance		0.395	0.172
Social Assistance		0.620	0.262
Labor Market Programs		0.236	0.289

[1] Depth – the average benefits received by each beneficiary, relative to the poverty line; computed as [Total SP expenditures/Total actual beneficiaries]/poverty-line expenditures

[2] Breadth – the proportion of the total potential beneficiaries who are actual beneficiaries of SP; computed as Total actual beneficiaries/Total potential beneficiaries

Source: ADB (2013)

and the Pacific or for Southeast Asia. In general, the country's SPI by component is lower compared to the region's average except for labor market programs.

In terms of depth of social protection (SP),[29] the country's overall depth is 0.368, higher than the average for SEA (0.284). This means that SP expenditure per actual beneficiary, relative to the poverty line is 36.8 percent, about 8.4 percent higher than SEA's average. By component, the depth ranges from 0.082 for social assistance to 1.056 for social insurance; higher than SEA's average except for labor market programs. The latter implies that the group of beneficiaries reached through social insurance programs is fairly small compared to social assistance and labor market programs.

In terms of breadth, the country's overall breadth of social protection is 0.231, meaning that only about 23.1 percent of the potential beneficiaries of social protection actually received any benefits; about half of SEA's (47.4 percent). By component, the country's actual coverage of potential beneficiaries of social protection is low compared to SEA's except in labor market programs where it is comparable. The proportion ranges from 17.2 percent for social insurance to 28.9 percent in labor market programs.

3.2 Assessment at the subcomponent level

3.2.1 Universal health care

A recent assessment of the health sector noted several significant developments towards universal health care (Pantig, 2013). Progress is not limited to increased coverage but also in innovative ways of financing its expansion. The government has recently succeeded in convincing Congress to pass a law increasing the taxes on 'vice' goods such as alcohol and tobacco and designating the proceeds entirely for financing the universal health care program. Given that the source of financing is stipulated in a law, there is a high probability that the program will be sustained.

In terms of width, the population covered by health insurance has dramatically increased by about 21 percentage points over a period of five years. Data from two National Demographic and Health Surveys (NDHS) showed that health insurance coverage rose from only 42.0 percent in 2008 to about 63.0 percent in 2013. The biggest expansion is in PhilHealth's coverage of indigents, increasing from 21.1 percent in 2008 to 42.0 percent in 2013. This increase is attributed mainly to the policy to automatically enroll in PhilHealth all Pantawid beneficiaries, with premiums paid for by the program starting in 2011. This policy continues, with coverage doubling within a matter of three years (4.4 million households as of the end December 2014).

Table 6.4 shows the number and distribution of PhilHealth members and their dependents as of end of June 2014. Indigents account for more than 55 percent of the total number of beneficiaries.

There is a significant rise in treatment-seeking, increasing from 7.9 percent in 2008 to 10.7 in 2013. There are also increases in the use of public facilities such as rural health units (RHUs), city health units (CHUs), and barangay health stations (BHSs). The NDHS data show that between 2008 and 2013 the use of RHUs/CHUs/BHSs increased from 33.6 percent to 48.1 percent while the use of private clinics declined from 19.2 percent to 11.7 percent. Travel time to health facilities or health providers was shortened from 38.7 minutes in 2008 to 33.6 minutes in 2013.

Unfortunately, it was also observed that while benefit payments for sponsored programs increased, last hospital visit data still showed a very low utilization rate of PhilHealth coverage. The second wave evaluation report of CCT, for instance, showed that even though coverage of CCT beneficiaries is almost universal (92 percent), the utilization of coverage in the last visit to the hospital is only 19 percent (DSWD and World Bank, 2014).

In terms of depth, improvements were observed with the implementation of the no-balance billing policy for indigents. Average hospitalization cost in public facilities declined. However, those in private hospitals increased. The support value remained low at 31.5 percent for hospital cost and 5.4 percent for medicines and supplies (NDHS, 2013). Ulep and dela Cruz (2013) using data from the Family Income and Expenditure Survey (FIES) also showed that from 2000 to 2012 out-of-pocket expenditures grew in real terms by an average annual growth rate of 21 percent. The lack of medicines and other medical supplies in these facilities may have undermined the no-balance billing policy for indigents.

As to the health insurance premium of 2.5 percent of salary base, payment is split between the employee and the employer for paying members. For indigents, the PhP2,400 per annum premium is by law paid for by government out of the proceeds from the 'sin taxes'. The secure financing provides this program a much

Table 6.4 Philippines' number of PhilHealth members and dependents (as of June 30, 2014)

Sector	Members (millions)	Dependents (millions)	Total beneficiaries (millions)	Percent of total beneficiaries
Members in the formal economy	13.0	14.0	27.1	33.2
Private	10.9	10.2	21.1	25.8
Government	2.1	3.8	5.9	7.3
Household help	0.1	0.0	0.1	0.1
Enterprise owner and family drivers	0.0	0.0	0.0	–
Members in the informal economy	3.3	3.8	7.0	8.6
Migrant worker	0.7	0.6	1.3	1.6
Informal sector	2.0	2.5	4.6	5.6
Self-earning individual	0.5	0.6	1.1	1.4
Organized group and others	0.0	0.0	0.0	–
Indigents	14.7	30.4	45.1	55.4
Sponsored members	0.4	0.4	0.8	1.0
Lifetime members	0.8	0.6	1.5	1.8
TOTAL	32.2	49.3	81.5	100.0

Note: – = nil or negligible
Source: PhilHealth (2014)

greater chance of being sustained. Table 6.5 shows the distribution of premium collection and benefit payments for 2013 by sector. As of 2013, those employed in the private sector, those sponsored by the LGUs and the NHTS-PR, and the individually-paying members together account for 76 percent and 77 percent of premium collected and benefits paid, respectively.

3.2.2 Social protection for children

The main social protection program for children in the Philippines is the Pantawid Pamilyang Pilipino Program or Pantawid. In 2009, the program had 700,000 household-beneficiaries with a budget of PhP 6.6 billion. Since then, it has grown to cover 4.4 million households with a budget of PhP 62.6 billion (Figure 6.5). The two waves of rigorous evaluation of the program (DSWD and World Bank 2013, 2014) showed that it is on track on its primary intermediate objectives of keeping children healthy and in school. The longer term question is whether the program will be sustained to meet its objective of breaking the intergenerational poverty cycle through investment in human capital. Unfortunately, there is no clear answer to this question.

In terms of width, the Pantawid initially targeted poor households with children 0 to 14 years old. In order to achieve its objective of building human capital, the program expanded its coverage in June 2014 to include children up to

Table 6.5 Premium collection and benefit payments: January-December 2013 (PhP billion)

Sector	Premium collections	Percent distribution	Benefit payments	Percent distribution
Government employed	9.1	16.4	7.2	12.9
Private-employed	24.9	4.9	14.2	25.5
Sponsored program (by LGU and NHTS-PR)	16.9	30.5	18.0	32.4
Individually-paying program	3.1	5.6	10.4	18.7
Overseas Workers Program	1.2	2.2	1.7	3.1
Lifetime program	-	-	4.1	7.4
TOTAL	55.4	100	55.6	100.0

Source: (Philhealth 2015)

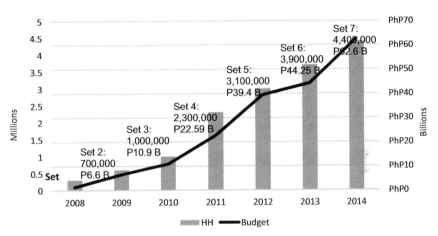

Php: Philippine Persos

Figure 6.5 Philippine CCT household targets and budget (2008–2014)

Note: Php = Philippine Persons
Source: DSWD

18 years old to cover secondary education. As of August 2013, a total of about 7.37 million children aged 0 to 14 years old from about 3.95 million households benefitted from the program (Reyes et al., 2015). With the expanded coverage, an estimated 1.7 million children between 15–18 years old are projected to receive cash benefits for secondary education (Paqueo et al. 2013).

In terms of breadth or services provided, the Pantawid has been providing grants for enrolment in pre-school and elementary since 2008 and up to secondary level starting 2014 for up to a maximum of three children per beneficiary.

As part of the program, pregnant mothers and children aged 0 to 5 are provided essential health services (such as check-ups and immunization) during the mandatory monthly visits to a health facility while children aged 6 to 14 years are subjected to deworming. The Pantawid also provides PhilHealth coverage to program beneficiaries and their dependents.

As a result of the Pantawid, net school attendance rate increased from 89 percent in 2008–2009 to 95 percent in 2012–2013 while dropout rates declined from 11.7 percent in 2008 to 5.2 percent in 2013 (David and Albert, 2015). Data from the DSWD and World Bank recent assessments of the Pantawid also indicated a positive impact on enrolment rates. Among the program beneficiaries, the enrolment rates were as follows: 54 percent for children 3–5 years old, 98 percent for children 6 to 11 years old, and 95 percent for children 12–15 years old. There is, however, mixed results for health services. Delivery rates in health facilities and attendance by a health professional were increasing while immunization rates were declining (DSWD and World Bank, 2014).

In terms of depth, the Pantawid provides a maximum benefit of PhP1,600 per month or about PhP19,200 annually per household beneficiary (assuming two children in pre-elementary/elementary education and one in secondary education) or about 20 percent of poverty threshold for a family of five in 2012.[30] This provides an indication that poor families cannot rely on the cash grants alone. Another measure is whether the cash grant is sufficient to replenish whatever is lost from children working because they have to be in school. Some indication can be provided by looking at whether the program was successful in preventing child labor among the beneficiaries. The common reason why children are out of school is because they augment family income by taking on paid work or doing activities that would earn them some income. Analysis of the evaluation data provides some evidence of the program's impact on child labor. In particular, the analysis showed that while the incidence of child labor did not decline with the program, the number of hours spent on paid work declined (Orbeta et al., 2013; DSWD and World Bank, 2014).

The Pantawid is funded through annual appropriation by the Philippine government from loan proceeds from multilateral institutions such as the World Bank and ADB and from grants from the Department of Foreign Affairs and Trade of Australia. There is a strong opposition to the program, as indicated by debates every time its budget is presented in Congress. The opposition criticized the program as a dole-out and pointed out that providing work opportunities for the poor would have been a better strategy. Proponents, however, have argued that the program is not a dole-out but is a source of critical investments in keeping children of the poor healthy and in school, securing a better future for them. In addition, providing work opportunities for the poor continues to be an important concern. The unwavering support of the former President Benigno Aquino III to the program saved it from being reduced or even aborted. These factors make the sustainability of the program uncertain. Its strong performance in delivering its primary objectives as shown by the rigorous evaluation may, however, result in its having a strong case for funding.

3.2.3 Social Protection for working age population

Orbeta (2010) pointed out that the Philippine social insurance programs by law virtually cover all formal sector workers with at least one program covering any conceivable contingency except for unemployment (Table 6.2). Actual coverage, however, is far from universal.

In terms of width, it may be safe to assume that all government workers with employer-employee relationship[31] are covered but not so with private sector workers as shown in Table 6.6. By SSS law, the eligible population includes private sector wage workers, the self-employed, OFWs, and more recently non-working spouse and household helpers. A comparison of the number of contributing members to the statutorily covered population in over two decades shows that the coverage for wage workers ranged from only 36 to 48 percent and in the last five years has not exceeded 40 percent nor has it shown a definite increasing trend. The coverage for own-account workers is at most 17 percent while those of OFWs is at most 22 percent, with an increasing trend. This problem of low coverage had already been recognized in the early 1990s (e.g. ILO, 1996 and WB, 1995). To date, however, the problem still remains.

With respect to informal sector workers, Manasan and Orbeta (2012) pointed out that existing social protection laws extend coverage to practically all including self-employed workers, household helpers, separated members, and non-working spouses. Getting them to register with the SSS, however, has been a constant challenge.

In terms of breadth, existing institutions involved in delivering social protection to the working population cover almost all contingencies including illness, work-related injury or disability, maternity, old age, or death (Table 6.2). Any short-term contingency can also be addressed by general-purpose salary loans

Table 6.6 Estimated SSS coverage of private sector workers in the Philippines

Year	Contributing SSS Members (millions)			Workers (millions)			Estimated coverage (%)		
	Employed	Voluntary	OFWs	Private wage & salary workers	Own account	OFW deployed	Private wage & salary workers	Own account	OFW deployed
	[a]	[b]	[c]	[d]	[e]	[f]	[a]/[d]	[b]/[e]	[c]/[f]
2000	5.5	1.3	0.1	11.5	10.5	0.8	48	13	11
2005	6.1	1.5	0.1	16.4	12.3	1.0	37	12	11
2010	7.4	1.6	0.2	19.8	12.4	1.5	37	13	17
2011	7.7	1.6	0.3	21.2	12.6	1.7	36	13	16
2012	8.2	1.9	0.3	21.6	12.0	1.8	38	16	18
2013	8.7	2.1	0.4	22.2	12.2	1.8	39	17	22

Source of basic data: PSA, LFS – Private sector workers, Own account workers; POEA – OFW Deployed; SSS/BLES – Contributing SSS members

which both the SSS and GSIS offer. Even for specific risks, like calamities and economic crisis, government often mandates SSS and GSIS to open special loan windows for affected members. A major limitation, however, is the absence of unemployment insurance. While several proposals have been presented, there is still no agreement on this issue as of 2016.

In terms of depth, Orbeta (2010) shows that a significant share of the benefits paid by both SSS and GSIS are in pensions. Employees' compensation for work-related injuries accounted for a relatively small share. There is no known assessment of how sufficient this coverage is for affected workers. Moreover, despite the increase in health insurance coverage, the out-of-pocket expenditure for hospitalization has been rising.

Social protection for the working age population is funded from contributions shared by the employee and the employer. As long as the premiums are determined correctly, the program will have sustainable funding. Of course, if that fails, the SSS and GSIS will need to resort to sovereign guarantee or other methods to obtain funds from the national government.

3.2.4 Social Protection for the elderly

Social protection for older persons includes pension benefits for retirees, a social pension program for indigents, a lifetime PhilHealth coverage for retirees and all senior citizens, and other social services designed for them.

In terms of width, the government strives to provide social protection for all senior citizens. All retirees who have contributed at least 120 months to the GSIS or SSS are eligible to receive pension benefits starting at age 65, the mandatory retirement age. However, Table 6.7 shows that in 2012 only 31 percent of households[32] whose heads are 60 years and above receive pension income Although the situation leaves much to be desired, this already represents a 7 percent increase within six years from 24 percent in 2006 (Orbeta, 2010).

For indigent senior citizens (60 years and above) with no pension from either SSS or GSIS or regular support from other family members, a social pension program was established under the Expanded Senior Citizen Law (RA 9994) in 2010. In 2012, DSWD covered 185,914 indigent seniors or only about 22 percent of the 841,750 heads of poor households who are 60 years and above estimated using FIES 2012. Starting 2015, the DSWD budget allocation will allow it to cover 939,609 indigent seniors who are 65 years and above.

In terms of breadth, aside from pension benefits for qualified SSS and GSIS and a social pension for indigent senior citizens, older persons are provided with a lifetime PhilHealth coverage. In addition, SSS and GSIS retirees are provided death benefit assistance. By law (RA 9994) all senior citizens regardless of economic status are entitled to economic assistance in the form of discount privileges for basic needs as follows: 20 percent for medicines and food in restaurants, 5 percent in basic necessities, 5 percent in electricity and water bills, and 50 percent

Table 6.7 Philippines' mean annual pension and per capita income for households with heads 60 years and older, 2012

Age of HH	With pension income (%)	Mean annual pension income (Php)	Ratio of pension income to total income (%)	Mean annual per capita income	Mean household size
60–64	25	18,728	5	69,412	4.5
65–69	33	25,661	8	66,250	4.2
70–74	32	21,542	8	63,071	3.8
75–79	34	20,845	9	61,780	3.7
80–84	41	28,515	11	66,711	3.4
85–89	39	32,563	12	68,927	3.7
90+	39	35,189	12	83,210	3.0
60 and above	31	22,287	7	66,476	4.1

Notes: Average per capita income: PhP 58,583
Poverty Threshold (per capita):
Min: PhP 15,891
Max: PhP 24,693
Source: author's calculations using PSA FIES 2012

discount on electricity, water, and telephone in group homes. Priority lanes in services are also provided for seniors.

In terms of depth, Orbeta (2010) noted that the pension formulas for SSS and GSIS members are likely yield a replacement value (ratio of pre- to post-retirement income) between 40 and 50 percent for members with 20 years of service, and between 60 and 75 percent for those with 30 years of service.

Table 6.7 shows that, on the average, pension income represents only 7 percent of the total income received by households headed by seniors implying that they can not be fully dependent on pension for their needs. It is notable from the table that the average per capita income of households headed by seniors is above the average per capita income, implying that on average they may not be poorer than the rest of the population.

In the case of indigents, the monthly social pension of Php500 represents only 32 percent of the PhP1,578 monthly per capita poverty threshold in 2012. RA 9994 provides for the review of the amount of pension by Congress, in consultation with the DSWD, every two years. To date, however, no assessment has been made.

Pensions of SSS and GSIS members are paid from the accumulated funds of the institutions. Both of these institutions have sovereign guarantees if ever they cannot pay their obligations. Thus, there is a strong likelihood of sustainability of the program. In the case of the social pension program, funding is appropriated annually from the national budget. Its sustainability, thus, is dependent on the priorities of the government leadership. While the law already exists, experience in the past few years indicates that implementation can lag behind because the appropriated budget is insufficient to cover the statutorily eligible population.

4. Future strategies and initiatives

The initiatives discussed here are drawn mainly from the ABND policy matrix which is the product of discussions of Government agencies, UN Agencies and NGOs. This is the most comprehensive review of social protection in the country using the SPF framework. The exercise begun in June 2014 and completed by December 2015. Initial results, however, are already publicly available (ILO, 2015). A summary of the options proposed is provided in Box 1. The total *incremental* cost of SPF from 2015–2020 (ignoring political economy, and implementation and transition costs) it is estimated between 0.65 to 2.45 percent of GDP for the 'high scenario'. This rather large range requires more rigorous refined costing, with appropriate 'stress test', before formally adopting SPF. It should be noted that according to the World Bank, total tax revenue to GDP ratio for the Philippines in 2014 was 13.6 percent of GDP. Thus, if high-end of the 'high' scenario materializes, the country would need to create fiscal space equivalent to nearly one-fifth of its current tax revenue.

4.1 Universal health care

With PhilHealth coverage expanded with the indigent program, there are only few remaining members in the society and risks that are not statutorily covered. Actual coverage and utilization, however, is an entirely different story. Those on foster care are still left uncovered. For health risks, testing for HIV is still not covered by the PhilHealth package.

Actual coverage of informal sector workers is considered a problem. To improve the performance in this area, a subsidy to the health insurance premium is being proposed. This has to be tempered, however, by the fact that the 'informal' sector is a very heterogeneous sector which covers street hawkers to self-employed professionals who do not deserve a subsidy. It is possible that the poor in the informal sector may have already been covered by the indigent program.

Those that will potentially be left out are the non-poor informal sector workers. They may not be part, however, of a system that is collecting regular payments for health insurance. It is possible that this group may not require a premium subsidy but only a means for regularly collecting contributions. The Philippines has been experimenting in the KASAPI program of PhilHealth that taps community organizations as collecting agents (Manasan and Orbeta, 2012). Llanto (2007), however, pointed out, that the indigent program may be undermining this initiative as this is contributory while the indigent program is paid for by government. Another scheme mentioned by Manasan and Orbeta (2012) is the Automatic Debit Arrangement of the SSS where members maintain a savings account in participating banks where premiums can be automatically deducted and proceeds from services can also be credited.

The assessment indicated that the utilization rate of PhilHealth benefits is low. Thus, there is a need to improve the appreciation of benefit payments for health insurance which may not be that simple for the uninitiated. It was also mentioned that the support ratio is low as indicated by the high and still rising out-of-pocket cost (Ulep and dela Cruz, 2013). One of the reasons provided is the lack of supply of medicines and supplies in health facilities which necessitates beneficiaries to buy medicines and supplies from outside sources.

As to the sustainability of the indigent program, the analysis done in Pantig (2013) shows that the financing of premiums will be sustained because it is financed through the 'sin taxes'. But it was also pointed out that expenditures will surpass the premium payments indicating that there might be a need to change the premium rate in the near future. This may have to be tempered by the early indications that the utilization rate is rather low for the indigent program. The fiscal liability however would arise if benefit payment exceed contributions, and these will need to be funded.

4.2 Social protection for children

The CCT program (Pantawid) is covering the education and health needs of children of poor households. What the ABND process has identified as lacking is the feeding assistance at the critical 0 to 2 years. For this, a voucher system is being proposed for inclusion in the CCT benefits. This proposal has a lot of merit as literature has pointed out that malnutrition at this critical stage of life has negative long term impacts (e.g. Almond and Currie, 2010; Heckman, 2007). While the grants can certainly be used to improve the nutrition of children, there is an added merit to making it explicit that nutrition at the early stage of a child's life is a very important investment. This can be easily demonstrated by explicitly giving emphasis on this idea among poor families such as the beneficiaries of the Pantawid program. The proposed option has not yet been included in the costing exercise because of the lack of forecast of the number of children 0 to 2 years old among poor families.

4.3 Social protection of the working age population

The ABND process recognized the need for an unemployment insurance for private sector workers as there is one for the public sector workers. Although this need has been discussed as early as the 1990s, no agreement has been reached until today on how to finance it (ILS, 2013). Weber, in a 2010 study, proposed the introduction of unemployment insurance in the Philippines with a modest contribution of 1 percent each from workers and employers with benefits of 50 percent of AMSC up to 10 months. No government subsidy is required except perhaps for initial loans which can be repaid in a few years. The ABND process, on the other hand, proposed for government to subsidize the premiums.

Another gap that has been identified in the ABND process is the non-coverage of the self-employed in the employees' compensation program. In the case of the self-employed, two challenges for injury compensation have been identified, namely, determining what is work-related, and determining when work starts and when work ends.

Subsidy for SSS premium for the informal sector was also proposed. Comments to the proposal to subsidize the premium of health insurance for the informal sector mentioned above are applicable also here. What may be needed are innovative ways of collecting premium contributions. As it turns out, SSS are experimenting on several ways of improving coverage of the informal sector.

One innovative way of covering the informal sector tested by SSS is the Auto Debit Arrangement (ADA) where members can maintain an account in participating banks and premium payments can be automatically deducted and proceeds from benefits can be credited (Manasan and Orbeta, 2012). This appears to have not gain traction with prospective members. As of 2010 less than 1 percent of the contribution came from this facility. A new initiative with similar objectives is the AlkanSSSya ('piggy-bank') system where SSS partners with informal sector groups (ISGs) where their members can contribute PhP11 daily until they are able to accumulate the P312 contribution to meet the contribution for a PhP3,000 monthly salary credit. Unlike the ADA, this initiative is attracting considerable number of ISGs. As of 2013, the program was able to secure cooperation of 592 ISGs with 53,605 members with a total collection of PhP33.5 million (SSS, 2015, Annual Report).

4.4 Social protection for older persons

The proposals for social protection for the elderly discussed in the ABND includes: 1. raising the amount of pension of PWDs and 2. expanding the coverage of social pension from the current 77 years and above to the statutory covered population of 60 years and above. DWSD was able to secure in the 2015 budget an allocation that will enable them to cover senior citizens up to 65 years and above. Whether this level of expenditure can be sustained in the future is difficult to say. Unlike the indigent program, which is covered by the flow of sin tax revenues, provision for this program has to be requested every budget year.

Box 1 Scenarios proposed in the ABND Process for the Philippines and their costs

At the request of the Department of Labor and Employment the International Labor Organization (ILO) initiated in collaboration with national government agencies, UN agency partners and NGOs what is called the assessment based national dialogue (ABND) to craft a 5-year National Social Protection Plan. One of the outcomes of the dialogue is the costing scenarios of what are deemed as important initiatives to establish a Social Protection Floor (SPF). What follows is a description of the scenarios and the estimated incremental cost to the government for each of the four components of the SPF.

Universal health care. For health care, two scenarios involving the subsidy of the health premiums for the informal sector were created. One is a 30 percent government subsidy for the health insurance premiums for the informal sector – the low scenario. The other is raising the subsidy to 50 percent – the high scenario. Under the low scenario, the cost is estimated at about 0.02 percent to 0.05 percent of GDP from 2015 to 2020. The cost increases to about 0.03 percent to 0.08 percent or by about 50 to 60 percent more under the high scenario.

Social protection (SP) for children. Two scenarios, each consisting of a combination of three proposed SP programs for children, were simulated. The proposed programs include: 1. food and cereal voucher for 0–2 years old under Pantawid; 2. meal for all children in public schools under the school feeding program (SFP); 3. meal and bottle of milk for all children; 4. social pension of PhP500 per month for all PWDs who do not benefit from other pension schemes, indexed to inflation; and 5. social pension of P750 per month for all PWDs, indexed to inflation. The low scenario includes programs 1, 2, and 4 while the high scenario includes programs 1, 3 and 5. The estimated cost under the low scenario is 0.26 percent to 0.89 percent of GDP from 2015 to 2020 and about 50 percent more under the high scenario ranging from 0.39 percent to 1.33 percent of GDP.

SP for working age population. Two scenarios, each consisting of a combination of three proposed SP programs for the working age population, were also simulated. The proposed programs include the introduction of unemployment insurance, subsidy of SSS premium for those in the informal sector, and daily allowance for those enrolled in TESDA programs. The options include: 1. introduction of unemployment insurance with 30 percent government subsidy on premiums; 2. introduction of unemployment insurance with 50 percent government subsidy on premiums; 3. 30 percent government subsidy on SSS premiums for the informal sector; 4. 50 percent government subsidy for the SSS premiums for the informal sector; 5. daily allowance at poverty threshold, indexed to inflation for low income individuals enrolled in TESDA training courses; and 6. daily allowance at twice the poverty threshold, indexed to inflation for low income individuals enrolled in TESDA training courses. The low scenario includes options 1, 3 and 5 while the high scenario includes options 2, 4 and 6. The estimated cost of the low scenario ranges from 0.08 percent to 0.31 percent of GDP from 2015 to 2020 while that of the high scenario is estimated to range from 0.23 percent to 0.93 percent or about 188 percent to 200 percent higher.

SP for the elderly. In the case of the elderly, two scenarios consisting of a combination of two proposed programs each were simulated. These programs include covering the PWDs with social pension, raising the amount for the monthly social pension, and implementing the statutory coverage of the social pension of 60 and above. The specific program options include: 1. adding PhP500 to the usual monthly social pension of PWDs; 2. adding PhP1,000 to the usual monthly social pension for PWDs; 3. expanding the coverage of social pension to the statutory eligible population of 60 years and above from the current 77 years and above, indexed to inflation; and 4. increasing the monthly social pension to PhP750 covering the statutory population of 60 years and above, indexed to inflation. The low scenario includes options 1 and 3 while the high scenario includes options 2 and 4. The estimated cost of the low scenario ranges from 0.06 percent to 0.08 percent of GDP from 2015 to 2020 while that of the high scenario ranges from 0.09 percent to 0.11 percent or about 37 to 50 percent higher.

The total incremental cost for the four components of the SPF from 2015 to 2020 ranges from 0.36 percent to 1.32 percent of GDP under the low scenario and 0.65 percent to 2.45 percent of GDP under the high scenario (Figure B1). The latter is 81 to 104 percent higher than the cost of the low scenario.

5. Concluding remarks

The main progress of social protection system is in the area of health insurance coverage. The government has decided to pay the premium of the poor through the sponsored program. In addition, it has found secure financing for it through the 'sin tax' revenues which provides optimism that this initiative will be continued. For instance, in the 2014 Department of Health report on the utilization of the sin taxes, the payment for the indigent program is only PhP22.71 billion (51 percent) out of the incremental 'sin tax' revenue of PhP44.72 billion (DOH, 2014). This revenue is estimated to increase to PhP65.6 billion by 2020 (Manasan and Cuenca, 2015). Another important progress is the social protection for children with the Pantawid program. Sustainability, however, of this program may be in doubt judging from the debates in Congress over the program. Without continued very strong support from the executive department, this program may have been smaller in size or even stopped altogether.

Judging from the advance stage of preparation, the policy community is preparing the stage for the formal adoption of the SPF as an essential part of the social protection strategy of the country. While some of the proposals are straight forward such as expanding actual coverage of the social pensions to the statutorily covered population, others may need some refinements. For instance, the proposals to subsidize the SSS coverage of the informal sector may not be warranted until the system has exhausted the avenues for collecting contribution better. There is no telling as yet whether the low coverage of the informal sector is a case of lack of capacity to pay the premium or more because of the difficulty of paying contributions and getting benefits from the system. It should be recalled that it

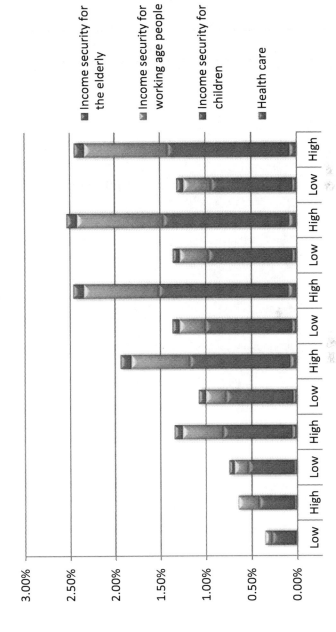

Figure B1 Costing scenarios of proposals to improve SPF in the Philippines as percentage to GDP, 2015–2020

Source: www.social-protection.org/gimi/gess/ShowProject.action?id=2507

was pointed out that the coverage of even the formal sector wage workers, is still low at below 40 percent, and no signs of rising. This can be taken as an indication that the contribution collection system even for the formal sector may be facing problems. To the credit of SSS, it has been experimenting on ways to improve the collection of the contribution from informal sector workers. Maybe they can also experiment on ways of spurring contributions from the formal sector workers. It can be argued that increasing the contribution of the formal sector worker should be given more priority before embarking on covering the informal sector workers. The guarantees proposed in the SPF, will always be easier and least costly to implement if formal sector workers are well covered when they are able to contribute to a social insurance system.

Notes

1   The NSCB defines the following poverty indicators as follows: Poverty incidence – the proportion of families/individuals with per capita income/expenditures less than the per capita poverty threshold to the total number of families / individuals;

Poverty gap – refers to the income/expenditures shortfall (expressed in proportion to the poverty threshold) of families/individuals with income/expenditure below the poverty threshold, divided by the total number of families/individuals;

Poverty threshold – the minimum income/expenditure required to meet basic food and non-food requirements;

Severity of poverty – the total of the squared income/expenditures shortfall (expressed in proportion to the poverty threshold) of families/individuals with income/expenditures below the poverty threshold divided by the total number of families/individuals www.nscb.gov.ph/poverty/Glossary.asp

2   NEDA-SDC Resolution No. 1, s. 2007 defines the four components as follows:

1. Social insurance programs seek to mitigate risks of loss of income and unemployment due to illness, injury, disability, retrenchment, maternity, old age, and harvest failure, among others. To benefit from these programs, members pay a premium over a given period of time. At the community level, this component includes micro- and area-based schemes such as micro-insurance and social support funds.

2. Social welfare programs seek to support the minimum basic requirements of the poor and reduce risks associated with unemployment, resettlement, marginalization, illness, disability, old age and loss of family care. These programs include direct assistance in the form of cash or in-kind transfers to the poorest and marginalized groups and social services such as family and community support, alternative care, and referral services.

3. Social safety nets are urgent responses for vulnerable groups affected by economic shocks, disasters, and calamities. These responses include emergency assistance, price subsidies, food programs, employment programs, retraining programs, and emergency loans.

4. Labor market programs aims to enhance employment opportunities and protection of the rights and welfare of workers. Measures that enhance employment include trade policies and skills development and training while the latter include compliance with labor standards such as minimum wages or health and safety in the workplace.

3   PhilHealth was established through RA 7875 as amended by RA 9241 and RA 10606 or the National Health Insurance Act of 2013.

4 RA 10351 "An Act Restructuring the Excise Tax on Alcohol and Tobacco Products by Amending Sections 141, 142, 143, 144, 145, 8, 131 and 288 of RA 8424. Otherwise Known as the National Internal Code of 1997, as amended by RA 9334, and for other purposes"

5 With the case rate system of PhilHealth, all hospital confinements are paid through a case-based payment mechanism.

6 Type Z-Benefits of PhilHealth specifies specific amounts ranging from PhP15,000 to PhP600,000 for various types of sickness or illness specified by PhilHealth.

7 PhilHealth's Primary care benefit: Package 1 include diagnostic examination (CBC, urinalysis, fecalysis, sputum microscopy, fasting blood sugar, lipid profile and chest x-ray) and primary preventive services (consultations, visual inspection with acetic acid, regular blood pressure measurements, breastfeeding education, clinical breast examination, counselling for lifestyle modification and smoking cessation). Package 2 includes outpatient drugs for diabetes, hypertension and dyslipidemia.

8 Sickness benefit is equivalent to a daily sickness an allowance equivalent to 90 percent of the member's average daily salary credit for a maximum of 120 days per year or 240 days in a single hospitalization. The benefit is granted provided the member has paid at least 3 months of contributions within the 12-month period immediately before the semester of sickness (RA 8282, Sec. 14 and 14-A). (www.sss.gov.ph)

9 ECC medical benefits cover: a) all fees and other charges for hospital services, medical care and appliances immediately after an injury or illness and during the subsequent period of disability and b) rehabilitation services consisting of medical, surgical or hospital treatment, including appliances to injured and handicapped employees (PD 626). (ecc.gov.ph)

10 Medical services for veterans are fairly comprehensive, including cardiac bypass.

11 The Program conditionalities are as follows: 1) Pregnant women should avail of pre-and post-natal care and should be attended by a trained health professional during childbirth; 2) Parents should attend family development sessions; 3) Children aged 0–5 years should receive regular preventive health check-ups and vaccines; 4) Children aged 3–5 years should attend day care or pre-school classes at least 85 percent of the time; and 5) Children aged 6–14 years should receive deworming pills twice a year and be enrolled in elementary or high school, with at least 85 percent attendance.

12 Commonwealth Act 647 "An Act to Grant Maternity Leave Benefits to Married Women Who Are in the Service of the Government or Any of Its Instrumentalities" (June 14, 1941)

13 RA 8291, Sec. 15–19 for GSIS; RA 8282 Sec. 13-A for SSS; EO 126 for OWWA

14 Separation benefit of not less than PhP12,000 for those with at least three years but less than 15 years of service or a cash benefit plus old age pension for those with at least 15 years of service.

15 Monthly cash payment is equivalent to 50 percent of AMC payable for a period of two to six months depending on the length of contributions made prior to unemployment or involuntary separation

16 Primary beneficiaries include the spouse and a maximum of five children less than 21 years old or disabled for SSS and less than 18 or less than 21 years old or disabled children depending on the retirement mode for GSIS.

17 A lump sum amount is granted if the number of contributions prior to the contingency is less than three years for SSS and less than 15 years for GSIS. The lump sum is based on the member's average monthly compensation and years of service but not less than PhP12,000 (GSIS) or based on the monthly pension and the number of monthly contributions paid or 12x the monthly pension whichever is higher (SSS). The monthly pension is equal to 100 percent of the old age pension divided between the spouse and up to five children. Primary beneficiaries of an

active GSIS member with 15 years of service who dies, in addition are entitled to an 18 months lump sum.

18 Those who entered government service prior to August 1, 2003 are covered with an LEP while those who entered after that date and those whose policies have matured are covered with an ELP.

19 The loan ceiling is PhP200,000 per individual borrowers and PhP100,000 per group at 9 percent interest rate per annum.

20 The maximum amount for loans is P125,000 per member, payable in monthly instalments for 1–2 years at zero interest.

21 Benefits under five GSIS retirement programs: 1) RA 660 "Magic 87" – both annuity and lifetime pension; 2) RA 1616 (Gratuity/Optional Retirement – a refund of GSIS premiums with 3 percent interest on the personal contribution plus gratuity benefit equivalent to one month's salary for every year of service, but not to exceed 24 months; 3) PD 1146 – a choice between a basic monthly pension guaranteed for five years or cash payment or combination of both; 4) RA 8291 – a five-year lump sum with a pension for life after the five-year guaranteed period or a cash payment and a lifetime pension starting upon retirement; 5) RA 9946 – a monthly pension equal to the basic pay plus the highest transportation and representation allowance (www.gsis.gov.ph)

22 Veterans include all personnel who rendered military services for the Philippines during the revolution against Spain, the Spanish-American War, World War I, World War II, the Philippine Expeditionary Forces to Korea, and the Philippine Civic Action Group or Philippine Contingent in Vietnam (RA 7696).

23 For Filipino veterans who served in the United States Army Forces in the Far East (USAFFE) during World War II, a one-time $9,000 lump sum settlement was granted under the American Recovery and Reinvestment Act of 2009. In addition, the US Department of Veterans Affairs provides additional regular benefits to Filipino veterans living in the US at a full-dollar rate and at a half rate for those living outside the US using the same eligibility rules as those applied to US veterans.

24 Under RA 9994 senior citizen or elderly refers to any resident of the Philippines at least sixty (60) years old; indigent senior citizen refers to any elderly who is frail, sickly or with disability, and without pension or permanent source of income, compensation or financial assistance from his/her relatives to support his/her basic needs.

25 RA 10351 'An Act Restructuring the Excise Tax on Alcohol and Tobacco Products by Amending Sections 141, 142, 143, 144, 145, 8, 131 and 288 of RA 8424. Otherwise Known as the National Internal Code of 1997, as amended by RA 9334, and for other purposes'.

26 RA 9994 'An Act Granting Additional Benefits and Privileges to Senior Citizens, Further Amending RA 7432, as amended, Otherwise Known as "An Act to Maximize the Contribution of Senior Citizens to Nation Building, Grant Benefits and Special Privileges and for other Purposes'.

27 SPI is used to assess the progress on social protection relative the country's level of income per person. It is also used to assess the nature and effectiveness of a country's social protection programs. Overall SPI is the weighted sum of the SPI social insurance, social assistance and labor market interventions (ADB 2013).

28 The SPI for social insurance includes pensions, health insurance, and unemployment benefits. For social assistance, SPI includes assistance to the elderly, health assistance, poverty programs, and child welfare. For labor market programs, SPI includes training and skills development and public works schemes.

29 Depth is estimated as (Total SP expenditures/Total actual beneficiaries)/poverty-line expenditures.

30 The annual national per capita poverty threshold in 2012 is 18,935 (PSA).
31 Those without employer-employee relationships include job-orders, which is a common practice now in government offices when it became difficult to get approval for permanent or contractual positions. Unfortunately, there is no estimate as to the number of such positions and individuals involved. Nonetheless, the estimate of the labor force of 7.8 percent of employed workers in government out of the 38.665 million in April 2014 round of the LFS can be expected to include these employees because there are based on household surveys.
32 Ideally this should be individuals 60 years and above. Unfortunately, no data is available to compute this at the individual level.

References

ADB (Asian Development Bank) (2013). *The Social Protection Index: Assessing Results For Asia and the Pacific*. Available at www.adb.org/sites/default/files/publication/30293/social-protection-index.pdf

Almond, D., and J. Currie (2010). Human Capital Development Before Age Five, in Orley Ashenfelter and David Card (eds.) *Handbook of Labor Economics*, Volume 4b,Chapter 15, pp. 1315–1486.

CMA (Center for Migrant Advocacy) (2012). *Bilateral Labor Agreements and Social Security Agreements*. Available at https://centerformigrantadvocacy.files.wordpress.com/2012/06/bilateral-labor-agreements-and-social-security-agreements1.pdf]

David, C., and J. Albert. (2015). *How Has Basic Education in the Philippine Fared and What Else Needs to be Done?* PIDS Policy Notes 2015–08.

DOH (Department of Health) (2014). *Sin Tax Law Incremental Revenue for Health Annual Report*, Available at www.doh.gov.ph/content/sintaxutilizationreportasofoctober22014.pdf

DOLE (Department of Labor and Employment). Available at www.dole.gov.ph

DSWD (Department of Social Welfare and Development). Available at www.dswd.gov.ph

DSWD (Department of Social Welfare and Development) and the World Bank (2013). *Philippines Conditional Cash Transfer Program impact evaluation 2012*.

DSWD and World Bank (2014). *Keeping Children Healthy and in School: Evaluating the Pantawid Pamilya Using Regression Discontinuity Design Second Wave Impact Evaluation Results*.

ECC (Employees Compensation Commission). *ecc.gov.ph*

GSIS (Government Service Insurance System). Available at www.gsis.gov.ph

Heckman, J. (2007). The Technology, and Neuroscience Of Human Capital Formation. *Proceedings of the National Academy of Sciences*, 104(33), 13250–13255.

ILO (International Labor Organization) (1996). *Report to the Government On Social Protection: Options and Recommendations For Reforms and Development*.

ILO (International Labor Organization) (2012). *Social Security for All: Building Social Protection Floors and Comprehensive Social Security Systems*.

ILO (International Labor Organization) (2015). *Philippines: Assessment Based National Dialogue on Social Protection, Employment Promotion and Disaster Management*, Available at www.social-protection.org/gimi/gess/ShowProject.action?id=2507

ILS (2013). *Country Report on Unemployment Insurance: Philippines*. ILS (Institute for Labor Studies) Discussion Paper Series.

Llanto, G. (2007). *Protecting the Vulnerable Through Social Health Insurance: PhilHealth's KASAPI as a Strategy*, PIDS Policy Notes 2007–03.

Manasan, R., and J. Cuenca. (2015). *Multi-Year Spending Plan for the Department of Health: 2016–2020*. Report prepared for the Department of Health.

Manasan, R., and A. Orbeta, Jr. (2012). Expanding Social Protection Coverage to Informal Sector Workers, in DSWD, UNDP, NEDA, *Strengthening Social Protection Components and Strategies in the Philippines: A Compilation of Social Protection Think Papers*, Department of Social Welfare and Development.

Matula, J. S. G. (2007, February). *Social Security Protection Of OFWs Through the SSS*, Paper presented at the FFW Symposium on Migration, Davao City, Philippines. Available at www.ffw.org.ph/bin/DEPARTMENTS/ . . . /**OFW**Briefing_Matula.ppt

NEDA (National Economic Development Authority) (2014). *The Philippines: Fifth Progress Report Millennium Development Goals*.

Orbeta, A. Jr. (2010). Social Protection in the Philippines: Current State and Challenges, in M. Asher, S. Oum, and F. Parulian (eds.) *Social Protection in East Asia – Current State and Challenges*, Jakarta: Economic Research Institute for ASEAN.

Orbeta, A. Jr., V. Paqueo, and C. Sphor. (2013). *Does Pantawid Foster Dependence or Encourage Work? Evidence From a Randomized Experiment*, Paper prepared for the 12th National Convention on Statistics, October 1–2.

Paqueo, V., A. Orbeta, Jr., T. Castaneda, and C. Spohr. (2013). *After Five Years of Pantawid, What Next?* PIDS DP 2013–41.

Paqueo, V., A. Orbeta, Jr., L. Lanzona, and D. Dulay. (2014). Labor Policy Analysis for Jobs Expansion and Development, in *Philippine Institute for Development Studies 2013 Economic Policy Monitor*. Philippine Institute for Development Studies.

Pantig, I. (2013). Sustainability Of the National Government Premium Subsidy For Indigents. *Philippine Journal of Development*, 72(1 and 2), 36–65.

PhilHealth (2015). Available at www.philhealth.gov.ph

PSA (Philippine Statistics Authority) [Philippines] and ICF International (2014). *Philippines National Demographic and Health Survey 2013*. Manila, Philippines, and Rockville, Maryland, USA: PSA and ICF International.

PSA (Philippine Statistics Authority) (2015). *Official Concepts and Definitions For Statistical Purposes*. Available at www.nscb.gov.ph/poverty/Glossary.asp

PVAO (Philippine Veterans Affairs Office) (2015). *Veterans Hospitalization Program*. Viewed 21 April 2015 at Server.pvao.mil.ph/SiteVhp.aspx

Reyes, C. A. Tabuga, C. Mina, and R. Asis (2015). *Promoting Inclusive Growth through the 4Ps*. PIDS Research Paper Series 2015-01.

SSS (Social Security System) (2015). Available at www.sss.gov.ph

Ulep, G., and N. A. dela Cruz (2013). Analysis of Out-Of-Pocket Expenditures in the Philippines. *Philippine Journal of Development*, 72(1 and 2), 93–123.

Villar, F. (2013). *The Philippine Social Protection Framework and Strategy: An Overview*, Paper presented at the 12th National Convention on Statistics, October 1–2.

Weber, A. (2010). *Social Protection in the Case of Unemployment in the Philippines*. International Labor Office.

World Bank (1995). *Philippines: An Agenda for the Reform Of the Social Security Institutions*. Report No. 13400-PH

World Bank (2014). *Snippets From the Benefit-Incidence Analysis of the Pantawid Pamilyang Pilipino Program*, Presentation at the Public Forum on the 2014 Impact Evaluation of Pantawid Pamilyang Pilipino Program, Oracle Hotel and Residences, Quezon City. November 17.

7 Social protection system in Thailand

An assessment

Srawooth Paitoonpong, Phacharawadee Tasee, and Pimrumpa Waisuriya

1. Introduction

Before the Asian financial crisis in 1997, Thailand exhibited an average real growth rate of 11.3 percent during the 1987–1991 period and 8.1 percent during the 1992–1996 period. The growth rate went down to -1.4 and -10.5 percent in 1997 and 1998, respectively, and averaged 3.9 percent in 1999. With such an economic performance, the proportion of the poor living below the poverty line declined from 42 percent in 2000 to 12.6 percent in 2012 (NESDB, 2014, 2). Thailand has experienced moderate growth since then. According to the World Bank, Thailand's real GDP growth averaged 2.1 percent during the 2013–2015 period. There have nevertheless been significant improvements in social development, including access to education, health, and other social services.

The objectives of the study are:

1. To review social protection programmes in Thailand and analytically link these to the fiscal implications under a few scenarios of expansion of social protection floor (SPF) to meet selected sustainable developments goals (SDG).
2. To review social protection mechanisms in Thailand and suggest policy measures and initiatives to improve their effectiveness.
3. To assess policy and organisational coherence among healthcare, social pension, child benefits, and other elements of Thailand's SP system.

The study is designed to contribute to the emerging debate on social protection in Thailand and elsewhere.

The study is based on literature review, secondary data, and, where possible, primary data from interviews, workshops, and seminars. The literature review covers the studies and related policies and a critical review of the study of the United Nations/Thai Royal Government (UN/TRG) Joint Team on Social Protection[1] regarding fiscal implications of future social protection initiatives (Schmitt et al., 2013).

The rest of the chapter is organized as follows. Section 2 gives an overview of the SP programmes in Thailand; Section 3 assesses the SP system and identifies fiscal implications under a few scenarios of expansion of SPF. Section 4 discusses future strategies and initiatives. Section 5 concludes.

2. Social protection system in Thailand: an overview

Thailand had achieved several important MDG targets before the 2015 time frame, including goals on the eradication of poverty and hunger, as well as goals on education, gender equality, and health. These early achievements have allowed Thailand to pursue the more ambitious and challenging Millennium Development Goals Plus (MDG+) with prospects for achievement in several areas (National Voluntary Presentation, 2014). This publication contains achievements of Thailand with respect to different MDGs.

In connection with the SDGs, Thailand has expressed its framework into seven focus areas of the post-2015 Development Agenda and its development goals as follows (NVP, 2014, 14–15): raising quality of people, enhanced opportunity, improved quality of education, access to information, labour productivity and social protection, improving values and preparation for the elderly, inclusive growth, green growth, and good governance.

Social protection in Thailand covers a wide range of schemes and sectors of population. Principally composed of contributory social insurance schemes, non-contributory tax-financed schemes (both targeted and universal), and partially subsidised voluntary social insurance schemes. These primarily cover civil servants and their dependents and workers in the formal sector. Vulnerable and poor people generally have access to ad hoc means-tested programmes. Universal social protection schemes in Thailand include the Universal Health Coverage Scheme and an old-age allowance scheme (Paitoonpong, 2012, 13).

Social protection in Thailand is rights-based as contained in the Thai Constitution, B.E. 2550[2]; the Social Security Act, B.E. 2533; the National Health Security Act, B.E. 2545; the Quality of Life Promotion Act for persons with disabilities, B.E. 2550; the Old Age Act, B.E. 2546; and the National Education Act, B.E. 2542. It is also aligned with the strategic plan on social welfare for the Thai society (2012–2016) and with Thailand's Eleventh National Economic and Social Development Plan 2012–2016 (Schmitt et al., 2013, iv). The Thai government has continued efforts to strengthen the social protection system, the savings system, and community welfare as it protects rights and provides welfare services, and develops the quality of life of the disadvantaged, the disabled, the elderly, and women and children (Government Policy, 2014, Section 3.3). The policy on healthcare is to lay a foundation to develop and strengthen public health, emphasizing inclusiveness, quality, and efficiency (Government Policy, 2014, Section 5).

The social protection system is scattered across programmes such as the Government Officials' Pension System, the Government Pension Fund, the Civil Servants Medical Benefit Scheme, the Workmen's Compensation Fund, the Social Security Fund, the Private School Teachers' Welfare Fund, the Universal Health Coverage Scheme, the National Savings Fund, the Universal Non-contributory Allowance for People with Disabilities, the Universal Non-contributory

Allowance for Older People, the Compulsory Migrant Health Insurance, the Education for All Policy, and several private provident funds.

2.1 Healthcare

2.1.1 Universal Coverage Scheme

The Universal Coverage Scheme (UCS) provides healthcare for persons not covered by the non-contributory Civil Servants Medical Benefit Scheme, Social Security System (SSS), or other government schemes provided by the government. UCS provides essential medical treatment ranging from outpatient and inpatient treatment, maternity care, childbirth, dental care, preventive care, and emergency care. Beneficiaries must register and choose a regular service unit which serves as one's entry point except in emergency cases. Specialised-care patients are referred to a higher-level hospital at no extra charge. Financed by general tax revenues, the UCS budget is coursed through the National Health Service Office (Schmitt et al., 2013, 10).

2.1.2 The Civil Servants' Medical Benefit Scheme

The Civil Servants' Medical Benefit Scheme (CSMBS) was established by the Royal Decree on Medical Benefit, B.E. 2553, issued pursuant to the Act on Stipulation of Payment Rules in Accordance with Budget, B.E. 2518. This non-contributory scheme covers civil servants and permanent employees, pensioners, the military, foreign employees paid by the government and whose employment contract does not specify a condition on medical service and their dependents (legitimate children, spouse, and parents). The scheme does not cover employees of local governments and state enterprises, temporary or fixed-term government contract workers, or pensioners who chose to receive a lump sum payment. Benefits include inpatient and outpatient treatment in public hospitals, specific private hospitals, or, in emergency cases, any other private hospitals (ibid, 5).

2.1.3 Social Security System Medical Benefits

Healthcare insurance of private sector employees as well as regular migrant workers is covered by the Social Security System Medical Benefits (SSSMB). Their dependents, however, are not covered by the scheme. SSSMB is compulsory and contributory. Section 33 of the scheme covers non-occupational injury or sickness benefits and maternity. The Workmen's Compensation Fund of the SSS covers work-related injuries and sickness. Although SSSMB provides a relatively comprehensive benefit package, certain medical treatments are not covered (Schmitt et al., 2013, 6, 26–27). Patients select a health provider within the contracted network of hospitals.

Medical benefits for employees of state enterprises are dealt by individual state enterprises and may differ in terms of agreements or regulations from one state enterprise to another (TDRI, 2013, 3–5).

2.1.4 Compulsory Migrant Health Insurance

Irregular migrant workers registered under Section 13 of the Foreign Workers Employment Act, B.E. 2551 are covered by the Compulsory Migrant Health Insurance (CMHI) programme. CMHI targets undocumented migrant workers who are registered (under the government's amnesty program) and does not cover dependents. Irregular migrant workers are required to apply for work permit or grace periods to stay in Thailand temporarily. The medical services provided are similar to UCS. The insured migrant pays 1,900 baht (B) per year (Schmitt et al., 2013, 28).

In some migrant-intensive areas, irregular migrant workers and their dependents have to rely on out-of-pocket treatments, hospital exemptions, assistance from non-governmental organisations, or purchased health cards (Chamchan and Apipornchaisaskul, 2012, 56).

2.1.5 Long-term care

Long-term care refers to long-term nursing and personal care of people with physical, functional, or mental restrictions (WHO 2007, 6). Provided in residential institutions, day-care centres, or at home, daily living activities include self-care activities such as bathing, dressing, eating, getting in and out of bed or chair, moving around, using the toilet, and controlling bladder and bowel movements. Caregivers monitor patients to avoid worsening of daily living activities. Long-term nursing and personal care exclude basic medical and social services, but are often provided in combination with these.[3]

Thailand is an aging society with an elderly population of 8.4 million in 2010. This is estimated to rise to 12.6 million in 2020. In 2011, the average proportion of the elderly with functional limitations in activities in daily living was 3.7 percent.

Thailand's long-term care system includes tax incentives such as Parental Care Expenses Deduction and Parent's Health Insurance Expenses Deduction and Care Services. The latter include 12 homes for the elderly provided by the national government, 13 homes for the elderly provided by local governments, home-care volunteers, sub-district health-promoting hospitals and village health volunteers, home healthcare for the elderly, and various long-term care pilot projects. In addition, there are Friends-Help-Friends projects by the Senior Citizens Club and a financing scheme at community level for long-term care through the Tambon Health Fund under the community-based integrated approach (Figure 7.1) (ibid.).

2.2 Children

2.2.1 Free education

Under the Constitution, B.E. 2550, children in Thailand are entitled to 12 years of free education. Nine years of education is compulsory for children (6–15 years old) under the National Education Act, B.E. 2542, with amendment No. 2, B.E.

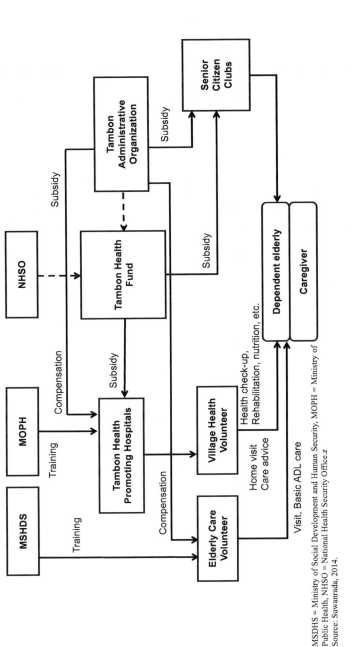

Figure 7.1 Thailand community-based integrated approach to older people's long-term care

Notes: MSDHS = Ministry of Social Development and Human Security, MOPH = Ministry of Public Health, NHSO = National Health Security Office

Source: Suwanrada, 2014

2545. Extended to 15 years in 2009, the free education from preschool through high school and vocational education covers formal, non-formal, and informal education and applies to all children, including stateless and ethnic minority children and children of migrants. The policy covers tuition fees (100 percent for public schools and subsidies for private schools), textbooks, learning materials, school uniforms, and activities that promote quality improvement among students.

2.2.2 Universal child allowance

A person insured under SSS is entitled to a child allowance of B400 per child aged 0–6 years for a maximum of two children.

The Royal Thai government has recently approved as a pilot project a non-contributory child allowance of B400 per month for a child from birth to one year old, starting 1 October 2015 to 30 September 2016. Eligible are families with incomes of not more than B30,000 a year (Thai TV 3, 20 January 2015 [in Thai]).

2.3 Retirement benefits

2.3.1 Government officials[4]

Government officials (including civil servants, permanent and temporary government employees, but not including the military) are covered by many social security benefits, including old age, healthcare, and child-related benefits. Civil servants enjoy the Government Officials' Pension System, the Government Pension Fund (GPF), and the CSMBS. The first is Thailand's oldest pension system for the public sector as enacted in the Pension Act in 1902. The act was later amended to award pensions only to government officials. In 1939, the amended act was replaced by an act for civil servants and another for military servants. In 1951, the Pension Act superseded the previous one and was used for central government officials until about 1996 (Kanjanaphoomin, 2004). Due to strains on the government budget, the government pension has, since 1996, been transformed into the GPF under the Government Pension Fund Act 1996.

Prior to the introduction of the GPF, a retired government official could choose between a lump sum payment and a pension based on his/her age at retirement, length of service, and disability using the following formula:

Pension = [(years of employment) x (last salary received)]/50

The lump sum payment was equal to the last salary received multiplied by the number of years of employment. The government pension is transferable to the children or other relatives of the pensioner.

GPF is mandatory for government officials except for those who were in service before 27 March 1997, and who chose the old pension scheme and are eligible for pensions according to the Government Pension Act 1951 only. In December 2003, GPF had 1.2 million members with a fund of B230 billion (Kanjanaphoomin, 2004, 13–14). In 2013, the number of GPF members was the same but with a fund of B632.5 billion (GPF, 2013, 68).[5]

Different from the benefits given to civil servants are the benefits to government employees, permanent government employees, and temporary government employees or fixed-term contract workers. The government employee system was established in 2004 to replace permanent government employees as well as civil servants as such government employees are employed by contract, mostly short-term and are not entitled to the SP benefits given to civil servants (OCSC, 2012, 2). Government employees are required to join SSS with five percent contribution with equivalent contribution from the employing agency and 2.75 percent from the government. The social benefits for permanent government employees, on the other hand, are under the Comptroller General's Department under the Ministry of Finance and include lump sum payment, medical benefits for them and their spouse, children, and parents, and education allowances for their children (CGD, 2012).

Permanent government employees can join the provident fund on a voluntary basis by contributing three percent of their salary. The employing agency pays another three percent (ibid., 52). Temporary government employees[6] do not have any medical or retirement benefits except for work-related injuries or sickness. They also receive benefits under SSS since they are required to join it (ibid., 91).

2.3.2 State-enterprise employees

All state enterprise pension systems (defined benefit systems) have been transferred to the provident fund according to the Provident Fund Act of 1987. Under this scheme, employees of state enterprises will receive a lump sum from the provident fund upon retirement. Medical benefits are dealt individually by state enterprises and differ in agreements or regulations (TDRI, 2013, 3–5).

2.3.3 Private sector employees

2.3.3.1 SOCIAL SECURITY FUND

Private sector employees are protected by SSS and the Workmen's Compensation Fund (WCF). SSS, established by the Social Security Act, B.E. 2533, provides mandatory insurance (Section 33) for employees in the private sector and regular migrant workers. SSS also provides voluntary insurance (Section 39) of workers previously covered by SSS Section 33 and who are willing to continue the insurance (such as newly self-employed or retired persons) and voluntary insurance (Section 40) covering self-employed or informal economy workers

Section 33 of SSS covers persons employed in non-agricultural establishments who are 15 years of age and above. Under the scheme, employers who have at least one employee must register their employee(s). The insured are entitled to non-occupational injury or sickness (healthcare), maternity, invalidity, death, unemployment, old age, and child allowance benefits. The employer and employee pay equal contributions of five percent of the worker's salary whereas the government contributes an additional 2.75 percent for a total contribution of 12.75 percent of the worker's salary.[7]

SSS Section 39 covers individuals previously insured under Section 33, who have paid contributions for not less than 12 months, ceased to be employees but wish to continue being insured. For a contribution of B432 per month (nine percent of the reference salary set at B4,800)[8], the insured are entitled to six types of benefits: non-occupational injury or sickness, maternity, invalidity, death, old age, and child allowance.

2.3.3.2 THE WORKMEN'S COMPENSATION FUND

The Workmen's Compensation Act, B.E. 2537, mandates any employer who has at least one employee in any type of business to contribute to the Workmen's Compensation Fund (WCF). The scheme covers employees in the formal private sector and regular migrant workers. The insured are entitled to benefits in case of work-related injuries, death, sickness, and disappearance. The benefits provided by WCF include monthly indemnities, medical and rehabilitation expenses, and funeral expenses. WCF is administered by the Social Security Office.

2.3.3.3 PROVIDENT FUNDS

The Provident Funds Act was enacted in 1987 to encourage private sector employees to save for their retirement. The fund is a voluntary benefit scheme between employers and employees who set up a fund committee to oversee the provident fund. The committee is composed of representation from the employer and elected representatives of the employees with a fund manager selected by the committee. The Securities and Exchange Commission is the regulatory authority of the scheme. Employees' contributions are not lower than 3 percent but not exceeding 15 percent of their wages (Provident Fund Act, 1987, Section 10). The employer's contributions must not be less than the employee's contributions. This requirement, however, was revised through the amendment of Provident Funds Act 1987 in 2015.

Employees receive a lump sum at the termination of their employment or retirement. Segregation of the fund as a distinct legal entity from the company is required. Contributions to the provident fund by employees and employers are tax deductible and benefit payment is tax exempted.

2.3.3.4 THE PRIVATE SCHOOL TEACHERS' WELFARE FUND

The Private School Teachers' Welfare Fund (PSTWF) was introduced in 1974 through an amendment to the Private School Act, 1954. In 2008, the Royal

Thai Government enacted the Private School Act in which the PSTWF became a private entity run by a board of directors chaired by the permanent secretary of the Ministry of Education. PSTWF provides a provident fund, welfare benefits, and financial assistance to private school directors, teachers, and staff. Monthly contributions (not more than three percent of salary) are paid by the teacher, the school (equal to the member's contribution), and the Ministry of Education (twice the member's contribution).

2.3.4 Informal economy workers

Informal economy workers – self-employed workers or family workers who are not covered by any social security system – are protected by SSS Section 40. Although partially subsidised by the government, this scheme is not embedded in the law and is subject to change with government policy. Since 9 December 2014, the scheme offers:

1. Package 1 – Sickness, invalidity, and death benefits (monthly contributions: B70 by the insured and B30 subsidy).
2. Package 2 – Sickness, invalidity, death, and old-age (lump sum) benefits (monthly contribution: B100 by the insured and B50 subsidy).
3. Package 3 – Old-age pension (monthly contribution: B100 by the insured and B100subsidy).www.sso.go.th/wpr/content.jsp?lang=th&cat=762&id=4002; 10 February 2015)

The scheme does not provide healthcare benefits, which are already provided by UCS.

2.3.5 Migrant workers

Low-skilled migrant workers from Cambodia, Lao PDR, and Myanmar can enter Thailand through a memorandum of understanding between Thailand and these three countries. Without work permits, they can enter as "registered migrant workers" or "nationally verified" or undocumented or irregular migrant workers.

Migrant workers under the memorandum of understanding and those with nationally verified status receive a two-year work permit and are entitled to the same social security rights as those of Thai workers under the WCF and the Social Security Fund (Section 33). In practice, however, most migrant workers fail to satisfy the conditions contained in Circular RS0711/W751 requiring them to possess a passport or nationality registration documents and for their employers to have registered and paid contributions to WCF.

2.4 The elderly

The government policy promoting the quality of life of the elderly and their appropriate employment or activities include promoting home care, nursing home, and hospital care through cooperation among the public sector, the private sector, the community, and family as well as the fiscal system (Bureau of Empowerment for Older Persons, www.oppo.opp.go.th/pages/law/law_06. html, 20 February 2015).

2.4.1 Old-age living allowance (OAA)

The old-age living allowance (OAA) is a universal non-contributory social assistance provided by the government since 1993, on a temporary basis, to provide income for the poor elderly. The allowance was later provided through the Old Age Act, B.E. 2546, which came into effect in 2009 through the Regulation on Disbursement of Old Age Allowance, B.E. 2552. The scheme grants B500[9] per month to persons who are 60 years old or older, have registered and submitted an application to the local government to receive the old-age allowance, have their domicile registered in the local government district where they applied for the allowance, and who receive no other regular benefits from the government, including pension, care in a government welfare shelter, or other income or benefits (except persons with disabilities or with HIV/AIDS).

Since October 2011, the government has applied a stepwise program to increase the monthly allowance to B600 for those aged 60–69 years, to B700 (70–79 years old), to B800 (80–89 years old), and to B1,000 (90 years old and older) (Schmitt et al., 2013, 11).

2.4.2 The National Savings Fund (NSF)

The fund, stipulated in the National Savings Fund Act, B.E. 2554, started operation in August 2015 with a status of a juristic person, independent entity which is not a government agency nor a state enterprise (FPO, 2011). The fund is aimed at encouraging workers in the informal sector to save with government contribution in an amount determined by the member's contribution and the member's age. Financing comes from the government and contributions from members. The intended beneficiaries are citizens aged 15–60 years old, not enrolled in other funds receiving contributions from the government, and not under the pension system of the government or the private sector. In essence, the fund covers workers in the informal sector, workers employed on daily or weekly basis, temporary state-enterprise employees who are not SSS members, temporary government employees, students, and local politicians. Workers enrolled under SSS Section 40 (informal workers) can be transferred to the National Savings Fund (NSF) on voluntary basis (NSF, 2015).

A member has to save at least B50 at a time but total savings may not exceed B13,200 per year. The government progressively contributes based on the age of the member: 50 percent of the savings but not exceeding B600 per year for members aged 15–30 years old, 80 percent but not exceeding B960 per year for those aged 31–50 years, and 100 percent but not exceeding B1,200 per year for those more than 50 years old. The NSF member will obtain the following benefits: lifetime pension upon reaching the age of 60, a lump sum of own savings and interest in case of disability before the age of 60, the government's contribution and interest upon reaching the age of 60, accumulated savings and interest in case of quitting before the age of 60, and, for the member's beneficiaries, all the member's savings plus the government's contribution and interest in case of death (NSF, 2015).

2.5 People with disabilities

Citizens with disabilities are entitled to a universal non-contributory disability allowance of B500 baht per month as established by the Quality of Life Promotion Act for Persons with Disabilities, B.E. 2550, that went into effect in 2010. Eligible are Thai nationals with disabilities domiciled in the district of local government per census, who have a disability card per Persons with Disabilities' Quality of Life Promotion Act, B.E. 2550, and are not being taken care of by a government welfare shelter. The allowance is administered by the Tambon Administrative Organization under the Ministry of Interior (ibid., 10).

2.6 People living with HIV/AIDS

People living with HIV/AIDs are entitled to AIDS Patient Allowance of B500 a month except for patients in Bangkok, who receive B3,000 a year. The allowance, given since 2004, is a universal non-contributory policy[10] and is administered by the Tambon Administrative Organization under the Ministry of Interior and the Bangkok Metropolitan Administration (for Bangkok patients).

Due to space limitations, other social assistance by the government and private insurance companies and provident funds are not mentioned here. For more information, see Schmitt et al., 2013, 15; Paitoonpong, 2012, 16.

3. Social protection system: an assessment of current schemes and future scenarios

This section assesses the existing SP system in Thailand, focusing on outputs/ outcomes and financial inputs, efficiency and effectiveness, and the extent of demand/supply gap. The assessment is divided into Social Protection Index (SPI), general assessment (in terms of coverage, types of benefits, level of benefits, financing level, demand – the supply gap of different SP system components), and fiscal implications of the SP system components (financing mix, out of pocket, risk-pooling arrangements, sustainability of funding). The assessment is based mainly on reviews of existing assessments by the Asian Development Bank (ADB), the Thailand Development Research Institute, and the United Nations / Royal Thai Government Joint Team.

Thailand's overall SPI in 2009 was 0.119, while the depth SPI and breadth SPI were 0.153 and 0.777, respectively. The above suggests that the average benefits from SP is 15.3 percent of the poverty line and the proportion of actual beneficiaries reached 77.7 percent of the potential beneficiaries.

Table 7.1 Thailand social protection expenditure and beneficiaries by category, 2009

	Social insurance	Social assistance	Labour market programmes	All SP programmes
Total SP expenditure (billion baht)	250.0	67.6	7.2	324.8
Beneficiaries (million)	36.5	22.4	0.6	59.5
Reference population (million)	45.5	23.1	8.0	76.6
25% of GDP per capita (baht)	35,583	35,583	35,583	35,583
SPI	**0.092**	**0.025**	**0.003**	**0.119**

Notes: GDP = gross domestic product, SP = social protection, SPI = social protection insurance

Source: Wedel, 2012, 26

For Thailand, use of SPI to assess the SP situation should be done carefully, for two major reasons. First, SPI is sensitive to the definition of coverage of SP and some schemes may not be counted. For example, skills training is included in SPF but not clearly for SP. Second, the use of 25 percent of GDP per capita to represent the poverty line is not appropriate for comparison over a time span since, because of the formula, when GDP per capita changes, the SPI inversely changes automatically (since Z and GDP per capita are the denominators of SPI). For example, Thailand's SPI declined from 0.119 in 2009 to 0.095 in 2010 (ADB, 2013 and http://spi.adb.org/spidmz/index.jsp, 1 March 2015) mainly due to the rise in GDP per capita from US$4,151 in 2009 to US$5,139 in 2010.

3.1 An assessment of the current social protection system in Thailand, fiscal costs, and financing

Table 7.3 provides fiscal costs of social protection programmes in Thailand for the year 2013. Unless otherwise noted, the fiscal cost data in this section is from Table 7.3.

Thailand's present healthcare has covered almost a hundred percent of the country's population. Yet the coverage figures alone do not mean there is no problem with the system. As mentioned in the previous section, the healthcare system in Thailand consists of three major schemes: the Civil Servants' Medical Benefit Scheme (CSMBS), the Social Security System's Medical Benefits (SSSMB), and the Universal Coverage Scheme (UCS) or the National Health Security Program. Each has been developed and implemented for different groups of beneficiaries. There also exist other schemes such as those for employees of the Bangkok Metropolitan Administration and 7,000 enterprises by local administrations and the state. Moreover, many private companies and public enterprises establish their own health schemes for their employees (Table 7.3).

Table 7.2 Thailand: numbers of people with different healthcare coverage schemes (in million persons)

	2005	2006	2007	2008	2009	2010	2011	2012	2013
UCS	47.34	47.54	46.67	46.95	46.95	47.73	48.12	48.62	48.61
SSSMB (Section 33 & 39, WFC)	8.74	9.2	9.58	9.84	9.67	9.9	10.17	10.33	10.77
CSMBS	4.15	4.06	5.013	5	4.96	4.92	4.96	4.97	4.98
Veteran / Private school teachers	0.13	0.23	0.24	0.24	0.23	0.52	0.64	0.61	0.49
Local officials									0.10
Population with coverage	60.45	61.04	61.63	62.02	62.39	63.06	63.89	64.53	64.96
Unregistered population	2.36	1.36	0.78	0.52	0.33	0.41	0.03	0.06	0.08
Total eligible population ᵃ/	62.81	62.39	62.41	62.55	62.7	63.47	63.92	64.59	65.04
% Population with Coverage	96.24	97.84	98.75	99.15	99.5	99.35	99.95	99.91	99.88
CMHI (for CLM migrants)	0.27	0.28	0.30	0.31	0.32	0.18	0.11	0.11	0.12

Notes:
ᵃ/ Not including displaced persons and Thai diaspora.
CLM = Cambodia, Laos, Myanmar, CMHI = Compulsory Migrant Health Insurance, CSMBS = Civil Servants' Medical Benefit Scheme, SSSMB = Social Security System Medical Benefits, UCS = Universal Health Coverage Scheme, WCF = Workmen's Compensation Fund.
Source: National Health Security Office, 2013

Among the three major programmes, CSMBS was created to finance the provision of healthcare services for civil servants and their families, who totalled roughly 5 million. SSSMB aims to provide health and social welfare assistance for roughly 10.8 million private employees while UCS is designed to be the healthcare scheme for those not eligible under the first two programmes. Membership stands at around 49 million. The various healthcare schemes indicate not the strength but the weakness of the system. Particularly, a study by the Thailand Development Research Institute (2013) points out the problems of quality and fairness with uneven benefits across groups of the system.

In 2013, the government budget for public health was B254.9 billion or 2 percent of GDP, increasing 15.7 percent from 2012 (BOB 2013a).

3.1.1 Fiscal costs and financing of healthcare

The national costs of the healthcare system in 2013 were B426.1 billion while the fiscal costs (national costs excluding out-of-pocket costs) are B338.7 billion. The total costs of health insurance borne by every scheme are B426.1 billion. The schemes borne by the government include the costs for CSMBS and UCS. The funding is from various sources as shown above. The cost to the government was the public health budget of B254.9 billion which include other expenses on community and social development (BOB, 2013a, 52).

Health insurance for employees of state enterprises is managed by individual state enterprises making up three methods of benefit claiming: directly through the state enterprise of employment, through SSS, and through the comptroller department of the Ministry of Finance. The average cost of healthcare benefits of state enterprise officials was B2.5 billion per year in early 2000 (Srianan, 2002, 23–27).

3.1.2 Efficacy of healthcare

According to the Thailand Development Research Institute (2013), the existing multiple programmes are rather problematic as they lead to inequality of health benefits and inefficiency due to duplicated administration and management. The three healthcare programmes of Thailand are administered by the Ministry of Finance, the Ministry of Public Health, and the Ministry of Labour, which manage CSMBS, UCS, and SSSMB, respectively.

Under SSSMB, insured persons are obligated to regularly pay health insurance premiums to benefit from insurance co-payments from their employers and the state, whereas beneficiaries of CSMBS and UCS are not. Members of the fee-for-service CSMBS system are allowed to obtain healthcare services in public hospitals nationwide, while SSSMB and UCS beneficiaries can obtain services only in hospitals or health centres where they have previously registered under the per-capitation payment system. Patients under the fee-for-service healthcare scheme (CSMBS) normally obtain better services than those under per-capitation schemes (SSSMB and UCS). Also, different schemes often use different diagnosis-related groups. Different reimbursement rates

Table 7.3 Fiscal costs* of social protection in Thailand, 2013

Programme	Source of funding	Costs	
		Billion baht	*% GDP*
Healthcare		**426.1**	**3.58**
CSMBS	Government	*85.9*	
USC	Government	*157.3*	
SSS+WFC	Tripartite contribution	*41.6*	
Out of pocket	People	*87.4*	
Non-USC	Government	*54.0*	
Children		**285.3**	**2.40**
Free education	Government	*284.7*	
Child allowance	Government	*0.6*	
Working age population		**248.6**	**2.09**
GOPS**	Government	*124.0*	
GPF	Gov't +Worker	*22.1*	
State-enterprise employee-PF ***	Gov't +Worker	*n.a.*	
SSS 33	Tripartite contribution	*63.3*	
SSS 39	Gov't + worker		
SSS 40	Gov't + worker		
WCF	*Employer*	*2.0*	
Provident Fund	Worker+ Employer	*37.3*	
The Elderly (OAA)	**Government**	**58.7**	**0.49**
People with disabilities (Allowance)	**Government**	**7.5**	**0.06**
People Living with HIV/ AIDS (Allowance)	**Government**	**0.4**	**0.0**
Grand total		**1,026.6**	**8.63**

Notes: *National costs; fiscal costs = national costs minus non-government costs; ** Assuming fiscal costs = government expenditure budget; ***Is included in PF; GDP 2013 is 11.9 billion baht (NESDB, 2015a).

CSMBS = Civil Servants' Medical Benefit Scheme, GDP = gross domestic product, GOPS = Government Official Pension System, GPF = Government Pension Fund, HIV/AIDS = Human Immune-Deficiency Virus/Acquired Immune Deficiency Syndrome, OAA = old-age living allowance, SSS = Social Security System, USC=Universal Coverage Scheme, WCF = Workmen's Compensation Fund.

Sources: National Health Security Office, 2013); Jitsuchon, 2011; Bureau of the Budget, 2013b; Social Security Office, 2013; Workmen's Compensation Fund, 2013

lead to different service quality. In terms of efficiency, the administrative separation of the health insurance system into three schemes leads to higher costs for the health services providers (hospitals) and the payers (public agencies) (TDRI, 2013).

3.1.3 Programs for children

Thailand's 15-year basic education programme is universal, covering 11.64[11] million students from kindergarten to the upper secondary education and vocational education. The fiscal costs in 2013 were B284.7 billion, accounting for 2.39 percent of GDP.[12] Financing is solely from government revenues through the Ministry of Education. The free education includes the costs of tuition, textbooks, uniforms, education accessories, and student development activities.

3.1.4 Child allowance

The Royal Thai Government has already initiated a pilot project to provide an allowance of B400 per month to children 0–1 years old from families with less than B30,000 per year income. The programme did not start until 1 October 2015. Eligible under this scheme are 93,658 children; the programme's estimated cost was B0.6 billion per year at its start. The United Nations / Royal Thai Government Joint Team study (Schmitt et al., 2013) has provided various projections on who should be covered, with ages ranging from 0–3, 4–6, and 7–14 years. The number of children aged 0–3 years was 2.3 million and those aged 0–6 years was about 4.5 million in 2014. The fiscal implication of this goal is presented in section 3.3.

3.1.5 Programs for working age population

Government officials are relatively well protected because their protection system started a long time ago; another reason which seemed to be often neglected is that government officials had very poor salaries. The medical and retirement benefits are incentives for working for the government. The old pension scheme (GOPS) was not sustainable and the government has incorporated the GPF scheme, which is a contributory system.

The Government Official Pension Fund (GPF) is financed by the government. In 2013, the government allocated B124.0 billion for pensions or lump sum payment of retired government officials (BOB, 2013a, 3).

In 2013, of the Government Pension Fund's 1,188,937 members, 28,846 retired and received lump sum pensions amounting to B20.4 billion (GPF, 2013a, 68). With operation costs assumed to be 0.26 percent (B1.6 billion) of the fund (B632.5 billion), the fiscal costs of GPF in 2013 were B22.1 billion.

In 2013, the government's contribution to GPF was B20.9 billion, with additional B32.9 billion coming from members (GPF, 2013a). Net income from investments of GPF funds was B22.6 billion, taking the total financing for 2013 to B76.5 billion.

3.1.6 State-enterprise employees

Employees of state enterprises are required to enroll in the provident funds of their agencies. Because the provident funds of state enterprises are managed individually, there are no data on the fiscal costs of their funding. It is noted that contributions to provident funds for employees of state enterprises are voluntary and not all state enterprises have established provident funds. There is need to address this data gap in Thailand's social protection system.

3.1.7 Private sector employees

Wage employees in private establishments are required to insure with SSS and
WCF. In 2013, around 9.8 million persons were insured under SSS (Article 33)
and 8.9 million under WCF. WCF differs from SSS in that only work-related
injuries, sickness, or disappearance are paid and contribution is borne solely
by employers. There are 14.1 million wage employees in 2013. SSS and WCF
schemes cover about 69 and 63 percent of the population at risk, respectively.
The coverage therefore can be regarded as moderately high, but some improvement is still desirable.

Table 7.4 shows the fiscal costs and financing of SSS.

Table 7.5 shows the fiscal costs and financing of WCF.

Table 7.4 Thailand fiscal costs and financing of Social Security System, 2013

	billion baht	*percent*
Fiscal costs		
Benefits	57.3	90.5
Operation expenses	4.8	7.6
Others	1.2	1.9
Total	*63. 3ᵃ/*	*100.0*
Financing		
Contributions ᵇ/	135.7	73.6
Interest	34.8	18.9
Others	13.9	7.5
Total	*184.5*	*100.0*

Notes:
ᵃ/ The costs as well as the financing are inclusive of SSS Articles 39 and 40.
ᵇ/ Inclusive of government contribution of about 30 percent.
Source: Social Security Office, 2013

Table 7.5 Thailand fiscal costs and financing of Workmen's Compensation Fund, 2013

	billion baht	*percent*
Fiscal costs		
Benefits	1.7	85.0
Operation expenses	0.2	10.0
Others	0.1	5.0
Total	**2.0**	**100.0**
Financing		
Contributions ᵇ/	3.9	73.6
Interest	1.4	26.4
Others	0.0	0.0
Total	**5.3**	**100.0**

Source: Workmen's Compensation Fund 2013

3.1.8 Voluntary provident funds

In addition to SSS and WCF, private sector employees can also join the provident funds of their establishments. In Thailand, provident funds are voluntarily established by agreement of employees and employers and registered under the Provident Fund Act, B.E. 2530, to encourage savings and financially secure employees and their families in the event of termination of employment, resignation from the company or from the provident fund, retirement, disability, and death. A fund may be set up and registered as a single fund for employees with a sole employer or a pooled fund for employees with more than one employer and/or multiple investment policies. As required by law, the investment policy of a provident fund to be registered must comply with the rules and regulations of the Securities and Exchange Commission.

In 2013, there were 2.6 million fund members with nearly 14,000 employers (SEC, 2015), and main annual costs reaching B57.5 billion and B1.9 billion, representing benefits payouts to employees and employers, respectively. Funding from employees' contributions reached B43.6 billion, whereas employers contributed B50.3 billion. Data on investment returns of these funds are not available.

Included in the statistics are members from state enterprises.

3.1.9 Informal workers

Informal workers are those not covered by any of the government social security programmes, particularly the self-employed, family workers, home workers, and non-wage farmers. At present, they can enrol in SSS (Article 40 or 39). There were 1.1 million informal workers under SSS Article 39 and 1.6 million under SSS Article 40 in 2013. Because of problems with the SSS Article 40 scheme, Option 3 (old-age pension), the government is enforcing the National Saving Fund, which had been suspended for political and technical reasons.

According to the survey by the National Statistical Office, about 24.8 million were classified as informal workers in 2012. In 2013, however, there should be about 19.8 million informal workers, according to the Labour Force Survey, Round 3. Thus, the proportion of informal workers covered by SSS Articles 39 and 40 (2.65 million) is about 10 percent of the total.

3.1.10 Migrant workers

In 2014, 3 million migrant workers and dependents were from Cambodia, Lao PDR, and Myanmar, with about 1.3 million classified as legal through the process of national verification and the memorandum of understanding between Thailand and those three countries. In 2013, about 400,000 migrants were insured with SSS while no figure was available for those insured under WFC. Under SSS, migrant workers are not eligible for maternity, child support, unemployment, and old-age benefits due to the nature of their employment and migration status.

3.1.11 The elderly

The elderly (60 years old and above) are entitled to OAA. The allowance is universal except for government pensioners.[13] There were 7.35 million elderly persons in 2013 and the cost of financing the scheme was B58.7 billion (BOB, 2013a). The OAA is administered through the Local Administration Organizations under the Department of Local Administration Promotion, the Bangkok Metropolitan Administration, and the Pataya Metropolitan Administration. The financing is from the government budget as shown in Table 7.6.

The registration for availing allowance, however, opens only once a year in November.

3.1.12 National Saving Fund (NSF)

The total number of intended beneficiaries may be projected at around 35 million, consisting of 24 million informal workers and 11 million people aged 15–60 years not in the labour force (Office of Fiscal Economics, 2011). Financing is entirely from the government. No data on actual beneficiaries and fiscal costs is available as the fund just started in August 2015.

3.1.13 People with disabilities

At present, persons with disabilities receive B800 per month. Eligibility is means-tested, for those whose income is less than the poverty line of B1,243 per month. There are 1.25 million (approximately 74 percent) disabled receiving allowances out of the total of 1.69 million (DEPD, 2015). The government budget for this programme was B7.5 billion in 2013, accounting for 0.06 percent of GDP (NESDB, 2015b).

3.1.14 People with HIV/AIDS

Persons living with HIV/AIDS are entitled to an allowance of B500 per month under the People Living with HIV/AIDS programme. The number of eligible persons is not known because many of them do not want to disclose their medical

Table 7.6 Thailand old-age living allowance by administration, 2013

Administration	Number of older persons ('000)	Budget (billion baht)
Local	6,828.6	54.6
Bangkok Metropolitan	513.9	4.1
Pataya Metropolitan	6.1	0.05
Total	7,348.6	58.75

Source: Bureau of the Budget, 2013d

condition. In 2013, 68,616 persons with HIV/AIDS received the allowance. Programme cost was B413 million and was funded by the government.

3.2 *Assessment of long-term financial implications*

There are four major studies on the assessment of financial implications of social protection in Thailand:

1. National Dialogue Based on Social Protection Assessment: Toward a Nationally Defined Social Protection Floor in Thailand, by the UN/RTG Joint Team (Schmitt et al., 2013).
2. Toward Social Welfare System for All in 2017 Report, submitted to the Thai Health Promotion Foundation (THPF) by Jitsuchon et al. (2011), Bangkok: Thailand Development Research Institute.
3. The Development of Guidelines for Health Insurance System Governance Report   (*Krong-karnkarn-pattananaew-thangapibarnraboblak-prakunsukhapharb*), by the Thailand Development Research Institute (TDRI) (2013), Bangkok (in Thai).
4. An Analysis of the Policy Impact of the Population Projection of Thailand, B.E.2553–2583, Report, by Wapathanawong, P., Pramote Prasartkul, and Sureeporn Punpuing (eds.) (2013), Nakornpratom: Institute of Population and Social Research, Mahidol University (in Thai).

The first is the most comprehensive and direct in terms of future SP programmes in Thailand and their coverage. The second, done earlier than the first study, covers similar SP programme but using a different methodology in setting up the goal based on a survey of the desires of stakeholders (the UN/RTG Joint Team based its assessment on the ILO Rapid Assessment Protocol in developing an assessment matrix for the desired goals of social protection). The third one focuses on health insurance system governance whereas the fourth is primarily interested in the implications of the new population projections on development.

In view of the comprehensiveness of the UN/RTG Team assessment – done collectively at the national level and recognised by the Royal Thai Government[14] – and due to the constraints of the present study, we review only the UN/RTG Team assessment to illustrate the fiscal implications of social protection.

In Thailand, SP was chosen as one of the six key areas of partnership between the Royal Thai Government and the UN system within the United Nations Partnership Framework. This partnership, for 2012–2016, focuses on enhancing Thailand's capacity to provide universal basic SP and higher levels of benefits through contributory schemes, with the overall objective of ensuring the financial and institutional sustainability of the system. The International Labour Organization (ILO) assigned a team of technical specialists to carry out the 'Social protection assessment based national dialogue: 'Towards a nationally defined social protection floor in Thailand' in accordance with the Social Protection Floors Recommendation, 2012 (No. 202) as adopted at the 101st International Labour Conference in June 2012.

From June 2011 to March 2013, the UN/RTG study team applied the Assessment-Based National Dialogue exercise to review the SPF situation and how it could be extended to all members of society in Thailand. It engaged line ministries, UN agencies, social partners, civil society organisations, academia, and other relevant stakeholders to assess the SP situation in Thailand, identify policy gaps and implementation issues, and draw appropriate policy recommendations to achieve a comprehensive SPF in Thailand (Schmitt et al., 2013, 21). The report provides a holistic description of existing social protection schemes and programmes and policy.

The ABND consists of three major steps (Schmitt et al. 2013, 19–20):

1. Step 1: Developing the assessment matrix (inventory of existing SPF to identify policy gaps, implementation issues, and a number of recommendations for the design and implementation of further SP provisions with the aim of guaranteeing, at a minimum, the SPF to all the population.)
2. Step 2: Rapid Assessment Protocol (RAP). Using the ILO/RAP,[15] the costs of the proposed SP provisions are estimated and projected over a 10-year period.
3. Step 3: Finalisation. The recommendations are shared with government representatives, workers and employers, and non-governmental organisations to validate assumptions and recommendations and to prepare for the next steps which may include feasibility studies for the design of new schemes, expansion of existing schemes, and establishment of coordination mechanisms.

The UN/RTG Team projections are on child allowance, various schemes for informal workers, and OAA providing scenarios in comparison with status quos up to 2020.

RAP is a simple methodology that builds on single-age population projections, single-age estimates of labour force participation rates along with a relatively crude economic scenario determined by assumptions of overall GDP growth, productivity, inflation and wages, and interest and poverty rates. The nominal and real GDP and GDP deflator used the 2005–2009 historical data from the National Income of Thailand. For 2010–2020, the UN/RTG Team uses TDRI's projections for nominal and real GDP as well as the GDP deflator (Schmitt et al., 2013, 53). The total government revenues, grants, and expenditures are based on historical data and projections. The current global scenario if subdue growth and trade-flows, suggest care in using the macro-economic assumptions of the UN/RTG study.[16]

The main variables are historical population data and projections, labour force participation rates, minimum wage, poverty line, poverty rate, nominal and real GDP and GDP deflator, headline inflation, unemployment rate, employment per sector, government total revenues, grants, expenditures, informal sector workers undertaking training, and inpatient care utilisation by informal economy workers.

RAP uses the recommendations formulated in Step 1 (assessment matrix) for specific SP provisions that need to be introduced or further expanded. The costs of these provisions were calculated and projected over the 2012–2020 period in

terms of percentage of GDP and government expenditures to provide preliminary indications of the affordability of the proposed SP provisions and the fiscal
space. However, the results of the costing exercise remain simplistic and do not
replace in-depth feasibility and actuarial studies.

3.2.1 The results of RAP assessments for social protection floor[17]

The UN/RTG Team study skipped the RAP step on healthcare since the assessment conclusion is that the SPF for healthcare had been achieved. Nevertheless,
there were some recommendations on health issues such as those formulated
to reduce fragmentation of the health system, ensure the long-term financial
sustainability of the system, and guarantee the gender sensitivity of the entire
healthcare system both in policy and practice (Schmitt et al. 2013, 30). These
recommendations, however, require additional in-depth studies beyond the RAP
assessment. The RAP assessment, therefore, has been conducted for the issues of
children, working age, and elderly as follows[18]:

Table 7.7 summarizes the estimates of the ***additional*** fiscal costs of various
social protection measures studied as compared to the 2012 base year. These
projections do not include additional healthcare costs, or other programs not
studied by the UN/RTG team.

3.2.2 Children

To complete the SPF for children, the main recommendation is to implement a
universal or targeted child support grant. The recommendation was translated
into six scenarios, with each scenario offering support grants of B400 – B500.
This is quite low, according to global standards; a child support grant should
amount to US$0.67 x 1.25 per day or around B750 (Schmitt et al., 2013, 55).
The main reason for the low grant is to avoid creating disincentives for workers
contributing to SSO schemes.

Each scenario differs in the child support grant (B400 – B500) and age coverage (0–3, 0–6, 0–12, 0–14 years). The administrative costs (5–15 percent)[19] and
the fund would be under the authority of the MSDHS; the distribution would be
administered by the local administrations under the supervision of the Ministry
of Interior.

As shown in Figure 7.2, by 2020, there will be 2.813 million beneficiaries
with total additional cost of B17.3 billion for the low scenario, compared to
9.5 million beneficiaries with total additional cost of B72.9 billion for the high
scenario. The total additional cost of the low scenario will be 0.08 percent of
GDP whereas the total additional cost of the high scenario will be 0.34 percent
in 2020 (Schmitt et al., 2013, 58).

3.2.3 Working age population

The recommendations for the working-age population are to establish a maternity allowance, a sickness benefit scheme for workers in the informal economy,

Table 7.7 Thailand status quo and projected costs of recommended social protection

	Status Quo 2012, billion baht	Additional Costs by 2020		
		Billion Baht	% of GDP	% of Government Revenue
Children: Universal child support grant				
Scenario 1: for all children aged 0–3 (B400 per month)	15.0	17.3	0.08	0.39
Scenario 2: for all children aged 0–6 (B400 per month)		30.7	0.14	0.69
Scenario 3: for all children aged 0–12 (B400 per month)		58.3	0.27	1.31
Scenario 4: for all children aged 0–6 (B500 per month)		38.4	0.18	0.86
Scenario 5: for all children aged 0–12 (B500 per month)		72.9	0.34	1.63
Working age population: Workers in the informal economy				
Scenario 1: Maternity allowance for all female informal workers	8.6	2.0	0.009	0.045
Scenario 2: Sickness benefit for all informal workers	0.8	2.8	0.013	0.062
Scenario 3: Vocational training programme for informal workers with allowance for the poor	0.3	60.0	0.2807	1.34
Scenario 4: Additional B500 for people with disabilities in the informal economy between 15 and 59 years of age	7.6	2.7	0.0125	0.06
Elderly: Universal non-contributory allowance for older people				
Scenario 1: With inflation indexation of the benefits	100.1	21.8	0.1	0.49
Scenario 2: With benefits expressed in percentage of the national poverty line	100.1	118.7	0.56	2.66

Notes: (1) GDP used is GDP at current prices projections by Jitsuchon. (Schmitt et al, 2013,53). The nominal GDP was assumed to grow at 6.5 percent from 2012 to 2017. The actual growth rates (at market price) are 9.3 percent for 2012, 4.5 percent for 2013, and 1.9 percent for 2014 (calculated from NESDB data). (2) The status quo of Child Allowance programme calculated from civil servants, scholarship, and formal sector: child allowance (Sections 33–39).
GDP = gross domestic product.
Sources: data from Schmitt et al.; International Labour Organization work file on RAP (Courtesy of Ms. Jittima Srisuknam, 2 March 2015)

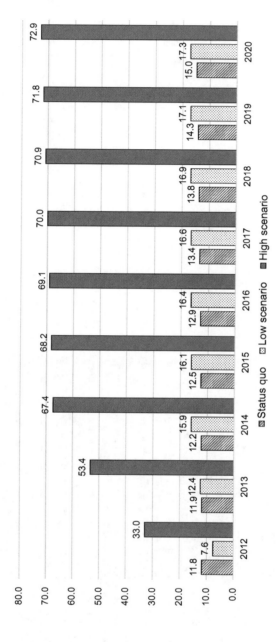

Figure 7.2 Thailand projected universal child allowance up to 2020 (billion baht)

Source: estimation by authors from data obtained from the International Labour Organization, Bangkok

to expand and adapt the vocational training programme for them, and to give additional B500 for people in the informal economy with disabilities and between 15 and 59 years of age. Four scenarios are projected:

1. Scenario 1: Maternity allowance for all women working in the informal economy. This aims to compensate all working women in the informal economy for loss of income during pregnancy and after delivery. This scheme would provide a cash benefit equal to three month's income at the level of the poverty line to ensure that the woman can maintain herself and her child in healthy conditions and with a suitable standard of living. The Ministry of Interior would manage the scheme and is in charge of registering newborn children. This scenario entails an additional cost of B2 billion or 0.009 percent of GDP by 2020.

2. Scenario 2: Sickness benefits for all informal economy workers. This scheme would guarantee compensation for loss of income due to sickness. The benefit is B200 per day starting on the first day of hospitalisation and without conditions on duration. This scheme will entail an additional cost of B2.8 billion or 0.013 percent of GDP by 2020.

3. Scenario 3: Vocational training programme for informal economy workers, including allowances for the poor. This scheme has a training component which provides one training every year to 20 percent of the target (or one training every five years to all workers in the informal sector), and a poverty-alleviation component in the form of cash benefits of B200 per day of training (two-thirds of the minimum wage) for participants who live below the poverty line. Training lasts 10–20 days depending on the education of workers; the scheme does not provide training for those with higher education. The introduction of a vocational training programme for informal economy workers and allowance for the poor will entail an additional cost of B60 billion or 0.28 percent of GDP by 2020.

4. Scenario 4: Additional B500 baht for people in the informal economy between 15 and 59 years of age with disabilities. The proposed scheme would add an additional B500 baht per person per month. The total benefit would be B1,000 per month indexed to inflation. It would be provided only to people with disabilities who are currently targeted by the B500 disability allowance and this will entail an additional cost of B2.7 billion or 0.0125 percent of GDP by 2020.

The target group are informal economy workers of Thai nationality (15–19 years of age); this does not include migrant workers. The scenario on vocational training costs eight times higher than the combined cost of the other three scenarios.

3.2.4 The elderly

To complete the social protection floor for the elderly, the main recommendation is to adjust the government's existing non-contributory allowance to guarantee a

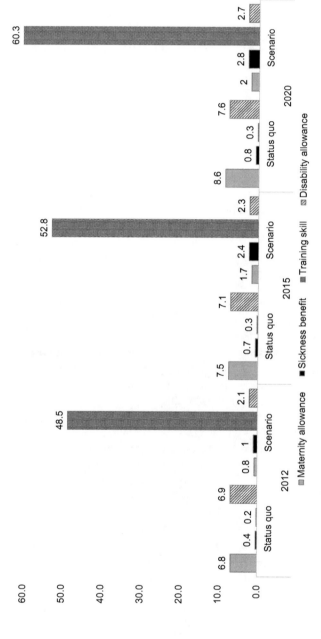

Figure 7.3 Thailand projected benefit scheme for workers in the informal sector up to 2020 (billion baht)

Source: estimation by authors from data obtained from the International Labour Organization, Bangkok

certain level of income security: that is, the amount of benefits should be indexed with inflation or expressed as a percentage of the poverty line. The target group includes all people 60 years of age and older except civil service pensioners. The non-contributory old-age allowance is considered a minimum income guarantee for the elderly. The scenarios for the elderly are as follows:

1. Scenario 1: Government's new policy for the universal non-contributory allowance for the elderly with indexing of benefits. The assumptions are the same as the status quo[20] except that benefits are indexed on inflation. This will entail an additional cost (compared to the status quo) of B21.8 billion or 0.10 percent of GDP (ibid., 68).
2. Scenario 2: Alternative non-contributory allowance for older people with benefits expressed in percentage of the nationally defined poverty line. This will entail an additional cost (compared to the status quo) of B118.7 billion or 0.56 percent of GDP (ibid.).

The fiscal implications from the UN/RTG Team study under various scenarios are summarised in Table 7.8. The financing is from government revenues.

4. Future strategies and initiatives

4.1 ABND recommendations

Some future strategies and initiatives on SPF for Thailand can be drawn from the recommendations that emerged from the national dialogue process (Schmitt et al., 2013, Ch. 4). Based on the process, the study had reviewed existing provisions and identified policy gaps and implementation issues before making recommendations for each programme on health, children, working-age population, and the elderly. The full recommendations (Schmitt et al., 2013, Chapter 4) are contained in a long wish list with a note that they require further in-depth study. Thus, the team did not calculate fiscal costs.

In the selected shorter version of the recommendations, the UN/RTG Joint Team recommends that, to close its social protection floor gap, Thailand should expand the existing SPF in the following dimensions:

1. To introduce a universal child support grant which would, inter alia, support parents and caretakers with the cost of raising children);
2. To extend maternity allowance to compensate all working women for loss of income during pregnancy and after delivery;
3. To extend sickness benefits to compensate all workers for loss of income during sickness;
4. To transform the existing vocational training system through a more efficient, targeted mechanism which would systematically reach 20 percent of informal economy workers every year and provide an allowance to trainees who are poor;

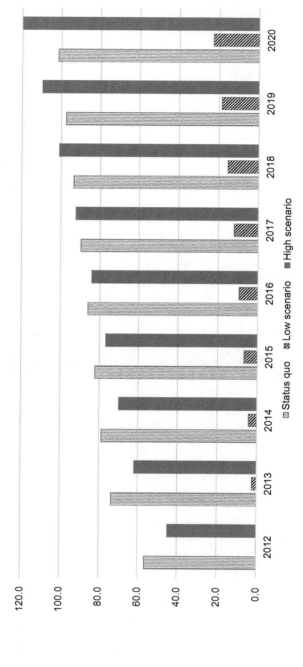

Figure 7.4 Thailand projected old age allowance up to 2020 (billion baht)

Source: estimation by authors from data obtained from the International Labour Organization, Bangkok

Table 7.8 Fiscal space (Status Quo, Low and High Scenarios Entirely Financed through Government Budget)

	2012	2014	2016	2018	2020
Balance (billion baht): Status quo	−345.7	68.9	158.9	274.2	424.8
Balance (billion baht): Low scenario	−406.2	−8.1	73.3	178.9	318.8
Balance (billion baht): High scenario	−468.8	−111.8	−40.3	52.5	181.1
Balance (% of GDP at current prices): Status quo	−3.1	0.5	1.0	1.5	2
Balance (% of GDP at current prices): Low scenario	−3.6	−0.1	0.5	1.0	1.5
Balance (% of GDP at current prices): High scenario	−4.2	−0.9	−0.3	0.3	0.8

Note: GDP = gross domestic product
Source: Schmitt et al., 2013

5. To increase the benefit package of the non-contributory disability allowance; and
6. To adjust the government's non-contributory allowance for the elderly.

The UN/RTG Joint Team proposes two possible combinations of schemes. The first is the "low scenario" and the second is the "high scenario". Based on these, completing the SPF would entail an additional cost of between 0.5 and 1.2 percent of GDP for the above programs alone by 2020 (Schmitt et al., 2013).

In 2015, according to the World Bank, Thailand's tax-to-GDP ratio was 16.5 percent. Thus, additional fiscal costs, even for these limited measures, would require fiscal management. If additional investments in infrastructure and higher operating costs are needed to implement the above measures, needed fiscal resources will be higher, as these have not been included in the above estimates.

4.1.1 Recent initiatives

Since the completion of the UN/RTG Team study, Thailand's social protection system has witnessed several initiatives. With reference to Appendix 1, the present study has the following observations.

4.1.2 Health

At present, the Royal Thai Government is moving to integrate the three health insurance systems (UCS, CSMBS, and SSSMB) by appointing a subcommittee to conduct the feasibility of the integration of the three health insurance systems with a view to reducing the inequitable benefits for the people. The subcommittee recently recommended that the government issue an act to reform the financing of the government's healthcare system, and monitor the services and benefits to the patients (*Post Today*, 20 May 2015). For other recommendations on health, the study team noted that they require further in-depth feasibility studies and/or can be implemented through specific technical cooperation projects (Schmitt et al., 2013, 30).

4.1.3 Children

With regards to C1 – the mandate to design and implement a universal child support grant for various age groups (0–3, 0–6, or 0–12 years of age) with the aim of child poverty reduction and support for parents by assisting with the cost of raising children – the Royal Thai Government has already started (on 1 October 2015) a pilot project providing an allowance of B400 per month to children 0–1 years old from families with income less than B30,000 per year. In connection with C2 – include a child support grant in the benefit package of the SSA Section 40 – SSA Section 40 is being reviewed for reform. C4 – improve the quality of the education system through enhancing workforce skills and promoting innovations – may be a part of the labour intervention programme but could be done under the formal education system.

4.1.4 Working age population

Recommendation W1 (to develop a combined benefit package composed of income support measures and mechanisms to increase employability and/or access to markets) should be studied more carefully, particularly regarding the occupational and educational structure of workers in the informal sector, and the training demand of the workers. More than half of informal workers are in agriculture. The target of 20 percent of workers trained a year may be too broad. In connection with Recommendation W4 (to review existing SSA Section 40 to cover more people with more adequate benefits), the government is working on the enforcement of the NSF, which may affect the reform of SSA Section 40. In addition, the TDRI is undertaking a study to integrate the existing various public pension systems (TDRI, 2015).

Recommendations concerning workers in the informal economy should be more carefully worked out. One reason is that the definition of informal workers includes those not covered by the public social security. Once covered by the SSS, they become formal workers and their number will reduce proportionately with the extent of SSS expansion. The second reason is that the definition includes workers in agriculture whose livelihood and skill needs are different from those of informal workers in the urban sector. Thus, the targeting of workers in the informal sector should be by economic sector. Third, the educational background of the workers in the informal sector will improve over the period from 2012 to 2020. This will affect the number of days of training and the cost of training.

4.1.5 Elderly

E1 (the recommendation to express the level of benefits of OAA as a percentage of the poverty line or to index the levels of benefits on inflation) may be redundant, although it makes the allowance more systematic. E2 (to legislate OAA to ensure systematic and predictable protection) can be done without additional fiscal costs. E3 (to design and establish a long-term social care insurance system in cash or in kind) is a matter of LTC, which may need attention. Regarding E4 (creating a National Savings Fund that would complement the OAA), the NSF has been promulgated.

4.2 Fiscal space

With regard to the ABND recommendation, the UN/RTG Joint Team has demonstrated the fiscal space of the expansion of SP in Thailand by comparing the estimated costs of the low and high scenarios with the government budget projection. The budget balance (revenues and grants minus expenditures) was then expressed in Thai baht and as a percentage of GDP for the status quo, the low scenario, and the high scenario. This provides an initial indication of the fiscal space, with an assumption that the proposed SP are financed entirely from the government budget. It should be emphasized that the Report of the UN/RTG team (Schmitt et al., 2013) explicitly states that "the results of the costing exercise remain simplistic and do not replace in-depth feasibility and actuarial studies" (p. xvii). These, however, have not been undertaken subsequently.

The study projects the additional fiscal costs (not including infrastructure costs) of the above set of measures as between 0.5 percent and 1.2 percent of GDP by 2020 (Schmitt et al., 2013). It then projects, rather curiously, that the low scenario would entail a deficit in the government budget until 2014, and the high scenario till 2017, but then there will be fiscal surplus until 2020, the end of the projection period. It should be emphasized that the study had assumed that Thailand's government budget would be in surplus from 2013, compared to a deficit equivalent to 3.1 percent of GDP in 2012. But *Thailand Budget in Brief* for the fiscal year 2016 projects a deficit equivalent to .8 percent of GDP (www. bb.go.th/budget_book/e-Book2559/FILEROOM/CABILIBRARY59/ DRAWER01/GENERAL/DATA0000/inBrief2016.pdf)

The above projections therefore need to be carefully re-evaluated before proceeding with any social protection initiatives.

Generally, fiscal space can be generated by enhancing the rate of growth and broadening its base, improving revenue performance, and managing expenditure to obtain better value for money (Asher and Vora, 2015). Similarly, fiscal space can be expanded by relocating public expenditures, increasing tax revenues, expanding social security coverage and contributory revenues, lobbying for aid and transfers (which is not applicable to Thailand), eliminating illicit financial flow, using fiscal and foreign exchange reserves, borrowing or restructuring existing debt, and adopting a more accommodating macroeconomic framework (Ortiz et al., 2015, ii).

In the case of Thailand, Jitsuchon et al. (2011, Chapter 7) proposed an approach to expanding Thailand's fiscal space through tax reform, management improvement, and development of a participatory welfare system. The tax reform can be done through one or a combination of ways: increase collection of income tax, increase value added tax, decrease corporate tax if revenue can be generated from other sources, expand the base for property tax, Fiscal space can be expanded by other means of revenue generation as well. The improvement of SP management can be done by applying targeting approach systems (instead of using universal coverage alone), avoiding duplication of programmes, and reducing populism programmes. The development of a participatory welfare society system can be applied through promotion of corporate social responsibility and promotion of civil society work in social protection.

5. Concluding remarks

This study has examined the SP system in Thailand to provide an analysis of Thailand's stage of SP implementation. It is noted that the concepts of SP and SPF are similar, with their main concern of providing basic SP for all. The report has reviewed Thailand's existing SP programmes, costs, and financing and has analytically linked them to the fiscal implications under a few scenarios of expansion of SPF to meet selected SDG goals. Thailand has developed a wide range of SP programmes which include social security, social assistance, and labour market interventions to serve people from all walks of life, from birth to death. Thailand's SP system is largely funded by the government and contributions from workers and the private sector. The total costs of the existing SP borne by the government and the public are about B1,026.6 billion in 2013, accounting for 8.6 percent of the GDP (Table 7.3). Its voluntary programmes such as provident funds are widely used as main sources of savings for old age, particularly for workers in the private sector.

The study reviews the scenarios assessed by the UN/RTG Team on Social Protection, which reveal that the major SPF gaps include children, workers in the informal sector, and disadvantaged people. A few additional schemes are recommended through the ABND assessment including introducing a universal child support grant, extending maternity allowance to compensate all working women for loss of income during pregnancy and after delivery, extending sickness benefits to compensate all workers for loss of income during sickness, providing skills training to 20 percent of informal workers by 2020, increasing the disability allowance, and adjusting OAA. The assessment indicates that closing such SPF gaps would entail an additional cost of B106.5 billion – 259.0 billion, or between 0.5 and 1.2 percent of GDP, by 2020. The policy and organisational coherence among pension, healthcare, social pension, child benefits, and other elements of the SP system has been observed.

The study notes Thailand's impressive record of MDG achievements and plans to address SDGs.

The study has argued that SP faces the problem of interpreting terms like "adequate", "minimum", "basic', 'essential", and so forth. Without clear definitions, they may be interpreted in many divergent ways without leading to "a life in dignity" (Mestrum, 2014). This may be the reason the UN/TRG Joint Team had to adopt the ABND approach to obtain a "nationally defined social protection floor". Such an approach is time-consuming and other countries may find it difficult to obtain consensus on SP. It is recommended, therefore, that a more universal concept be developed and applied.

The study supports the recommendations by the UN/TRG Joint Team, with exceptions. For example, the extension of more SP to workers in the informal sectors may face moral hazards due to lack of either efficient registration or good distribution system. It is recommended that before taking further action on these recommendations, more study and planning be conducted.

Improving and extending skills training to 20 percent of workers in the informal sector will incur relatively high costs, although there has been no study on the demand or need of these workers. Without knowing the actual demand for training, overlapping of programmes and waste of resources will happen.

Thailand has already taken some measures, such as child allowance, re-engineering of SSS Section 40, and the NSF. These improvements should be considered in the implementation of the recommended programmes.

In connection with the above, it should be kept in mind that sooner or later, every SP involves fiscal space risks, which need to be addressed. It is recommended that fiscal space be carefully studied, projected, and updated, particularly during times of crisis.

It should be emphasised that in the context of SP or SPF, looking at the coverage and financing issues is not enough since they deal with the quantitative aspect of SP. Indeed, there are quite a few pitfalls in SP implementation beyond fiscal space and/or sustainability. These include the quality as well as the inequality of SP, management, accessibility, governance, and even political instability. To improve the effectiveness of the existing SP system, it is recommended that concerned parties keep the basic concept of SPF regarding these matters and pay attention to and act on the qualitative aspect of SP. In the case of Thailand, at least three major issues on SP need further support to review and reform: inequality in the health insurance system, inequality in pension systems, and quality in schooling.

Finally, concerning SDGs, there are concerns whether these are aspirations or measurable goals, whether the goals are too comprehensive, whether baseline data of reasonable quality are available, etc. As such, it is recommended that concerned parties be made aware of fiscal implications of SPF/SDG commitments and of sustainability, fairness, and the criteria for spending less, spending well, and spending wisely.

Notes

1 Hereafter called the UN/RTG Joint Team. It consists of UN agencies, the Ministry of Social Development and Human Security (MSDHS); the National

Economic and Social Development Board, Thailand; the Ministry of Labour; the Social Security Office; the Ministry of Finance; and the civil society, and co-chaired by the International Labour Organization (ILO) and MSDHS (Schmitt et al. 2013, xiv, 22).

2 The Constitution was revoked in May 2014.

3 Basic medical services include help in dressing wounds, pain management, medication, health monitoring, prevention, rehabilitation, and palliative care. Social services are lower-level care, such as home help or help in instrumental activities of daily living, including homemaking, meals, transport, and social activities. Chronic care is a broader concept that refers to partnership between patients and families, healthcare teams, and community supporters, including medical, nursing, and social programmes. (WHO, 2007, 6–7).

4 There are four types of government agencies: ministerial agencies, state or public enterprises, public organisations, and government agencies in new form consisting of independent entity and juristic person funds or funds with legal entity (OPDC, 2008, 9). The latter two types are not discussed in the report because they are managed independently and access to data on their social protection (SP) and financial costs is difficult.

5 Government officials who started official duty before 27 March 1997 and chose to enroll in the GPF can undo the GPF membership and return to the GPOS under the law newly stipulated in late 2014 on "Returning to the Pension System under the Government Pension Fund Act, B.E.2494, more commonly known as UNDO Law" (GPF, 2013b).

6 Temporary government employees consist of those paid by government budget and those by local or agencies budget (CGD 2012, 56).

7 As a temporary measure to cope with the impact of the 2011 floods, the government, in 2012, reduced workers' and employers' contributions from five percent to three percent for the first six months and from five percent to four percent for the last six months of 2012.

8 To be increased, since the minimum wage is higher than B4,800 per month.

9 As of 12 January 2016, US$1 = B35.35.8 or B100 baht = US$2.8.

10 www.m-society.go.th/ewt_news.php?nid=11837, accessed on 21 February 2015

11 The number is calculated from BOB (2013b) and is less than the number reported by the Ministry of Education of around 12.9 million. The detailed costs of free education by level of schooling can also be found in Liumjaraskool (2012, 21).

12 The GDP figure used is the actual GDP (current price) in 2013 of B11,897 million (NESDB 2015a, 15).

13 There was some misunderstanding before as the elderly already receiving pensions from some sources are considered not eligible for OALA. The issue was decided by the Council of State which ruled that the elderly are eligible for both OALA and other pensions.

14 The launching event of the report was held on 10 May 2013 at the Government House with the presence of Prime Minister Yingluck Shinawat.

15 Details are discussed in Chapter 5 of (Schmitt et al., 2013).

16 As noted, Thailand's average real GDP growth during the 2013–2015 period was only 2.1 percent, and the immediate prospects are not robust.

17 Assumptions of the RAP Assessment are given in Schmitt et al. (2013, 55–67).

18 The projected costs of each scenario are those in addition to the status quo.

19 The administration cost of scenario 1–5 (target all children) is relatively low at 5 percent. Scenario 6 (targets only poor children) has an administration cost that is 15 percent higher than the universal scheme.

20 The levels of benefits increase with age: B600 for the elderly 60–69 years old; B700 for the elderly 70–79 years old; B800 for the elderly 80–89 years old; and B1,000 for the elderly 90 years old and above. The benefits are not indexed to inflation.

References

Asher, M. G., and Y. Vora (2015). *India: Social Protection Floor, Presentation for the Third Meeting of ERIA Project on Social Protection Floors*. 1 August 2015, Chiang Mai (PowerPoint presentation).

Asian Development Bank (2013). *The Social Protection Index: Assessing Results for Asia and the Pacific*. Manila: ADB.

BOB (Bureau of the Budget) (2013a). *Expenditure Budget Report Summary, 2013 FY*. Bangkok: Bureau of the Budget, The Prime Minister Office (in Thai).

BOB (Bureau of the Budget) (2013b). *Expenditure Budget Report FY2013*, Vol. 3, No. 8(1), Ministry of Education, Bangkok: Bureau of the Budget, The Prime Minister Office (in Thai).

BOB (Bureau of the Budget) (2013c). *Expenditure Budget Report FY2013*, Vol. 3, No. 1, Central budget, Bangkok: Bureau of the Budget, The Prime Minister Office (in Thai).

BOB (Bureau of the Budget) (2013d). *Expenditure Budget Report FY2013*, Vol. 3, No. 6, Ministry of Interior, Bangkok: Bureau of the Budget, The Prime Minister Office (in Thai).

Bureau of Empowerment for Older Persons. Available at www.oppo.opp.go.th/pages/law/law_06.html (accessed 20 February 2015).

Chamchan, C., and K. Apipornchaisaskul (2012). *A Situation Analysis on Health System Strengthening for Migrants in Thailand, Supported by World Health Organization and European Union*. Thailand: Institute for Population and Social Research.

Comptroller General's Department (CGD) (2012). *Handbook on Welfare Benefits for Government Permanent/Temporary Employees*. Bangkok: Ministry of Finance (in Thai).

Department of Empowerment of Persons with Disabilities (DEPD) (2015). *Statistics of Disabled People, 2015*.Disability Information Center, Available at: http://ecard.nep.go.th/nep_all/file/Stat_Mar58.pdf (accessed 1April 2015).

Fiscal Policy Office (2011). *National Saving Fund, Ministry of Finance* (PowerPoint presentation, in Thai).

Government Pension Fund (2013a). *2013 Annual Report*.

Government Pension Fund (2013b). *Presentation Issues*. 16th Anniversary, 21 June 2013 (PowerPoint presentation, in Thai).

Government Policy (2014). Available at www.cabinet.thaigov.go.th/bb_main31.htm (accessed 1 November 2015).

Jitsuchon, S. et al. (2011). *Towards Social Welfare System for All in 2017, Submitted to Thai Health Promotion Foundation*. Bangkok: Thailand Development Research Institute (in Thai).

Kanjanaphoomin, N. (2004). *Pension Fund, Provident Fund and Social Security System in Thailand*, International Conference on Pensions in Asia: Incentives, Compliance and Their Role in Retirement. Tokyo, February 23–24.

Liumjaraskool, N. (2012). *An Analysis of the Costs of Education of Households Under the Free Education Program*. Public Policy Study Institute, Chiangmai University (in Thai).

Ministry of Social Development and Human Security (2010). Available at: www.m-society.go.th (accessed February 2010).

National Economic and Social Development Board (2004). *Thailand Millennium Development Goals Report 2004*. Bangkok.

National Economic and Social Development Board (2014). *Report on the Analysis of Poverty and Inequality in Thailand in 2012*.Bangkok (in Thai).

National Economic and Social Development Board (2015a). *GDP in 4th Quarter 2013 and Economic Trend 2014*, Press Release, 17 February 2014.

National Economic and Social Development Board (2015b). *Number and Budget of People Receiving Old Age Allowance, Disability Allowance and AIDS Patient Allowance 1994–2014*. Available at: www.m-society.go.th/ewt_news.php?nid=11837 (accessed 14 June 2015).

National Health Security Office (2013). *Annual Report 2013.*Ministry of Public Health, Bangkok (in Thai).

National Saving Fund (2015). Available at: www.nsf.or.th (accessed 18 August 2015).

National Voluntary Presentation (2014). *For the Annual Ministerial Review (AMR) at ECOSOC 2014 On the Theme 'Addressing Ongoing and Emerging Challenges For Meeting the Millennium Development Goals in 2015 and For Sustaining Development Gains in the Future'*. Bangkok: NESDB.

Office of Civil Service Commission (2012). *Handbook For the Government Employee Administration*. Bangkok: Office of the Prime Minister (in Thai).

Office of Fiscal Economics (2011). *National Saving Fund*, (In Thai, Power point).

Office of the Public Sector Development Commission (OPDC) (2008). *Structural Organization of Government Agencies Under the Administration's Authority* (in Thai).

Ortiz, Isabel, M. Cummins, and K. Karunanethy (2015). *Fiscal Space for Social Protection: Options to Expand Social Investments in 187 Countries*, ESS Working Paper no. 48, Geneva: ILO.

Paitoonpong, S. (2012). *Social Protection in East Asia, in Asian Development Institute*. 6th Workshop on Social Protection in East Asia Proceedings, Seoul: Seoul National University.

Post Today (2015). 19 March 2015. www.posttoday.com (accessed 1 May 2015).

Provident Fund Act B.E. 2530. (1987).

Schmitt, V., T. Sakunphanit, and O. Prasitsiriphol (2013). *Social Protection Assessment Based National Dialogue: Towards a Nationally Defined Social Protection floor in Thailand*. Bangkok: ILO and the United Nations Country Team in Thailand (UNCTT).

Security Exchange Commission (2015). *Provident Fund Statistics 2014.* Licensing Department, Bangkok.

Social Security Office (2008). *Annual Report 2008*. Bangkok.

Social Security Office (2013). *Annual Report 2013*. Bangkok.

Srianan, N. (2002). *Healthcare Insurance System for Civil Servants and State Enterprise Officials*, Research Report No. 9, The Monitoring and Evaluation of Universal Health Coverage in Thailand, First Phase 2001/2002'. Bangkok: TDRI (in Thai).

Suwanrada, W. (2014). *National Experiences From Thailand Regarding Long-Term Care of Older Persons*, Regional Expert Consultation on Long-term Care of Older Persons, 9–10 December 2014, Bangkok: ESCAP.

Thai TV 3 (2015) (in Thai), January 20. Available at www.thaitv3.com; accessed on 10/2/2015

Thailand Development Research Institute (2013). *The Development of Guidelines for Health Insurance System Governance*. Bangkok (in Thai).

Thailand Development Research Institute (2015). *Integration of National Pension Systems, Brain-Storming Workshop*, 24 April 2015 (PowerPoint presentation, in Thai).

Wedel, Y. (2012). *Kingdom of Thailand: Updating and Improving the Social Protection Index*, Technical Assistance Consultant's Report, ADB.

Workmen Compensation Fund (WCF) (2013). Annual Report 2013. Available at: http://www.sso.go.th/wpr/uploads/uploadImages/file/AnnualReportBook 2556.pdf); accessed 1/4/2015

World Health Organization (WHO) (2007). *Financing Long-Term Care Programmes in Health Systems: With a Situation Assessment in Selected High-, Middle- and Low-Income Countries.* Geneva: World Health Organization.

8 Social protection system in Vietnam

An assessment

Nguyen Thi Lan Huong

1. Introduction

This chapter analyses Vietnam's social protection system in the context of global initiatives for social protection, and suggests options for reforming the system, including how to generate additional financing for the programs. Generating additional fiscal space has acquired greater importance due to less robust medium-term growth prospects for Vietnam.

In April 2009, the High-Level Committee on Programmes of the UN Chief Executives Board adopted the Social Protection Floor (SPF) as one of its Joint Crisis Initiatives, with the ILO and the WHO as lead agencies. This initiative encouraged countries to plan and implement sustainable social transfer schemes and essential social services. As this objective transcends the mandate of any single body or agency, the Initiative built a global coalition comprising UN agencies, the IMF, and the World Bank, as well as development partners and leading NGOs.

The SPF promotes income security through a basic set of guarantees (see Overview chapter). The term "guarantees" also implies that in principle benefit access is underwritten by effective legal entitlements, but leaves a maximum flexibility for national adaptation. In practice, however, such 'guarantees' are not easily enforced, at least not fully.

Transfers may be organised as universal benefits (as in the case of universal tax-financed pensions or a universal national health service), as social insurance schemes with near-complete population coverage (which may mean subsidised insurance coverage for some population groups), or a combination thereof; they may be conditional or unconditional, or organized as social assistance schemes that guarantee access to income security and health care only for those who have no other coverage. What is important is that everyone who is in need of income transfers or health services can access at least some transfers in cash or in kind and is not confronted with obstacles that effectively exclude them from coverage.

Classifying the components of the floor as guarantees could create flexibility that makes the concept of a social protection floor compatible with a variety of national social protection systems. It may be useful to review Vietnam's recent growth, demographic, and labor market trends.[1]

Vietnam's economic reforms undertaken during the period from 1986 to 2016 (and still ongoing) have played an important role in providing a solid foundation for economic growth, including creating better jobs and higher living standards, and poverty reduction. The data on economic indicators in the subsequent paragraphs are from the World Bank's Development Indicators (World Bank, 2016). Though the world financial crisis heavily affected Vietnam from 2009 to 2012, the country's GDP grew (in 2010 prices) at an annual rate of 5.8 percent from 2008–2014. The GDP per capita grew by 5.2 percent per year (in current value), with per capita income of US$3,133 in PPP terms.

In 2014, the population reached 90.7 million with an annual population growth of 1.1 percent (since 2008). Around 30 percent of people live in urban areas and nearly 70 percent live in rural areas. The share of elderly (aged 60 and above) increased rapidly from 7.7 percent in 2009 to 10.9 percent in 2014. At the same time, the number of children aged from 0–14 years decreased slightly from 21.5 percent of total population in 2009 to 21.0 percent in 2014. The disabled share of total population also decreased, from 7.8 percent to 7.4 percent.

In 2014, 53 million out of 54 million people in the labor force were employed. For the period 2009–2014, the total employment increased by 2.5 percent per year. In 2014, skilled labour was about 18.6 percent of total labour force. Notably, the number of underemployed and unemployed was reduced from 4.6 million people in 2009 to 2.5 million in 2014, resulting in the reduction of the corresponding rate from 5.4 percent to 2.4 percent for the same period. Taking unemployment alone, in 2013, total unemployment was 1.1 million, equivalent to 2 percent of the labour force. The contributory reasons for reduction of unemployment and underemployment included the introduction of an unemployment benefit program in 2009 as well as the vocational programs training people in rural areas.

The national poverty line increased from VND 299,320 per person per month for the period 2005–2010 to VND 590,000–740,000 for 2011–2015. In the last decade, economic growth and government support lowered the poverty rate from 11.3 percent in 2009 to 6.0 percent in 2014. However, there was a big gap between poverty rates among Kinh/Hoa and ethnic minorities. Vietnam has 54 ethnic groups. The poverty rate of ethnic minorities reached almost 40 percent. In 2014, ethnic minorities made up only 15 percent of total population but constituted 48 percent of the poor. In 2014, the rural poverty rate was 12.4 percent, 4 times higher than in urban areas.

Vietnam already achieved universal primary education in 2000 and for lower-secondary education in 2012. In 2014, attendance to pre-school by children of 5 years of age reached over 98 percent; primary education reached 98 percent; lower-secondary, 90 percent; and upper-secondary, 62 percent. Access to education has been increasing, especially for girls, children of ethnic minorities, children from poor households, and children with disabilities. Education in remote and ethnic minority areas has been remarkably improved.

In 2014, the mortality rate among children below 1 year of age was 15 percent. The mortality rate among children below 5 years of age was 22 percent. The malnutrition ratio among children below 5 years of age was 16.3 percent. The ratio of children who were stunted was reduced to 24 percent. In 2014, over 96 percent of pregnant women received tetanus vaccinations; 83.4 percent of pregnant women received medical check-ups; and more than 90 percent of children below 1 year old received full vaccinations. Life expectancy at birth was at 73.2 years in 2014. Some digestive diseases (typhoid, shigella), meningitis, and many infectious diseases, especially those that can be prevented by vaccination (diphtheria, pertussis, and meningitis) have been remarkably reduced.

The rest of the chapter is organized as follows. Section 2 briefly enumerates five factors which Vietnam needs to address as it aims to progress towards higher level of social development. This is followed by a discussion of the current social protection system in section 3. A brief discussion of SPF gaps in Vietnam is presented in section 4.

2. Factors impacting social development in Vietnam

There are five factors which Vietnam needs to consider as is aspires to progress towards higher levels of social development.

2.1 Socio-economic

As an emerging economy that is increasingly integrated into the global economy, Vietnam will continue to be exposed to global trends and external economic shocks. Further, the overall socio-economic development and changes in family structures (e.g., migrant workers who do not live with their parents or family) pose new challenges. In the future, the social protection system will have to target these new groups. As an example, implementing a general social assistance benefit for all people in need could merit serious consideration.

2.2 Demographic risks

The population in Vietnam has recently completed its transition from high to low mortality and fertility. The population is still young. In 2010, more than 26 percent were in the age group of 0–14 years and only 8.6 percent were older than 60 years. In 2014, 21 percent were aged 0–14 years, while 11 percent were older than 60 years. It is projected that the median age will increase from 27.9 years in 2009 to 40.5 years in 2049, an increase of 12.6 years in 40 years. At the same time the percentage of the elderly aged 65 and above will almost triple, from 6.4 percent in 2009 to 18.9 percent in 2049. These trends pose major challenges for the social insurance schemes.

With rapid ageing, the number of pensioners above 75 years of age will rise rapidly, requiring measures for what is usually referred to as 'eldercare'.

2.3 Informal economy

In 2014, around 11.4 million workers were covered by the social insurance scheme, accounting for only 21 percent of the labour force. This suggests that 4 out of 5 workers are not insured. Social health protection covers around

71 percent of the whole population, but its financing is primarily from the government subsidies. Moreover, according to the current estimates, nearly one million people enter the labour market every year, while the formal and agricultural sectors are unable to employ all these people. Even with impressive economic growth, around 25 percent of new entrants into the labour market end up in the informal sector. The informal economy is therefore expected to grow.

2.4 Inflation

Inflation poses a continuing challenge for the social protection system, even though the rate of consumer price inflation has dropped from 19.9 percent in 2008 to 9.2 percent in 2012 and further to 4.1 percent in 2014. On average, the annual growth rate of CPI has been 10.8 percent, much higher than the target of under 7 percent per year. The challenge lies in how an SP benefit allowance, especially for pensions, will keep pace with inflation in the future.

2.5 Climate change

Most of the population lives in low-lying river basins or coastal areas. Because of this, more than 70 percent of the population is estimated to be exposed to risks from multiple natural hazards, such as storms, typhoons, floods, flash floods, landslides, and droughts. In the last two decades, several hundred people died annually because of natural disasters. The official estimates suggest that annual economic loss was equivalent to 1.3 percent of GDP (PPP) or $3.6 billion in 2010. The overall social protection system will have to adapt to the burden of climate change in the next years. Due to population growth, socio-economic development, and rapid urbanization, the vulnerability of the population has continued to increase. This requires particular efforts in disaster risk reduction and social protection.

3. How the Social Protection Floor (SPF) is being approached in the country

Social protection has a long tradition in Vietnam. As early as 1945 – after its independence – the first measures were implemented. But in the period before Vietnam introduced extensive reform or renovation in 1986, the social protection system was focused on public servants, army personnel, and workers in state-owned enterprises. In the past few decades, social protection coverage has expanded to other groups.

In Vietnam social protection involves "the set of public (social insurance / social assistance) and private interventions (non-statutory or private measures) designed to reduce poverty and vulnerability; it comprehends the enhancement of capacity of people and society in protecting themselves against hazards and interruption or loss of income; and assures social stability, development, and equality.

The current social protection system has four pillars: 1. active labour market programs (employment, minimum income and poverty reduction); 2. social and health insurance policies; 3. social assistance programs; and 4. basic social services that are designed to improve and safeguard people's rights, especially the security rights of the poor, the rural population, and other vulnerable groups.

3.1 Social protection initiatives in Vietnam

The Constitution of the Socialist Republic of Vietnam and the Social Economic Development Strategies, 2011–2020 (SEDS) act as key sources for the overall future development of the country. The revised 2013 Constitution states that all citizens have a right to social protection. The Constitution mandates the state to guarantee basic programs and policies on social protection areas, for specific groups, particularly old people, people with disabilities, or orphans without family support.

Box 8.1   Current development in social protection policies in Vietnam

Legal framework	Main feature
The Resolution 15-NQ/TW of Central Committee of the Communist Party of Viet Nam on "Some issues on social policies during the period of 2012–2020"	Update the definition, structure, main direction, main components of social protection system to 2020
Viet Nam Constitution (revised 2013)	Confirm the task of Government to assure SP rights of the citizens and delivery of SP programs
Labour code (revised 2013)	More priority given to women; better role of government to better job
Law on Employment (2013)- first time introduced	New legal frame work for employment creations (public work program); Concerning employment in both formal and informal environment
	Further development of Unemployment insurance (cover all workers with labour contract from 3 month++;
	Introduction of public work program for poor

Legal framework	Main feature
Law on Health Insurance (2014)	To assure to universal coverage of health insurance by 2020; Large subsidize of government to vulnerable groups
Law on Social Insurance (2015)	Further develop compulsory SI (cover workers with labour contract from 1 month and above; enhance the compliance of business sector)
	Further development of voluntary SI (flexible in terms of contribution and benefits levels
Decision 1956/2009/QĐ-TTg on vocational training for rural workers until 2020 (2009 and revised 2013)	Gives priority to the people of social welfare, people with merits, poor households, near poor households, ethnic minority people, people with disabilities, and people with acquired lands.

Source: country sources, 2014

Besides the state, informal and family safety nets still play a major role in Vietnam. Accordingly, the Constitution acknowledges the important role of family and inter-generational support.

3.2 Social protection strategy for the years 2012–2020 (SPS)

Vietnam has a fairly extensive set of social security programmes in place. In 2012, the Government of Vietnam determined to develop a social protection system that is relevant to a middle-income country and the international standards in order to increasingly realize basic human rights. *It should be noted that, for the first time, the Communist Party of Vietnam announced its concern to develop social policies in Vietnam, which included two main areas: social protection and social policies for merit groups.*

The overall objective of SPS is to enhance the material and spiritual life of people with merits, striving for people with merits to have minimum living standards equal to or higher than the average standards in their areas by 2015 and to achieve social security for the whole population, ensuring minimum levels in income, education, housing, clean water, and information, making contributions to a gradual enhancement of incomes, ensuring secure living and the happiness of the people.

The main objectives of Social Protection 2012–2020 are shown in Box 8.2.

Box 8.2   The main objectives of social protection policy in Vietnam, 2012–2020

1. Implement the Law on Employment to cover all sectors. Pilot and develop public work programs. By 2020, the general unemployment rate should be below 3 percent and urban unemployment rate below 4 percent.
2. Increase, by 2020, the per capita income of poor households by 3.5 times compared to that of 2010. Reduce poverty rate by 1.5 percent – 2 percent per year and by 4 percent in poorest districts and communes.
3. By 2020, ensure that about 50 percent of labor force will participate in social insurance and 35 percent of work force contributes to the unemployment insurance.
4. Continue to expand the coverage with appropriate forms of support; gradually increase benefit levels of regular social assistance (RSA) in line with the availability of the state budget and with socio-economic development. By 2020, have more than 2.5 million beneficiaries of regular allowances, of which more than 30 percent receive social pensions.
5. Implement the emergency social assistance to timely support the people suffering from accidents, natural disasters, floods with losses in lives and to ensure the minimum levels of basic social services for the people, especially the poor, ethnic minority and disadvantaged people.
6. Ensure minimum education. By 2020, achieve net enrollment ratio of primary education at 99 percent, lower-secondary education at 95 percent; 98 percent of people from 15 ages up are literate, 70 percent trained workforce.
7. Ensure minimum health care. By 2020, more than 90 percent of children below 1 year old should have received full vaccination; rate of underweight and malnutrition among children under age of 5 reduced below 10 percent. Develop policies to encourage people, especially people with middle incomes, to participate in health insurance. By 2020, more than 80 percent of the population should participate in health insurance.
8. Ensure minimum housing.Address the challenges in land, planning, capitals, and procedures to enable businesses to implement social housing development projects. Provide incentives for enterprises to construct housing in industrial zones.
9. Ensure clean water. By 2020, 100 percent of rural population will have access to clean water, of which 70 percent will have access to clean water at national standards.
10. Ensure information access. By 2015, ensure that 100 percent of communes in mountainous, remote, border, and islands areas have radios and terrestrial television and 100 percent disadvantaged communes in border, safety zones, and coastal and island areas have communal radio stations.

Source: compiled by the Author from official source

The SPS is often asserted to be an engine of economic growth and development. This assertion finds rhetorical support among Vietnam's policymakers. The concept of social protection not only embraces social transfers but also brings into a consistent and comprehensive framework health care policies, labour market policies, social insurance policies, social welfare/assistance, poverty reduction programmes, and access to public social services.

4. An overview of social protection programs in Vietnam

4.1 Health care

The government aims to provide universal access to primary health care services and to also implement universal health insurance. The Ministry of Health (MOH) is responsible for policy development, while the Vietnam Social Security (VSS) is responsible for monitoring and disbursement of health insurance funds.

The government has implemented 1. the National Target Program on prevention of infectious and non-infectious diseases; 2. open vaccination; 3. reproductive health care; 4. children's nutrition and school health care; 5. the National Target Program on food safety; 6. the National Target Program on HIV/AIDS prevention and control; as well as many other measures on the enhancement of health care services and socialization of health care services.

The Health Insurance Law (1/7/2009), revised in 2013, aims at achieving universal health insurance by 2020. The promulgation of the Law on Health Insurance (HI) has shown the strong commitment of the government to fully or partly fund the health insurance contributions of vulnerable groups (i.e., the poor or near-poor, ethnic minority people, households with medium and lower incomes operating in agriculture, forestry, and salt industries, and beneficiaries of preferential social "treatment" and social assistance).

The total number of HI participants increased from 50.7 million in 2009 to 65.2 million in 2014. As a result, the coverage of HI expanded from 58.9 percent to 71.9 percent of the total population (VSS, 2015). The total number of compulsory HI increased from 46.1 to 58.4 million from 2009–2014, making up 89.5 percent of total HI beneficiaries in 2014. The number of participants in voluntary HI increased from 4.6 million to 6.8 million in 2014, but accounted for only 10.5 percent of total HI participants. According to the Ministry of Finance (2015), the revenues of HI rose rapidly due to the expansion of HI's participation and as the result of upward wage adjustments by the government. The turnover increased from VND 12.8 trillion in 2009 to VND 36.5 trillion in 2014. State subsidies have represented 45 per cent of total HI budget, around 1 per cent of GDP. The revenue of compulsory HI increased from about VND 8.9 trillion in 2009 to VND 20.1 trillion in 2014, with annual increase of 16.9 percent, but accounting for 55 percent of total HI turnover in 2014. The share of voluntary HI increased from 30.4 percent of the total in 2009 to 44.8 percent in 2014. HI revenue share significantly exceeds its share in total HI beneficiaries (10.5 per cent at the total in 2014) due to 1. the biased selection of the voluntary HI, with only people at high risk allowed to participate, and 2. the over-use of HI cards. Thus, we suggest that incentives need to be managed through better health governance.

There are a large number of special target groups who receive full or partial government subsidies. In 2009, the government subsidized payments for HI cards covering 23.5 million people, which account for 54.3 percent of total HI participants (15.9 were fully and 11.6 million were partly subsidized). In 2014, 38.8 million people were subsidized, accounting for 59.5 percent of HI, of whom 24.7 and 14.1 were fully and partly subsidized, respectively. According to official data, for the period 2009–2014, an average of 15.2 million people from poor and near- poor household was subsidized.

In 2009, the costs of subsidises on health insurance as a share of total health expenditure was 30.4 percent, but by 2014, it reached 38.9 percent (Table 8.1).

4.2 Social assistance

Social assistance (SA) is a pillar of social protection. SA provides benefits in cash or in kind, and this is a set of tax-financed social benefits to reduce poverty and vulnerability.

The SA policies in Vietnam are approached from a life cycle perspective and covered almost all beneficiary groups: children with difficult circumstances, working poor, elderly, and disabled.

Box 8.3 summarizes the social assistance policy system in Vietnam as the mix between the life cycle and the kind of beneficiaries.

Table 8.1 Select indicators of health care expenditure in Vietnam (million VND)

	2009	2010	2011	2012	2013	2014
Total expenditure	3,884	11,532	13,789	13,210	13,961	14,201
Cash monthly review (67/13)	235	567	750	1,285	1,631	1,738
Poor and ethnic minority,	2,376	5,042	6,207	5,894	6,051	6,216
Children under 6 year olds	0	2,980	3,446	3,886	4,043	4,094
Near poor	150	274	350	538	477	376
Students	1,123	2,669	3,036	1,605	1,758	1,774
Farmers participating in VSI	0	0	0	2	2	2
Subsidies /total health expenditure	30.4	57.7	59.1	39.7	41.5	38.9

Source: VSS, 2015

Box 8.3   Summary of policies and beneficiaries of regular social assistance by life cycle in Vietnam

No	Beneficiary group	Forms of assistance
1	**Children with difficult circumstances**	
	Orphaned both parents, abandoned children without nurturing source	Monthly cash transfer; tuition fee exemption; free health insurance card
	HIV infected people from poor households	
2	**Children under 6 years old**	
	Conditions as the group 1 from poor households	Support 70.000 dong/month/student for tuition fee
	Children of the public and non public staff who got industrial accidents or diseases enjoying the regular assistance allowance/near poor households	Reducing 50% of the tuition fee
	Children from the ethnic minority groups who are in nursery schools or public preschools	Assistance equivalent to 30% of the minimum wage/month
	Children under 6 years old	Fee health insurance card
3	**Children above 6 years old at primary school level**	
	For children the most economic difficult areas	15 kilograms of rice/month; Meal allowance: 40% MW; Housing allowance for students, 10% of MW
	Public primary schools	– Tuition fee exemption
	Children from the poor households in ethnic minority groups are studying in the schools of their villages	40% of MW
	Children in ethnic minority groups are studying in semi-boarding and boarding schools	equivalent to 60% of MW
	Poor households	Free health insurance cards
4	**Student in secondary schools and high schools**	
		15 kg of rice/month; Meal allowance: 40% of MW; Housing allow. for the students: 10% of MW
	Eligible conditions as the group 1 and 2, poor households, ethnic minority groups, especially difficult areas	Tuition fee exemption
	Eligible conditions as the group 1 and 2, poor households	Support VND 70,000 month/student for study expenses
	Eligible conditions as the group 1 and ethnic minority poor households	VND 120.000 per year per student for textbooks, and studying tools

No	Beneficiary group	Forms of assistance
	Children with disabilities	Reducing 50% of the tuition fee and contributions for school development
	Children from poor households in ethnic minority groups are studying in semi-boarding and boarding schools	60% of MW
	Children from poor households in ethnic minority groups are studying in semi-boarding and boarding schools at district level and semi boarding	100% of MW
	Poor households	Free health insurance cards
5	**Vocational training students/college and university students**	
	Students aged 16–18 years old studying intellectually or vocationally	Monthly cash transfer
	Vocational ethnic minority trainees at the boarding schools	Scholarship of 280.000 VND per student per month and other supports
	Children from ethnic minority, upland areas/parentless/ with disabilities / from poor households	Scholarship
	Ethnic minority students from poor households, studying at schools (university, college, professional and vocational secondary schools	100% of MW
	Poor households	Free health insurance cards
6	**People with disability**	
	People with serious disabilities having no ability to work or serve themselves.	Monthly cash transfer Free health insurance cards
	The people living with different mental diseases, have been treated repeatedly by health hospitals and clinics but have no improvement	
	HIV.AIDS infected people without working ability and from poor households	
	Single parent from poor HH with children under 16 years old; and children studying intellectually or vocationally under 18 years old.	Monthly cash transfer Free health insurance cards
7	**The elderly (from 60 years and above)**	
	Single elderly people from poor HH, elderly having no children or relatives to rely on, from poor households (by MOLISA poverty line).	Monthly cash transfer Free health insurance cards
	The elderly aged 80 years old and higher have no pension or social insurance allowance	

No	Beneficiary group	Forms of assistance
8	**Households**	
	Families and individuals who adopt orphans or abandoned children	Monthly cash transfer
		Free health insurance cards
	Households with two and more members with serious disabilities and having no capacity to serve themselves	
	Poor households	Electricity subsidy (46.000 dong/month)
	Ethnic minority households living in the areas uncovered by the electricity net	Monthly cash transfer of 46.000 dong

Source: MOLISA, 2014

The government of Vietnam is strongly committed to moving towards a social protection floor for all. As a result, a wide range of population has received the support. In 2014, the total beneficiaries were 64.2 million people, accounting for 41.4 percent of population (MOLISA, 2015).

The largest group of beneficiaries (around three-fifths) comprises those receiving health insurance subsidies, followed by education (around one-fifth), and social unemployment (around one-sixth). Those receiving regular cash payments had less than 5.0 percent share.

The budget for social assistance was 1.85 percent of GDP in 2010, but was reduced to 1.1 percent GDP in 2014 (MOLISA, 2015). This is mainly due to reduced expenditure on clean water and housing support, and on education, as the benefit levels have been increased slowly. In 2014, the largest share of total expenditure was on health insurance (33.6 percent), followed by the education subsidies (22.3 percent), and then on water and housing (12.8 percent) (MOLISA, 2015).

4.3 Social insurance

Social insurance is an emerging area of social protection in Vietnam. Initiatives to broaden coverage of social insurance included the inclusion of private sector employees in 1995, and the revision of social insurance for military and police forces. The recent period has exhibited acceleration towards a comprehensive system of social insurance.

The Social Insurance Law (SIL), introduced in 2009 (revised in 2014), has three areas of application: compulsory social insurance, voluntary insurance, and unemployment insurance. Box 8.4 provides a summary of the main characteristics of SI in Vietnam. Voluntary SI was introduced in 2006 and it has subsequently expanded, with maximum benefit reaching 75 percent of base salary. For compulsory SI, the contribution rate is 25 percent, which is a significant addition to the cost of formal employment. This may encourage less formal employment by some individuals and some employers.

In 2014, total number of SI participants was 11.5 million people: an increase of 5.1 percent per year from 2009. Nearly all of the contributors fall under the category "compulsory." The compliance rates for SI could be improved. In 2015, only 70 percent of the formal sector workers participated in the compulsory system. The participation of informal workers in voluntary system has been negligible at around 1 percent.

Box 8.4   Social insurance in Vietnam: key characteristics

Type of SI	Target group	Benefit schemes	Conditions to participate and benefits
Prior 1995			
Compulsory SI	Public Employees	05 benefits: sickness, maternity, work accident, occupational disease, survivorship and old age.	No contribution by employees. Government pay full benefits
From 1995–2003 (Follow SI Ordinary of Government Decision 12/CP dated 26/1/1995)			
Compulsory SI	Workers with labour contracts of 3 months in state agencies or foreign enterprises with more than 10 workers.	05 benefits: sickness, maternity, work accident, occupational disease, survivorship and old age.	based on the Pay As You Go principle, Defined benefit formula
From 2003–2006: Follow Government Decision dated 01/2003/NĐ-CP			
Compulsory SI	Workers with labour contracts of 3 months in all enterprises with more than 10 workers.	05 benefits: sickness, maternity, work accident, occupational disease, survivorship and old age.	based on the Pay As You Go principle, Defined benefit formula
Law on Social Insurance (2006)			
Compulsory SI (from 2007)	Workers with labour contracts of 3 months and above in all enterprises	05 benefits: sickness, maternity, work accident, occupational disease, survivorship and old age.	based on the Pay As You Go principle based on worker salary in labour contract

Type of SI	Target group	Benefit schemes	Conditions to participate and benefits
Voluntary SI (from 2008)	Workers in informal sector	02 benefits: survivor and old age pension	Contribution on worker income (not lower than MW)

Law on Social Insurance (2015)

Type of SI	Target group	Benefit schemes	Conditions to participate and benefits
Compulsory SI (from 2016)	Workers with labour contracts of 1 months and above in all enterprises	05 benefits: sickness, maternity, work accident, occupational disease, survivorship and old age.	based on the Pay As You Go principle based on worker salary in labour contract
Voluntary SI (from 2016)	Workers in informal sector	02 benefits: survivor and old age pension	Contribution on worker income

	Employees contribution	**Employer contribution**
Compulsory SI	8% of his/her salary;	17% (2 % to the sickness and maternity fund, 1% to the occupational accident and disease fund and 14% to the old age pension and survivor's fund).
Voluntary SI	22% of the income	Government might support to some groups (not identify yet)

Qualifying conditions for old age benefits

For both compulsory and voluntary SI:	The employee who has paid social insurance premiums for at least 20 years Reached the age of 60 for a man and 55 for a woman; or Reached the age from 55 to 60 for a man and from 50 to under 55 for a woman but worked at least 15 years in heavy, hazardous and dangerous occupations in the list issued by the Ministry of Labour, Invalids and Social Affairs and Ministry of Health or other conditions specified by Government.
Voluntary SI	Employees at retirement, but not have less than 15 years contribution can buy the missing years to until their social insurance premium payment period reaches 20 years.

Benefit level calculation

For the first 15 years contribution	45% of average salary of last 5 year salary if government employees 45% of average salary for the rest of workers
For each of additional year of contribution	Male: 2 % more but totally not exceed 75% of base salary Female: 3 % more, but totally not exceed 75% of base salary
Minimum benefits guaranty	For compulsory SI: Pension not lower than Minimum wage For voluntary SI: No guarantee

Source: MOLISA, 2013

Table 8.2 Vietnam: a summary of total revenue and expenditure for Social Insurance, all types, 2008–2014

	Years							Annual increase, (%)
	2008	2009	2010	2011	2012	2013	2014	
Total revenue (trillion VND)	30.9	37.6	50.0	62.5	84.7	106.9	130.8	28.1
CSI	30.9	37.5	49.9	62.3	84.3	106.3	130.1	28.0 s
VSI	–	0.1	0.2	0.3	0.4	0.6	0.7	
Total expenditure (trillion VND)	21.4	28.4	35.8	43.2	59.4	75.7	86.3	
CSI	21.4	28.4	35.8	43.2	59.4	75.6	86.1	26.8
VSI	–	–	–	–	–	0.1	0.2	26.8
Ratio expense/revenue, %	69.0	75.7	71.6	69.1	70.2	70.8	65.9	NA
CSI	69.0	75.8	71.8	69.3	70.5	71.1	66.2	NA
VSI	–	–	–	–	–	16.7	28.6	NA
								NA

Note: – = negligible; NA = not applicable
* Including the funding from government budget for CSI participants prior to 1995 (no contribution)
Source: VSS, 2015

There are three types of benefits under the SI: 1. Regular/monthly payment: for pension, survivor allowance and other monthly benefits; 2. The lump sum payments: for retirees, survivors (including funeral allowances), and workers with injuries or occupational diseases and retirees who do not meet the full 20 years of contribution; and 3. Short-term beneficiaries: this includes payments for sickness, maternity, labour accident, and professional disease.

In 2014, the share of total beneficiaries that received pensions was 23.5 percent (reduced from 37.9 percent in 2009); share of other regular payments (survivor and others) was 7.1 percent (also reduced from 12.4 percent); 62 percent received short-term payments (increased from 40.4 percent) and 7.5 percent received lump sum payments (reduced from 9.3 percent) (estimated from MOLISA, VSS 2015). Thus, short-term payments dominate among the beneficiaries. The total number of pensioners increased from 1.7 million people in 2009 to 2.2 million in 2014, implying an annual increase of 5.2 percent. Even then, only 22 percent of people aged 60 years and above benefitted from pensions (VSS, 2015). Extending pension coverage to the rest is still a challenge.

Two main sources of the revenue for SI are the contributions to CSI and VSI since 1995 and transfers from the government for CSI participants prior to 1995 (Table 8.2). During the 2008–2014 period, the SP revenue increased rapidly at an annual rate of 28 percent, reaching VND 130.7 trillion in 2014. Most of the revenue is still derived from the CSI.

4.4 Unemployment insurance

Since 2013, workers with labor contracts of twelve months and above have been covered. The workers contribute 1 percent of the monthly salary or remuneration; employers contribute 1 percent of the remuneration of the labourers who participate in unemployment insurance. The government supports 1 percent of the funding of the salaries and remuneration of labourers insured by unemployment insurance, which is transferred once a year. The fund is preserved and invested, with profits from it used to increase the fund. Box 8.5 summarizes benefits provided under unemployment insurance.

Box 8.5   A summary of four unemployment benefits in Vietnam

1. Unemployment allowance: The monthly unemployment allowance is equivalent to 60 percent of the average monthly salary or remuneration of six consecutive months before unemployment. The period of enjoying unemployment allowance is stipulated as follows: (i) three months,

if unemployment insurance premiums have been paid for between full twelve months and under thirty six months; (ii) six months, if unemployment insurance premiums have been paid for between full thirty six months and under seventy two months; (iii) nine months, if unemployment insurance premiums have been paid for between full seventy two months and under one hundred and forty four months; (iv) twelve months, if unemployment insurance premiums have been paid for full one hundred and forty four months and more.

2. Vocational Training Assistance: Persons who are on unemployment allowance shall be supported in vocational training for a period of no more than six months. The support level is equivalent to the level of expense for short-term vocational training in accordance with the law on vocational training.

3. Job seekers allowance: Persons who are on unemployment allowance shall be provided with employment consultancy and recommendation free of charge.

4. Health insurance: People who are on unemployment benefits are entitled to health insurance. Social insurance organizations shall pay health insurance premiums for persons who are on unemployment benefits. However, the time in which the person participated in the pension and survivors insurance is saved during the period when they are on unemployment benefits.

Source: MOLISA, Department of Employment, 2015

The total number of unemployment insured participants reached 9.4 million in 2014, equivalent to 17.5 per cent of the labour force. The ratio is much higher if only those in the formal labor markets are included. The number of unemployment insurance beneficiaries in 2014 was 0.5 million. In 2014, the total revenue from unemployment insurance was 11.8 trillion VND, while the expenditure was 4.5 trillion VND, implying that less than two-fifths of the revenue was paid as benefits. The actuarial studies regarding future receipt and benefit flows are not available. This gap needs to be addressed.

4.5 Labour Market Program (LMP)

Active Labour Market is one focal area of social protection in Vietnam. It consists of different instruments, such as vocational training, retraining, credit, rural labour migration, labour market and information. The targets of LMP are: the poor, the youth, rural workers, and other vulnerable workers.

The National Target Program on Employment (NTPE) was set up in 1992 under the Resolution 120/1992/NQ-HĐBT. The objective was to develop labour demand-supply connections and services to help the workers access labour market information. Especially in 2013, the government took the initiative to set up a platform for development of a legal framework for employment services, labour demand-supply connections, and to facilitate job searches.

Program to support education and vocational training

The purpose of the programs is to enhance human capital of vulnerable groups by providing subsidies for education, vocational training to enhance opportunities for disadvantaged people to promote employment, especially for poor households, households dependent on social welfare, and rural labourers.

Initiated in 1992, NTPE has played a significant role in creating jobs for vulnerable people. Up to 2009, every year, NTPE has enabled 0.2 million people to get employment, accounting for 15 percent of annual new employment created each year. Especially since 2009, when due to the economic crisis many people lost employment, NTPE has had an even more important role. In 2014, 2.2 million people benefited from the program, accounting for 0.31 percent of total employed people, with the cost estimated of 3,822 billion VND.

The evidence suggests that vocational programs have moderately helped the rural poor. In 2014, total beneficiaries reached 0.54 million people, accounting for 0.5 percent of total rural population or 1.5 percent of the rural employed population. There is, however, a need to give greater priority to vocational training, especially in rural areas.

Box 8.6   Summary of national target program on employment

NTPE policies include: preferential credits for business development and employment generation; development of labour markets information and public employment policy. The aim of NTPE is to create 200–300 jobs per year in order to reduce the unemployment rate under 5 percent for urban areas and increase productive time use for rural areas.

There are 4 projects included

1. *Employment creation support project:* using preferential credits in combination with training and job introduction, development labour market information to booster employment creation.
2. *Development of labour market information system project:* collection, update, process, analysis, utilization, dissemination, employment mapping, projection of labour markets and producing reports on labour

market trends. . . . Government initially manages and oversees the labour markets, supporting the connection of labour demand-supply.
3. Development of employment service centers project.
4. Staff development project.

Source: MOLISA, Department of Employment, 2015

5. SPF gaps in Vietnam: a brief discussion

In 2010, Vietnam received an official visit from Madam Michelle Bachelet, the UN Deputy President, to encourage implementation of SPF. In 2011, the ILO report on Vietnam SP was realised to show how much it would cost Vietnam to implement the concept of SPF.

For the years from 2012 to the current date, several efforts were made by the government to strengthen social protection systems in Vietnam: The Constitution 2013 has assured a rights-based approach on social protection; a new law was passed on employment (2012); a revised Social Insurance law was created (2014), a health insurance law was revised (2013) in order to close the gap between the current SP policies and the SPFs.

MOLISA, MOF and other government agencies are encouraged to work together on finding the solutions to closing the SPF gap. In 2014, the government borrowed from the World Bank to reform the social assistance program.

5.1 Health care and health insurance (HI)

There are no design gaps in terms of coverage which could be detected in the health insurance program. Government policies clearly state the objective to close the coverage gaps by 2020. The revised HI law was developed to achieve population coverage until 2020. There are, however, many implementation gaps. These may be stated as follows.

1. Access to health care is not equal among the population and the inequality is increasing (among income groups, ethnicities, locations, residential statuses, and gender). People in many urban areas and economically developed areas are facing the phenomenon of obesity among both children and adults.
2. The grassroots health care services face many limitations: although almost all communes have health care stations; many stations are degrading, and have shortages of medical staff, poorly qualified medical personnel, and unbalanced human resources.
3. The mobilisation of resources for health care has been limited.
4. The remaining direct and indirect out-of-pocket health care costs (48 percent) are exceeding affordability for poor households and vulnerable groups.

Moreover, the ratio of coverage among some population groups is low. By 2014, nearly 30 percent of the population had not yet participated in health insurance, of which 87 percent are near-poor, 66 percent are workers from cooperatives, and 47 percent are workers from private enterprises. Though children below 6 years old are fully subsidized, only 81.3 percent of them have been covered. Also, only 76 percent of students and pupils participate, despite subsidy levels for health card costs being 30 percent. The benefits and services of health insurance are limited. The state budget still has to bear most of the expenses for health insurance. Reimbursements through health insurance are easily abused due to corrupt practices in finance and medication.

5.2 Income security for children

The following gaps have been noted in the numerous programs targeted at poor children.

First, there is no general child benefit that provides for income security of children. Second, the existing social assistance programs for children exhibit low coverage due to tight eligibility criteria. Low levels of benefits are failing to ensure subsistence living standards and sustainable poverty reduction. There are some overlaps among the beneficiaries, policies, and resources of poverty reduction programs.

In addition, implementation gaps also exist. These include inadequate coverage of migrant children; lack of awareness of policies and programmes; and absence of unified registry of beneficiaries for social assistance; fragmentation of the responsibilities for monitoring and evaluation are divided among different levels within MOLISA and DOLISA branches, with no consistent and standardized procedure at the national level; and the limited resources for implementation are dispersed between too many programs, adversely affecting outcomes.

5.3 Income security and employment opportunities for the working age population

The main gaps in policy are the limited capacity of the economy to generate employment; low job security due to technological and other factors; area-based social assistance programmes resulting in substantial protection gaps for workers in informal employment in urban and near-urban areas; unemployment insurance and maternity protection reaching only a minority of workers, particularly in the informal sector. Less than 20 percent of the working age population in 2014 was covered by maternity benefits; and labour market policies are underfunded, as indicated by only 0.14 percent of GDP spent on them in 2014.

Vietnam remains an agricultural and rural labour surplus market, with labour supply unevenly distributed. It has limited transition abilities. Moreover, the labour market information system fails to satisfy the needs of the employers and labourers, with no national database on labour markets. The ESCs are mostly located in the urban areas and provide limited information on demand, and so only small proportion of enterprises and workers find employment there. There is very limited support for workers migrating to industrial zones and urban areas. Many legal regulations even restrict the access of migrants to better employment and basic social services in the urban areas.

5.4 Social assistance

The main gaps are that many SA programs have very limited coverage and benefit levels (only one-third of poverty line)[2], particularly the disabled and single parents; effectiveness of some programs, for example electricity subsidies to poor households, is low. There is a lack of effective measures for people with chronic poverty, and for children and the vulnerable against shocks such as natural disasters, economic downturns, restructuring.

There are also implementation gaps with other SP programs, such as for children. Policy coherence and organizational coordination need to improve substantially.

5.5 Income security for the elderly

For contributory pensions, the main gaps are that despite the opportunities to join the social insurance scheme on a voluntary basis, there is no general income support for informal workers (close to 70 per cent of total employment)[3]; low compliance rate among enterprises leading to low coverage (one-fifth); and mismatch between contributions and benefits[4]

For non-contributory pensions, the main gap is the limited coverage of social pensions for persons aged 60–80. The level of benefits is also low, equal to around 25 percent of minimum living standards, even lower than the poverty line (for both rural and urban).

6. Estimating SPF costs in Vietnam

6.1 Estimated additional costs of completing the social protection floor

This section reports on the **additional** cost estimates for SPF in Vietnam, based on the report on "Costing and Financial Projections to Implement Social Protection Policies 2011–2020 for Vietnam", representing preliminary rapid assessment undertaken by the UN country team and MOLISA/ILSSA team, jointly. The exercise covered only a **limited** set of SP measures, and not the full impact of age-related additional pensions, health care, and other expenditures.[5]

The main objective of the report was to support the implementation planning of social protection strategy in Vietnam by using the SPF approach and tools. This was done by taking stock of the social protection situation through a mapping exercise of all existing and planned social protection schemes, actors, institutions, strategies, legislations, assessments, and studies; carrying out a quantitative and qualitative analysis of the social protection system and strategy, in terms of covered population, benefit levels and adequacy of benefits, availability and quality of social services, good practices and weak points, priority needs, potentials and constraints; and facilitating a dialogue in order to identify priority areas for government interventions, based on the stocktaking exercise and on the design and costing of the corresponding programs and schemes. We also undertook a fiscal space analysis to support decision making.

6.2 Social protection floor rapid assessment matrix

The assessment matrix is a tool to analyse to what extend existing and future social protection provisions match the benchmarks set by the four guarantees of the social protection floor and to support the identification of policy priorities to complete the floor. The matrix analyses the present (and future) social protection situation, and identifies design gaps and implementation gaps.

The steps to facilitate the implementation of social protection for Vietnam were identified as follows:

1. to define the policy options that Vietnam has planned to implement for next years to achieve universal coverage for the people;
2. to use SPF RAM to estimate the cost of the different policy options, in order to project the government budget.
3. forecasting Vietnam's socio-economic development by the year 2030 to facilitate projection of costs of SPF.

The costing exercise was designed to provide a rough estimate of cost in Vietnamese dong as well as in percent of GDP and government expenditure of ***additional*** social protection provisions in order to develop a comprehensive social protection floor in Vietnam. It follows that well considered policy decisions on social protection cannot be based on recognizing only the additional costs of the limited measures examined.

The main limitations of any such studies (as identified in the Thailand chapter in this volume) also apply in this case. In particular, such Rapid Assessment results are not a substitute for more detailed actuarial and other analysis if the intention is to use the conclusions for policy formulation and implementation.

The ILO Report listed the selected policy options that Vietnam could choose to implement within the next several years.

6.3 For beneficiaries receiving monthly cash: three options

Option 1 (baseline case)

*   There is no change in the policy on beneficiaries, but the benefit level will be adjusted with annual CPI.

Option 2: higher benefits are given to income security for the elderly and children and to those working in the informal sector

- The benefit to be adjusted with SPI, and
- Expanding the number of beneficiaries to cover the following:

    - For the elderly: Extend the existing non-contributory social pension for individuals 75 years old and above (instead of the current practice of 80 years old and above)
    - For the children: Extend the child allowance for all poor children aged 0–15 years old (instead of poor children with special circumstances)

Option 3: Base on option 2, but increase the level of benefits 1 from 20 percent of minimum living standards (now) to 40 percent of minimum living standards. For support of basic social services, the options considered were:

- For health insurance: Follow government plan to expand the coverage for health insurace;
- For education exemption: Follow current government policies to support;
- For electicity support: Follow current government policies to support;
- For housing, clean water: Follow current government policies to support;

For unemployment insurance, the options considered were follow current government policies to support (1 percent of contribution on unemployment insurance).

Options for support for working people to participate in voluntary social insurance was 30 percent of the eligible persons participating in voluntary social insurance.

6.4 Result of forecast of beneficiaries

Option 1: baseline case

1. Total number of social assistance targets according to Decree 67, 13 and 136

There is no change in the policy regarding beneficiaries and benefit levels, but the benefit level for targets according to Decree 67,13,136 are to be adjusted with annual CPI.

In this option, the monthly cash received will follow the current policies (decree 67/2007/ND-CP, 13/2010/ND-CP, 136/2013/ND-CP), so the number of beneficiaries would increase slowly (under 2 percent per year). The poor households will depend on the change of poverty line for the period 2016–2020, 2021–2025, and 2026–2030.

The total number of beneficiaries will reach 2,799 million people in 2015, then 3,037 million in 2020 and 3,737 million in 2030. The coverage will be 3.06 percent of population in 2015 and 3.62 percent of population in 2030 (Table 2.4). Among the beneficiaries:

- The share of the elderly aged 80 years old and older takes 57.1 percent in 2015, but it reduces slightly to 49.2 percent in 2030.
- The total number of disabled people (severely disabled people; people with mental illness and families having 2 or more people with serious disabilities), increased from nearly 1 million people to 1.62 million in 2030. This group accounts for the second largest proportion, takes 35.7 percent in 2015, increased to 43.1 percent in 2030.
- The total number of children (parentless children, abandoned children, children having no parents and families, orphans, adopted) reduced from nearly 70 thousand to 49 thousand in 2008, resulting in decrease of children's share for 2.4 percent to 1.5 percent of the total beneficiaries for the same period.

2. Basic social service

As noted, besides the regular cash transfer, government has subsidised other target groups, for health care, education fees, textbooks; electricity, drinking water, and housing. Thus, the number of people receiving HI cards and health care services reached 39.0 million in 2015 and is projected to increase to 44.4 million in 2030, equivalent 43 percent of total population.

Between 2015 and 2030, the total workers getting subsidies for employment insurance will increase from 10.1 million to 19.3 million. The corresponding share of population will increase from 11 percent to 18.7 percent for the same period.

3. For supporting workers to participate in voluntary social insurance

If support is provided only to farmers, the number will increase from 0.4 million (0.4 percent of population) in 2015 to 9.4 million (9.1 of population) in 2030.

4.3.2 Option 2: expanding beneficiaries

1. Total number of social assistance targets according to Decree 67, 13 and 136

The eligibility of beneficiaries is adjusted:

1. The elderly from 75 years old can benefit from monthly social assistance, instead of from 80 years old as before; and
2. The coverage of the child beneficiaries would be all children below 15 years in poor households (instead of only children with difficult circumstances).

Official projections are that the number of children below 15 years old, under the poor household category, will be 0.8 million in 2015, but will increase to 1.2 million in 2030.

The number of elderly aged 75 years old and older without pension or social insurance allowance will increase from 2.18 million people in 2015, to 2.6 million in 2030.

The total number of social assistance targets according to Decree 136/2013/ND-CP would be 4.3 million in 2015 and increase to around 6 million in 2030, far higher than in Option 1.

The share of population for all social assistance targets under Decree 13/2010 would be around 4.75 percent in 2015 and 5.84 percent in 2030.

2. *The total beneficiaries from social services, unemployment, and voluntary social insurance under option 2 will be the same as in Option 1.*

4.3.3 Option 3: combination of expanding beneficiaries and adjusting benefit levels, according consumer price index

This option is combination with Option 2 (expanding the beneficiaries) and expanding the benefit levels.

As indicated, the benefit levels for social assistance targets according to Decree 67,13 and 136 will be increased from 20 percent of minimum living standards to 40 percent.

1. *Total number of social assistance targets according to Decree 67, 13 and 136 will the same as in Option 1.*
2. *The total beneficiaries from social services, unemployment, and voluntary social insurance under option 2 will as the same as in the option 1 and 2.*

Option 3 is closed to achieving fuller progress toward SPF goals, so it is recommended. Table 8.3 summarizes social protection expenditure for the 2012–2014 period. The share of expenditure on social protection increased from 5.9 percent of GDP in 2012 to 6.6 percent in 2014. The government expenditure on social protection was 18.7 percent of the total in 2012 and 21.5 percent in 2014.

Table 8.4 provides macroeconomic and other projections for Vietnam underlying the projected results for the three options. The real GDP growth is estimated to remain high at around 7 percent, and inflation rate to remain constant at 6 percent between 2015 and 2030.

Table 8.5 summarizes the estimated costs of the three options, with Option 3 predictably costing much more relative to GDP in all years. But the costs as a portion GDP declines rapidly between 2015 and 2030, while absolute VND costs increase. Thus, for Option 3, absolute costs increase from 62.2 trillion VND in 2015 to 158.9 trillion VND in 2030, while corresponding share of GDP declines from 1.43 percent to 0.61 percent, only 43 percent of the 2015 level. This is

Table 8.3 Vietnam's government spending on social protection, 2012–2014

	2012	2013	2014
1. Total, trillion VND			
Gov. spending on social protection	190.9	210.2	259.8
GDP, current price	3,245.4	3,584.3	3,937.9
Total government expenditure	1,022	1,115	1,217
2. %			
Gov. expenditure on SP/GDP	5.9	5.9	6.6
Gov. expenditure on SP/total Gov. expenditure	18.7	18.9	21.4

Source: ILSSA Estimation

Table 8.4 Projection of some selected socio-economic indicators till 2030 for Vietnam

Year	2015	2020	2025	2030
CPI (%)	6	6	6	6
GDP growth (%)	6	6.8	7.2	7
GDP current price (trillion VND)	4,340	7,863	14,170	26,106
Population (thousand people)	91,583	96,179	100,129	103,161
Population in working age (thousand people)	70,189	74,060	78,066	82,170
Workforce (thousand people)	54,747	58,507	62,453	66,147
Employed workers (thousand)	53,478	57,150	61,005	64,613
Poor household rate (%)	4.4	4.18	6.88	3.97
Minimum wage (thousand dong)	1,150	1,500	2,100	2,550
Urban poverty line	800	1070	1432	1916

Source: ILSSA calculate, 2015

Table 8.5 Estimated *additional* costs for 3 options in Vietnam

	2015	2020	2025	2030
1. Total costs, trillion VND				
PA 1:	43.0	55.5	81.6	112.9
PA 2	56.9	73.1	105.3	149.4
PA 3	62.2	79.3	112.2	158.9
2. % of GDP				
PA 1:	0.99	0.71	0.58	0.43
PA 2	1.31	0.93	0.74	0.57
PA 3	1.43	1.01	0.79	0.61

Source: ILSSA calculations

Table 8.6 Estimation of government revenue and expenditure till 2030 for Vietnam

	2015	*2020*	*2025*	*2030*
% of Government expenditure/ GDP	30.7	30.5	30.3	30
Government expenditure (trillion VND)	1,332	2,398	4,293	7,832
% government revenue/GDP	27.4	27.6	27.7	27.9
Government revenue (trillion VND)	1,189	2,170	3,925	7,284
Government expenditure +SPF (trillion VND)	1,394	2,477	4,406	7,991
% Gov. expenditure+SPF/GDP	32.1	31.5	31.1	30.6
Gov. deficit, % (without additional costs of Option 3)	3.3	2.9	2.6	2.1
Gov. deficit because of SPF, % if Option 3 Accepted	4.7	3.9	3.4	2.7
additional deficit %	1.4	1.0	0.8	0.6

Source: ILSSA calculate, 2015

a curious result requiring further analysis. In particular, simulation studies are needed which vary macroeconomic and other assumptions.

Table 8.6 shows the forecast of the impact of closing the gaps in the current system and SPFs. The revenue-to-GDP ratio is projected to increase only slightly, from 27.6 percent of GDP in 2020 to 27.9 percent in 2030, while corresponding figures for government expenditure exhibit a slight decline, from 30.5 percent in 2020 to 30.0 percent in 2030.

As a result, the government deficit will be reduced from 3.3 percent in 2015 to 2.9 percent in 2020 and further to 2.1 percent in 2030. The basis for projecting overall government expenditure and revenue, however, is not explained.

With the introduction of the SPFs (Option 3), the impact on government deficit is more serious from 2015–2025, but then the burden is projected to be reduced sharply. This is due to the projected *additional* cost falling sharply from 1.4 percent of GDP in 2015 to only 0.63 percent in 2030. It simply mirrors the results of Table 8.5. No reasons have been advanced for this curious result.

- In 2015: the additional cost would be 1.4 percent, leading to government deficit being increased to 4.7 percent;
- In 2020, the additional cost would be 1 percent, and government deficit will be 3.9 percent.
- In 2025, the additional cost would be 0.8 percent, and government deficit will be 3.4 percent.
- In 2030, additional costs will be less, only 0.6 percent of GDP, and the government deficit will be less, about 2.7 percent.

6.5 *Measures needed to fund the projected SPF costs*

The additional costs and deficits would be reduced with introduction of the following measures:

1. Vietnam needs to increase the participation of taxpayers

The personal income tax contributes only 0.5 percent of GDP.[6] According to the OECD report,[7] the tax system in Vietnam is rather progressive but only a minority of income earners (14 percent-17 percent) in the top deciles are required to pay taxes. There is therefore a strong case for reforming the taxation system (covering more income groups, as well as improving tax payment compliance), to help gain revenue from the income tax. *Expanding social protection, and higher retirement age, could increase social security contributions and tax revenue.*

Increase of social protection coverage from 21 percent of the labour force to 50 percent in 2020 could lead to an increase of the revenue from SP contributions, which can be used by government to make SP more sustainable;

- Higher retirement age could increase the tax contribution, as those with seniority in government benefitting from this measure have incomes subject to income tax.
2. Focus on broad-based high economic growth.
3. Budget reform

Such reforms could focus on enhancing revenue and rationing unproductive expenditure (such as reducing the subsidies on electricity to poor households); narrowing tax exemptions; broadening revenue base, as by introducing tax on property; and curtailing non-efficient spending; rationalize tax and customs tariff deductions and exemptions; and improve expenditure management to obtain better outcomes from the same budgetary expenditure.

4. Taking effective measures to address contingent liability and fiscal risk from the banking sector, strengthening of the state enterprises, and increases in non-tax revenue are possible avenues to generate fiscal space in this category.

The above will, however, require much greater focus on improving Vietnam's public financial management.

Vietnam has made considerable progress toward social protection goals. But it faces continuing challenges in expanding coverage and improving benefit levels, while continuing to sustain high growth in a challenging domestic and global economic and socio-political environment.

Notes

1 All the data are from Vietnam's official sources.
2 Vietnam, Ministry of Labour, Invalids and Social Affairs, Draft 10 Social protection strategy. Period 2011–2020 (Hanoi, 2010) and associated detailed calculations (ILSSA)

3 The current Law on Social Insurance covering compulsory social insurance, voluntary social insurance and unemployment insurance has created opportunities for workers, especially those in the informal sector, to participate in social insurance. However, notably due to a lack of communication as well as mechanisms and policies to assist informal sector workers, only a few join the social insurance scheme on a voluntary basis. Most voluntary social insurance participants are those who used to participate in compulsory social insurance for few years, and they continue participating in voluntary social insurance to satisfy the minimum condition of a twenty year contribution to be eligible for a pension (Draft Social Protection Strategy 2011–2020, Hanoi 2010)

4 According to the law, the pension premium from 2014 is 22 percent and the benefit is 75 percent, which means the accumulated premium of the employee is inadequate to pay for 10 years' benefits. The ratio between the contributors and the beneficiaries is reducing quickly.

5 For analytical and empirical discussion of age-related fiscal costs in selected Asian economies, see Asher et al. (2016).

6 ILO, World Development Indicators (http://data.worldbank.org/data-catalog/world-development-indicators/ accessed February 2011).

7 OECD, Social Cohesion Policy Review, see Chapter 8 References section in this volume.

References

Asher, M. G., and F. Zen. (2016). *Age Related Pension Expenditure and Fiscal Space Modelling Techniques and Case Studies from East Asia*. London: Routledge.

ILO, *World Development Indicators*, Available at http://data.worldbank.org/data-catalog/world-development-indicators(accessed February 2011)

ILSSA/GIZ (2012). *Social Protection Book (2012)*.

MOLISA (2010). *Draft Social Protection Strategy, Period 2011–2020*. Hanoi: Ministry of Labour, Invalids and Social Affairs.

OECD (2013). *Social Cohesion Policy Review in Vietnam, 2013*.

Vietnam, ILSSA (2013). *Development Of the Social Security System in Vietnam Until 2020*.

Vietnam, ILSSA (various years). *Labour and Social Trend*, Annual Report.

Vietnam, Ministry of Health (2014). *Resolving Social Issues in the New Situation*.

Vietnam, Ministry of Labour, Invalids and Social Affairs (2012). *Report on the Implementation of Social Protection Policies For Social Policy Beneficiaries*.

Vietnam, Ministry of Labour, Invalids and Social Affairs. www.molisa.gov.vn/vi/Pages/chitiettin.aspx?IDNews=20415

Vietnam Social Security (VSS) (2015). http://www.baohiemxahoi.gov.vn/

World Bank (2014). http://www.worldbank.org/en/news/press-release/2014/08/07/support-to-reform-and-innovation-in-vietnams-social-assistance-program; (2) http://projects.worldbank.org/P123960?lang=en

World Bank (2016). *World Development Indicators*. Available http://data.worldbank.org/data-catalog/world-development-indicators

Index

Note: Page numbers in *italic* indicate a figure and page numbers in **bold** indicate a table on the corresponding page.